UNLOCKED

Assessment as the Key to Everyday
Creativity in the Classroom

KATIE WHITE

Solution Tree | Press

a division of
Solution Tree

555 North Morton Street
Bloomington, IN 47404
800.733.6786 (toll free) / 812.336.7700
FAX: 812.336.7790

email: info@SolutionTree.com
SolutionTree.com

Visit **go.SolutionTree.com/assessment** to download the free reproducibles in this book.

Printed in the United States of America

Library of Congress Cataloging-in-Publication Data

Names: White, Katie, 1970- author.
Title: Unlocked : assessment as the key to everyday creativity in the
  classroom / Katie White.
Description: Bloomington, IN : Solution Tree Press, 2018. | Includes
  bibliographical references and index.
Identifiers: LCCN 2018030288 | ISBN 9781947604513 (perfect bound)
Subjects: LCSH: Learning--Evaluation. | Students--Rating of. | Creative
  ability--Study and teaching. | Motivation in education.
Classification: LCC LB3051 .W48847 2018 | DDC 371.26--dc23 LC record available at https://lccn.loc.
gov/2018030288

Solution Tree

Jeffrey C. Jones, CEO
Edmund M. Ackerman, President

Solution Tree Press

President and Publisher: Douglas M. Rife
Editorial Director: Sarah Payne-Mills
Art Director: Rian Anderson
Managing Production Editor: Kendra Slayton
Senior Production Editor: Tara Perkins
Senior Editor: Amy Rubenstein
Copy Editor: Ashante K. Thomas
Proofreader: Jessi Finn
Text and Cover Designer: Abigail Bowen
Editorial Assistant: Sarah Ludwig

ACKNOWLEDGMENTS

After every venture into the realm of writing, it is important for me to stand back and acknowledge the experiences and the relationships that have led to a single book. For this work in particular, the words merely attempt to capture what feels like a lifetime of creative learning alongside the people in my life.

First of all, I must acknowledge my art students. I started teaching art classes when I was eighteen years old, and all the years of working with young artists have taught me so much about the creative process—how it flourishes and how it collapses in on itself. I am so grateful for all the children, youth, and adults who helped me figure out how to encourage innovation and risk taking while still having fun.

I also wish to acknowledge other groups of students. There were those who sat in my mathematics classes when I tried zany ways of making sense of things. There were students who learned alongside me in science classes when we tried, failed, and tried again. There were the students who trusted me in English language arts classes as we explored ways to write well, weaving stories out of life's experiences. Teachers are learners first, and I am so grateful for all the learning I did in my classrooms over the years. Creativity followed me everywhere, and my students were always up for the challenge.

I have to acknowledge the Solution Tree team, who exercise tremendous patience as I work through my own creative process. Always thorough and encouraging, and always helping me bring a coherent message to my work, I thank this team for everything they do, from editing, to cover design, to publicity. This book would not be a book without you.

Lastly, I have to acknowledge my highly creative family, who not only live with but also support my creative inclinations every day. From my mom, who is the most creative person I know, to my literary father, to my musician husband, to my incredibly creative daughters (in pretty much every way possible), my life is full and rich and wonderful because of you.

Solution Tree Press would like to thank the following reviewers:

Kristi Bundy
Sixth-Grade Teacher
Ashland-Greenwood Middle School
Ashland, Nebraska

Kathy Nimmer
English Teacher, Constructional Coach
William Henry Harrison High School
West Lafayette, Indiana

Jeff Byrnes
Principal
Mountain Meadow Elementary School
Buckley, Washington

Amber Webb
Stage I Teacher
The Roeper School
Bloomfield Hills, Michigan

Sarah Carter
Mathematics Teacher
Coweta High School
Coweta, Oklahoma

Tracy Williams
Principal
W.G. Mallett School
Farmington, Maine

Megan Grube
Director of Curriculum, Instruction,
    and Technology
Grand Isle Supervisory Union
North Hero, Vermont

Visit **go.SolutionTree.com/assessment** to download
the free reproducibles in this book.

TABLE OF CONTENTS

Reproducible pages are in italics.

5

Unlocking Expression **143**

6

Unlocking Reflection and Response **169**

ABOUT THE AUTHOR

 **Katie White** is coordinator of learning for the North East School Division in Saskatchewan, Canada, and an educational consultant. With more than twenty years in education, she has been a district and in-school administrator, a learning coach, and a K–12 classroom teacher.

Katie was an integral part of her school division's multi-year journey through renewed curricula and standards-based assessment and reporting. She helps develop and utilize strong assessment and grading practices that support teaching and learning in classrooms. Her focus is on helping educators develop a personalized understanding of the connections between curriculum, assessment, and instruction. Katie has developed multiple supports for teachers and administrators as well as facilitators of school-based professional learning. She is a co-moderator of the All Things Assessment (#ATAssess) Twitter chat and a frequent contributor to the *All Things Assessment* blog (http://allthingsassessment.info/blog).

Katie received a bachelor of education and master of education in curriculum studies from the University of Saskatchewan.

To learn more about Katie's work, visit www.kwhiteconsulting.com, or follow her @KatieWhite426 on Twitter.

To book Katie White for professional development, contact pd@SolutionTree.com.

INTRODUCTION

Early in my career as a teacher of senior art, when I had large classes, I talked myself out of using one-on-one formative assessment and feedback strategies, such as conferencing, to advance creative thinking, because I figured I simply did not have the time. Furthermore, I wondered what the other students would do when I was speaking with individuals about their work. How could I make sure all students completed my assignments and cared for my art materials when I was working with a single student? So, in the beginning, I skipped conferences, simply assigned student artwork a summative grade, and called it a day. However, I began to change my mind as the years progressed.

The turning point happened in a senior art class. I sensed that some of my quieter and more reluctant students were connecting with a painting unit I was teaching on watercolor painting. As they built confidence and technique, I had the urge to speak to some of them about what they were experiencing. So, I began to conference with my students. I structured an activity that invited independent exploration, and I let the learners know that I wanted to speak with them individually about their ongoing efforts. I made sure every student was able to work on his or her own and then I began calling students, one at a time, out into the hallway, where I had hung their work.

I began by asking them which aspect of their work gave them the most pride, based on the skills we had been practicing. I followed with a question about which part of their work most surprised them. I then asked them what they might do differently if they could have another try at the painting on the wall. The conversations were organic, productive, and criterion referenced. I learned so much about my students and their thinking. I also found the space and time to honor their learning. This was so powerful.

I especially remember a session I had with a particular student. He was definitely one of the quietest in my class, and he was a year older than the other students in the room. School was not a place where he experienced tremendous success, and I had the sense that he was just trying to graduate so he could get on with "real life." I believe he enrolled in my elective course because he thought it would get him one credit closer to graduation (and it did). He was always unfailingly polite but very reserved. I am not sure I could have told you much about him as a person, even after having him in my class for a month.

When he joined me in the hallway for his conference, he looked a little terrified, unsure of what was going to happen. I began by expressing how grateful I was for his efforts in trying a new kind of painting. He honestly looked as if hearing a positive comment like this was a completely foreign experience—he immediately smiled and began to talk about how interested he was in the quality of watercolor paint. Our conversation flowed from that point on, and he easily reflected on his processes and set goals for his next piece. What struck me the most was the power of a formative assessment and feedback session when in the hands of this learner. He shared more in those ten minutes than I heard from him in the preceding month, and our conversation ignited his creativity as he began to plan his next art piece. It completely confirmed my suspicion that assessment's role is to motivate and inspire. Most of all, it reminded me of the importance of student voice in the learning and assessment process. It is a lesson that has never left me.

Too many classrooms stifle, push down, or lock up creativity. Students receive assignments with little or no room to express themselves or explore their options; this lack of options locks them into stagnant routines. The implications of this stagnation in a classroom setting are immense. Without creativity and assessment processes that truly nurture inquiry and growth, we end up with systems filled with compliance and "right" answers. We run the risk of eliminating multiple viewpoints, critical thinking, and deep connections by rewarding the systematic movement of learners through prescriptive content. Teachers want more for students—we want students to feel the grit of learning; the struggle and challenge; the recursive nature of rich, authentic learning. We want them to feel the power of making their own decisions, the challenges when those decisions do not yet yield the hoped-for results, and the pride when they give students exactly what they wanted. We want students to recognize the power of revision, of returning to ideas more than once in order to deepen and extend thinking.

When we introduce creativity into all classroom settings, we unlock the potential for profound learning and development of valuable life skills. We can use creativity to teach resilience, to foster imagination, and to nurture stamina. We can invite students into processes that encourage them to see problems and topics from multiple perspectives. We can use creativity to reinforce critical thinking alongside curiosity and wonder. Creativity, and the assessment that supports it, encourages students to broaden their idea generation and revisit assumptions. Pete Hall and Alisa Simeral (2015) remind us, "The most successful individuals today are those who have the ability to reflect—those who are aware of what they know, recognize that what they know is always subject to change, and have the ability to undo and relearn knowledge. Therefore, they are able to revise their belief systems" (p. 47). Grant Wiggins and Jay McTighe (2005) go on to clarify the importance of the kinds of assessment that unlock creativity: "Self-understanding is arguably the most important facet of understanding for lifelong learning. Central to self-understanding is an honest self-assessment, based on increasing clarity about what we do understand and what we don't; what we have accomplished and what remains to be done" (pp. 215–216). The development of our learners into thinking human beings depends on the presence of creativity in our classrooms.

About This Book

The purpose of this book is to offer very tangible ways we can use assessment processes to unlock creativity in any classroom at any grade level. The kind of assessment I will describe in each chapter purposefully invites learners right into the middle of creative decisions by simultaneously inviting them right into the middle of assessment.

Assessment is the key that unlocks the creative potential so many students have learned to suppress in school, are unaware they possess, or over time have convinced themselves never existed at all. When we embed assessment within the creative process, it invites students to consider decisions they are making in relation to personally meaningful goals. It invites us, as their teachers, to observe their progress and the actions they are taking so we can respond carefully.

When we decide to develop creativity within our classrooms, we may feel the pull between the messiness of exploration and the desire to protect both our own and our students' sense of self-worth and need for control. We face the challenge of deciding what kind of feedback to offer every time a student shares a product with us; of determining to what degree we are going to ask him or her to re-enter the creative process, and to what degree we are going to let students make those decisions on their own. This process is complex and recursive, and we might not be familiar with this kind of complexity, this degree of revision, and this shift in the conversations we have about learning in our school system. Students, in turn, are used to a particular way of doing business when at school and often work on the premise of needing to get things done and complete tasks quickly. For this reason, if we are going to develop creativity in our classrooms, we need embedded assessment processes that help both teachers and students navigate the messiness of creativity. In making creativity flourish in our classrooms, we may first have to reconsider our assessment decisions and methods and examine how best to invite the kinds of assessment that actually support creativity in our learners.

Creativity and Assessment

Part of the challenge of this work rests in how we understand creativity—what it is, how it works, and how it is reflected in all areas of life. We can say the same for assessment. We may have two misunderstandings compounded exponentially and, as a result, both are sold incredibly short in our education system. Misunderstanding breeds misuse or omission. This is not only unfortunate but also outright dangerous. Educational psychologist Joseph S. Renzulli (2000) agrees, stating:

> *The sad fact remains that in spite of dozens of books about creativity, hundreds of research studies, and thousands of training programs and workshops, the development of creative potential is still largely an ignored aspect of a child's total repertoire of acquired behaviors. (p. 15)*

Without creativity developed using strong assessment processes, we cannot hope to develop learners who become deep thinkers, critical consumers, and empathic human beings.

Daniel Pink (2009) reminds us:

> *We know—if we've spent time with young children or remember ourselves at our best—that we're not destined to be passive and compliant. We're designed to be active and engaged. And we know that the richest experiences in our lives aren't when we're clamoring for validation from others, but when we're listening to our own voice—doing something that matters, doing it well, and doing it in the service of a cause larger than ourselves. (p. 145)*

I cannot overstate the importance of engaging in creative experiences that encourage this active engagement and passionate pursuit of meaning. Getting there, however, may require us to reimagine our ideas about creativity and assessment.

Reimagining Creativity

Being creative can be messy, unpredictable, and downright uncomfortable. It takes time and an unrelenting persistence in working toward desired outcomes, regardless of the cost. It cannot be packaged and sold in sterile boxes, locked away from the real lives of our students. That being said, educators must acknowledge that regularly engaging in creative processes and the assessment that supports this way of doing business takes tremendous courage, as Joan Franklin Smutny, founder and director of the Center for Gifted, and her colleague S. E. von Fremd (2009) assert:

> *Creative self-expression in its most basic elements determines how life is experienced, how problems are perceived, how duties are performed, how instruments are played, and how visions are realized. It demands openness and spontaneity, as well as the courage to fend off unreceptive responses of hard-nosed or narrow-minded thinking. (p. 293)*

This runs contrary to the design of our education system. Timelines and deadlines rule the day, and making time for discomfort and mess is unpalatable and seemingly impossible for many. However, the cost of not doing so is far greater. An education system void of creativity and the kinds of reflective and self-directed assessment that support it is a system that will fail to nurture learners' long-term emotional, intellectual, and social needs. It is a system that limits the potential of not only students and teachers but also the societies of which they are a part. As education scholar Katie F. Olivant (2015) shares, "A dichotomy has developed between what societies need from education and that which the education system is providing" (p. 115). Without creativity and the kind of assessment that fully supports it, we cannot hope to develop citizens who look for new solutions to problems, who innovate in the face of challenge, and who explore their need for expression and wonder as a way to nurture their mental health. Even decades-old research by Carl R. Rogers (1954, 1961), Abraham H. Maslow (1954), and Mihaly Csikszentmihalyi (1990) finds that doing creative work is one of the most significant experiences of a person's life. Our societies need more from an education system than simply revisiting information already discovered. Information is important, certainly, but inviting students to manipulate that information and reimagine it, revisit it, and build from it is critical for the health and growth of our societies as a whole.

To position the idea of creativity clearly in our thinking, consider the definition Sir Ken Robinson (2009) offers: "To be creative you actually have to do something. It involves putting your imagination to work to make something new, to come up with new solutions to problems, even to think of new problems or questions" (p. 63). Many people mistakenly believe creativity is limited to the arts, but Robinson's definition of creativity shows us that the creative processes exist in every field. Another misconception is that creativity belongs to the gifted and is the result of building something from nothing. In fact, creativity can occur in everyday moments by everyday people. For example, during meal preparation, when a cook adds new ingredients to a tried-and-true recipe, he or she is exhibiting creativity, or when an adolescent tries a new strategy while playing a video game, he or she is taking a creative risk. Looking at existing ideas in new ways is a creative act. Imagining a new perspective or mode of expressing an idea that already exists is a creative event. Creativity is the fuel that drives exploration and wonder. Thinking in new ways, asking new questions, and imagining new outcomes advance all manner of learning. Olivant (2015) concurs:

> *Creativity is crucial to personal and cognitive growth and to academic success. It is a concept that continues to merit a central position in education but tends to fail to attain the appropriate attention and support of policymakers and education leaders. (p. 127)*

Creativity is not simply about making something beautiful. Rather, it is about answering important questions, imagining possibilities, and solving challenging problems. By shifting our understanding of creativity, we can reimagine its place within our classrooms.

Creativity, in this sense, is a harkening back to the kinds of learning we did naturally when we were young. Smutny and von Fremd (2009) describe how students have lost this learning over time:

> *The creative world they lived in during their earliest years of learning as they touched, tasted, performed, molded, constructed, expressed, and explored their surroundings has lost its validity. They had to let it go in order to ply the more serious waters of skill acquisition and content mastery. (p. 5)*

However, this loss does not have to occur. We do not have to choose skill acquisition and content mastery over creativity. Creativity, skills, and knowledge can develop simultaneously. They are interdependent, with each serving to advance the other. Slight changes in the kinds of questions we ask and the manner of assessing in which we engage can propel creativity forward, with skill development and content mastery being integral parts of the creative process. This is truly a win-win situation for students.

Reimagining Assessment

As we begin this conversation, just as we need to share a common understanding of what *creativity* describes, it is important to be sure there is clarity about the term *assessment* as it appears in this book. There are certainly enough definitions of this word to keep a teacher busy any day of the week. However, Grant Wiggins and Jay McTighe (2005) define assessment as "techniques used to analyze student accomplishments against specific goals and criteria" (p. 337). This definition is a great starting point for exploring the kinds of assessment processes critical to unlocking creativity.

In order to develop our understanding more fully, let's imagine the word *techniques* in Wiggins and McTighe's (2005) definition is interchangeable with the word *processes*. In *Unlocked: Assessment as the Key to Everyday Creativity in the Classroom*, we will explore a number of assessment processes a teacher can apply each and every day to develop learners' creative potential. These include, but are not limited to:

- ◇ Daily formative assessment
- ◇ Self-assessment
- ◇ Peer assessment
- ◇ Constructive and targeted feedback
- ◇ Goal setting
- ◇ Long-term reflection and criteria setting

Through these processes, educators can nurture critical skills such as striving to seek new solutions, building stamina for multiple attempts, and developing strategies to engage in purposeful revision for each and every learner.

The word *analyze* is also critical in our understanding of assessment, because by analyzing artifacts of student thinking, we as educators can ask further questions, consider options, and make decisions about next steps. It is important to be clear about the criteria against which we measure success and challenge, and the act of analyzing performances and products is an essential part of the creative process. The key is to realize that students could conduct this analysis just as often as teachers could. When both teacher and student undertake the analysis, they deepen thinking and support the opportunity for further exploration.

The last part of this definition that needs some attention is the phrase *against specific goals and criteria*. Both goals and criteria for success are critical for learning and expressing oneself creatively. Students must ultimately own the goals and criteria, and teachers can use the forms of assessment in the preceding list to guide them in setting and reflecting on progress toward those goals.

Engaging in assessment processes that advance and nurture this kind of personal meaning making and creative exploration for students will ensure that we protect both assessment and creativity, not as add-ons, but as major players in new kinds of learning within our schools. In fact, deeply considering the relationship between assessment and creativity is the key to maximizing their potential and developing the very human beings who engage in these processes. Assessment and creativity are deeply and intimately connected and are critical to the development of enriching and complex learning experiences.

When working together, assessment and creativity have the potential to change the world both within and beyond the classroom. Together, creativity and assessment enhance the relationship between humans and their inner landscapes, fostering the search for new questions, new ideas, and new connections. They invite our students to think about solutions to problems greater than themselves and consider the needs of others and the world as a whole. When educators nurture creativity and assessment in their classrooms, they invite students to enhance the quality of their lives by moving past the mundane and the usual, and encourage them to look deeper, search wider, and explore multiple perspectives. When assessment fuels creativity, students move toward and through learning they didn't anticipate when they began. They set new goals and ask new questions, which move them in new directions. Without assessment, creativity stops, and without creativity, our classrooms stagnate, locked into routines.

While this book focuses on the kinds of assessment processes that move creativity and learning forward (formative assessment processes), it is important to note that assessment *of* learning, or summative assessment, is also part of the creative process.

There is a time when students finish brainstorming, exploring prototypes and scenarios, and adjusting, and learners are ready to verify whether the products and processes in which they engage accomplish their desired goals. Teachers will work alongside learners to take part in this verification, and it is from this process that students ask new questions and set new goals, and new learning emerges. This is exactly how assessment becomes *part* of learning and creativity, instead of sitting outside of it.

Many books that explore creativity imply but rarely name let alone unpack the process of assessment in terms of its essential relationship to creativity. Society has come to view assessment as separate from learning, and we have to rectify this if we are going to unlock all kinds of deep thinking, including creativity. Instead of assessment being something we do to learners, it has to be something we educators do *with* learners or something learners do with our guidance and support. Creativity comes from the creator. It is a very intrinsic process. As a result, the more often we can place responsibility and ownership with the students doing the creating, the better they will develop and refine these skills for the long term.

To be clear, using assessment to unlock creativity is not the same as assessing creativity, nor is it assigning creativity a value to use as a grade. It is about using assessment to invite deeper and original thought—to *advance* creativity. Assessment, in this context, means that we need to put the learning in the learners' hands and invite them to determine what they hope to accomplish and how they plan to do so.

How This Book Will Explore Creativity Through Assessment

Unlocked is based on my experiences as a classroom teacher, as a community art instructor, and as a teacher of teachers. It is grounded in the belief that only when learners own their learning can they reach their potential. This book will explore the relationship between assessment and creativity, providing practical ideas for connecting the two processes within any classroom setting, and share processes for engaging students in the continuous goal setting and establishing of criteria firmly embedded within the creative process.

Each chapter focuses on a key aspect of creativity in our classrooms. We begin with chapter 1, which examines the connection between creativity and assessment. Next, chapter 2 discusses the importance of establishing creative spaces that attend to learners' intellectual, emotional, and physical needs. Finally, chapters 3 through 6 explore the four critical stages of the creative process: (1) exploration (students explore concepts and questions), (2) elaboration (students expand on a concept or question, developing skills and conducting research along the way), (3) expression (students choose a form for their creative output around the concept or question they have chosen to focus on), and (4) reflection and response (students examine the product of their work and the feedback they receive and decide how to move forward).

The following recurring features will help make the connection between assessment and creativity clear and attainable in classroom settings.

◇ **Critical actions for teachers and students:** A description of necessary actions required to explore, elaborate, express, and reflect and respond while immersed in creative pursuits.

◇ **Select and reflect reproducibles:** Questions to guide student reflection when they are experiencing difficulty during a stage of the creative process. A reproducible list of supporting questions follows the discussion of each critical action. When we select a great question and pose it at the right time, we can move our learners' creative processes forward. These questions can serve as a catalyst for students to reflect on their creative processes during each stage of the creative process and sustain ownership for their decision making and problem solving.

◇ **The role of the teacher:** Important actions teachers must take to develop and sustain creativity in the classroom and practical ways to live out these actions.

◇ **Assessment and creativity stage:** A section that explores ways to ensure that assessment unlocks creativity at each stage.

◇ **Observation and self-assessment reproducibles:** Self-assessment tools for teachers to monitor the critical actions students must take during each stage and suggestions for how to respond when students experience difficulty.

◇ **Additional reproducibles:** Assessment templates and processes teachers and students can use immediately within the classroom to unlock creativity in each stage of the creative process.

Final Thoughts

In developing creative thinkers, we ask our students to consider what it feels like to learn, solve problems, innovate, and design. We ask them how it feels to be messy and experimental and to take risks, make mistakes, and solve problems. We want them to explore how it feels to wonder deeply and make connections in meaningful ways, curating variables to meet specific needs. We want learners who reflect on not only their products and performances but also the decisions they make as they engage in creative processes. Effective assessment processes move students through this learning, developing and refining both the knowledge and skills again, while also developing independence, autonomy, and creativity.

At the end of the day, we want schools where learners can explore complex learning in a variety of ways, with a strong focus on creative pursuits and inquiry. We need students to dig deeper and deeper into areas about which they are passionate—the kinds of learning we want from students will emerge out of this kind of exploration and wonder. To accomplish this, we simply have to trust the power of creativity and the students who engage in it, and we have to trust ourselves to craft classroom assessments that support this kind of learning.

The Integrated Nature of Assessment and the Creative Process

Imagine a physical education teacher invites his students into a creative process during a physical education class. He has spent a few weeks exploring a number of net games (for example, tennis, volleyball, table tennis), and the class is ready to use a creative process to determine degrees of understanding and skill. He decides he wants students to apply what they learn about net games to a new game of their own creation. The teacher invites them to choose equipment and design rules. He then offers them the chance to try the game with classmates, in order to identify strategies and tactics that advance their game. He asks students to create a scoring system and parameters for wins and losses.

During this creative process, the teacher engages in assessment with the students. During exploration, he might preassess students to determine the degree to which they understand what makes net games unique. He checks their understanding of rules during tennis, badminton, volleyball, and pickle ball. He ensures they have a grasp of the critical features of a net game. For those students who are struggling with this content, he offers additional instructional support and practice, so learners can successfully engage in the creative process in relation to this topic (building foundational domain knowledge).

Students may begin to brainstorm ideas for their own game, exploring the equipment in the storage room and talking with each other about their ideas. The teacher interacts with students at this stage, asking probing questions and handing out a list of the criteria that they need to attend to in their design (equipment, rules, scoring, and so on). At the end of exploration, students write their two best ideas on a goal sheet. They will narrow down their choices the next day.

When they arrive the next day, the students examine their goal sheets and talk with a partner about their two best ideas. Their partner offers them advice and asks further questions. (The teacher might introduce question starters to help students frame their questions, if this is new.) He observes the pairings and looks for signs of indecision or stalled conversation. He then joins groups, as needed, to support their efforts during the elaboration stage of their work. During this class, students choose their final idea and create a graphic organizer that allows them to articulate their decisions in relation to these criteria. In the middle of this class period, the teacher stops the students and invites them to reflect on what they accomplished so far and what they need to do next. He adds to the criteria (perhaps team positions or performance cues important to their game). Learners then re-engage in their work, enhancing their ideas and refining their thinking. They may watch videos or partner to explore equipment. At this stage, they are welcome to make changes on any decision. In fact, the teacher invites students to reflect on their own efforts in relation to criteria often, to ensure they are satisfied with their efforts. At the end of this class, students add their most recent decisions to their documentation. The teacher then prepares learners to commit to their games by the following day, so they can begin to determine how best to share ideas with the class. Students are encouraged to think about their designs in their spare time and make any changes they feel they need to, to enhance their games.

On the third day, students work together to determine the best ways to share their designs. Together, they post a number of options (in a video, on a game card poster, through paired presentations, for example) and students decide which method works best for them. The teacher works with those students who are struggling to decide and leaves others to create the method that is most meaningful for them. The teacher draws students' attention to the criteria throughout and invites a five-minute journal reflection, when students identify a strength and a challenge. In this way, the teacher can assess which students need additional supports, instruction, or both, and which are working independently with success. The teacher may notice that as students engage in expression, they want to continue to refine their games and add additional details. The teacher encourages this because he knows that the creative process is not neat and tidy; students see gaps and errors as they construct their method of expression and see their products through their peers' eyes.

The final step is sharing, combined with reflection and response. Students practice listening well and asking reflective questions, inviting learners to consider aspects of their design they hadn't considered previously. The teacher also builds in a celebration component, when students acknowledge their own strengths and those of their classmates. Meanwhile, the class uses the predetermined criteria to assess the products, allowing for one last effort at refinement if the feedback dictates. The products strongly reflect subject-area goals, and the class has invited additional kinds of learning through the creative process. The teacher has nurtured collaboration, reflection, communication, and critical thinking. As the class ends this creative endeavor, the teacher invites students to reflect one last time on their approaches during the creative cycle. The teacher may ask them to consider which of their strategies were most useful and which led to unsatisfactory results. He may invite them to consider what conditions support their creativity and how they might create these kinds of conditions next time. He places these reflections in their portfolios and refers to them the next time they work in creative ways.

When I want to spot creativity working hand-in-hand with assessment, I watch closely for confidence and uncertainty in students when they engage in solving a problem or creating a product. I celebrate both emotions because when students are feeling something in relation to their complex work, it means they are assessing their efforts and the results of those efforts in relation to a goal they have. Assessment experts Cassie Erkens, Tom Schimmer, and Nicole Dimich Vagle (2017) explain that "assessment cultivates student investment, a dual kind of reflection—on learning and engagement—where students persist through tasks and pursue higher levels of learning because they now believe that with effort, they can do it" (p. 135). Emotion signals investment, and investment means the seeds for creativity and problem solving are ready to grow.

In order to further explore how assessment connects to the creative impulse, we can examine some words we use in conjunction with creativity—*innovation, imagination, artistry, design*—all words that reflect the kinds of rich thinking we want to develop in our learners. We might also use the phrase *problem solving* in relation to creativity because it helps us see creative endeavors as an attempt to solve a problem that holds meaning for the creator. Psychologist R. Keith Sawyer (2006) confirms this, noting, "Many creativity researchers now believe that creativity involves both problem solving and problem finding" (p. 116). Creating a work of art is often solving a *visual problem* in order to reach a desired goal (achieving balance, emotion, or message, for example). Writing a narrative or descriptive text is solving the *problem of communicating meaning* through written language. Designing a prototype for a scientific question means solving the *problems of function and design*. In these examples, problems are not bad; in fact, they are catalysts for creative action. They are the reason people heavily create and invest in the process. In this way, understanding the relationship between creativity and assessment is understanding how creativity (or innovation, imagination, artistry, or design) connects to problems and how problems connect to investment in goals.

Indeed, creativity is lived out moment to moment and decision by decision. A final product may or may not reflect a desired goal, but the journey in getting to that product might be very creative. Understanding the relationship between the creative process and the assessment that supports the development of creative products is critical to understanding creativity in all its complexity. Enmeshed firmly inside creative processes are assessment processes that propel the person who is creating forward into the next stage of the creative process. Setting goals, assessing successes and challenges, seeking feedback, refining actions, and verifying and sharing efforts are all assessment processes that are essential to the creative process. When teachers use assessment skillfully, purposefully, and at meaningful times, they enhance the results of a creative endeavor.

In this chapter, we will address a number of myths about both assessment and creativity. We will more fully explore both creativity and assessment, as well as the threats and misconceptions that may exist within classrooms and school settings that make engaging in both challenging at times. We will also explore how students may experience creativity in different classroom contexts and subject areas and the assessment processes that support these experiences.

Myths About Creativity

As mentioned in the introduction, the myths that creativity only occurs in arts-related courses and the notion that only gifted people are capable of creativity are prevalent and often inhibit the development of this important skill in our schools. Mythology surrounds the topic of creativity, and this mythology can paralyze teachers in their pursuit of developing creative thinkers. Resting at the core of creativity's story is an either-or paradigm. Educators often feel like they need to choose between speed (getting through the content) and exploration (going where the learners want to go). They worry that they need to choose between classroom management (self-regulating and maintaining optimal learning conditions) and the free-for-all teachers imagine creative exploration requires (going where the learner wants, when the learner wants, how the learner wants). Educators wonder whether they have to give up their standards if they are going to develop creative learners. These false dichotomies set up teachers to make decisions that not only sell creativity short but sell rich learning short, too. When educators address these myths—the false dichotomies that inhibit them—they can begin to imagine classrooms where they develop self-regulated individuals who also explore ideas creatively.

Let's explore the myths about creativity, so we can begin to imagine how we might nurture environments that foster all the skills and knowledge we hope to develop in our learners. Following are nine pervasive myths teachers must be aware of to ensure they support all students' creativity.

1. **Either you are creative or you aren't:** Sadly, if you ask an adult whether he or she views him- or herself as creative, many will emphatically assert, "I am definitely not creative. I can't even draw a stick figure!" This illustrates a belief that people who aren't creative will always remain so. It also shows a narrow view of what creativity means. If we are going to work to develop creative learners, we have to believe it is possible to do so. Creativity is a

learned trait. Katherine E. Batchelor and William P. Bintz (2013) explain, "There is no creativity gene, a gene that individuals are born with that provides them with a predisposition for creativity. There is also no academic discipline that has an exclusive monopoly on creativity" (p. 10). People can develop creativity over time, in any number of contexts.

2. **Creative people generate quality results on their first effort:** This myth is the reason why so many people, adults and children alike, give up on creativity. The idea that creativity is absent of effort, trial and error, or failure is a harmful misconception, because when these things come to pass, frustration sets in and forward momentum stops. Instead of a perfect creative product emerging immediately, creativity is primarily conscious, hard work (Sawyer, 2006; Simonton, 1988, 1999). A truly creative effort requires the learner to return to ideas again and again, considering multiple perspectives, uses, adaptations, and applications. Assessment facilitates this iterative process, and it takes investment, revision, and time.

3. **Creativity is a solitary pursuit:** Often, as students experience the creative process, they share ideas with others, generate new questions, and provide alternate perspectives. Students may find themselves working with peers, asking for opinions and resources that can act as catalysts for further exploration. Gretchen Morgan (2015) states, "In a culture in which we are given permission to be inventive, a strong practice of learning from one another is required to accelerate our collective effectiveness and maintain trust" (p. 72). This social aspect of creativity speaks to the need for teachers to be mindful in learners' creative processes. Erkens et al. (2017) assert, "Teacher responsiveness to student dialogue, questions, comments, and work can lead to a deeper culture of learning" (p. 120). Teachers act as fellow seekers, critical friends, and experts at various times. They facilitate self-assessment, peer assessment, and research and invite authentic audiences and strong purposes for the work.

4. **Creative people break all the rules:** In this creativity myth, the rules or specific knowledge and skills within subject areas can get in the way of creativity; they are too constraining and static. People may believe that a "true" creator breaks the rules and pushes past convention. However, rules provide a necessary foundation and shared understanding upon which new ideas, strategies, and approaches can be layered. When students hold knowledge or skill in a particular subject area, that knowledge or skill becomes the language through which students express their creativity. The rules give learners something against which they can assess their creative efforts. They give students the scaffolding they need to reach new creative heights (Dacey & Conklin, 2004).

5. **Creativity happens entirely inside the mind, like a flash of inspiration:**
    Sawyer (2006) explains, "Creativity doesn't happen all in the head . . . it
    happens during the hard work of execution" (p. 386). Creativity is not just
    about idea generation. It is about monitoring and evaluating ideas and
    approaches and reflecting on inspiration and catalysts. Creativity happens
    over time, with mini-insight, interspersed between hard, persistent work.
    Not only will students benefit from creative processes, but they will also
    benefit from sustained, focused efforts over time. This is truly a win-win.

6. **Creativity is all about fun:** Creativity is not easy or peaceful. There are
    moments during the creative process that are downright uncomfortable.
    Results can be ambiguous, goals can shift, and ideas can falter, all in the
    name of exploring and elaborating on ideas. Educational consultant Patti
    Drapeau (2014) confirms, "Creative lesson components are not just feel-
    good activities. They are activities that directly address critical content, target
    specific standards, and require thoughtful products that allow students to
    show what they know" (p. 3). It is through effective assessment practices that
    teachers and learners can connect the creative processes being used to critical
    skills and understanding under development. The good news is the kind of
    resilience students develop as a result of engaging in creative processes will
    serve them for their lifetime.

7. **Creativity is a linear process:** This particular myth is one reason educators
    may not get to creative processes in their classrooms. If we believe that a
    student has to earn the right to be creative by learning prerequisite concepts
    and skills, then some students will never get to experience it. Ken Robinson
    and Lou Aronica (2015) explain—

    > *It is true that creative work in any field involves a growing mastery of
    > skills and concepts. It is not true that they have to be mastered before the
    > creative work can begin. Focusing on skills in isolation can kill interest
    > in any discipline. (p. 147)*

    Students can gain many of the skills and conceptual understandings we
    desire *through* creative processes.

8. **No one can measure or assess creativity; the quality of creative products
    is completely a matter of opinion:** When we walk alongside our students
    in their creative pursuits, we will utilize formative assessment processes
    to determine degrees of comfort with risk taking and creative progress in
    relation to student goals. We engage in feedback to propel learning forward
    and we utilize summative assessment to verify degrees of understanding and
    skill. Furthermore, we can also assess the development of creative skills. For

example, we can capture and assess the quality of questions students are generating or we can assess our learners' use of materials to create products. Students can receive feedback on their creative processes, not only for the products they are yielding but also for the degree to which their creative processes are allowing them to advance thinking and learning. In this way, students can transfer the creative skills they develop from one context to the next. John A. C. Hattie and Gregory M. Donoghue (2016) elaborate, "Transfer is a dynamic, not static, process that requires learners to actively choose and evaluate strategies, consider resources and surface information, and, when available, to receive or seek feedback to enhance these adaptive skills" (p. 12). The development of these skills and strategies is one of the key benefits of creative processes in our classrooms.

9. **Creativity is about off-the-wall or weird ideas:** This last myth relates to the misguided belief that students can only develop creativity through the arts. People expect creative products to look odd, discomfiting, or disorganized; it is often because society labels these kinds of products as creative. Creativity, in this case, acts as a justification for products or processes that may feel uncomfortable or unappealing. Some people may claim creative license as an explanation when they offer a process or product that others may not enjoy or accept. In contrast, creativity in its many forms might resemble a tidy mathematics problem, or a clear experimental process. Sawyer (2006) proposes that creativity is "the constant dialogue between unconscious inspiration and conscious editing; between passionate inspiration and disciplined craft" (p. 320). It might look like a well-crafted narrative essay or an organized community event. Creativity does not always look messy. In fact, a true benefit of creativity is its ability to yield refined, organized, logical results (Sawyer, 2006).

By exploring some of the myths surrounding creativity, we can begin to reimagine how creativity might live inside everyday classrooms. Recognizing that creativity is not only attainable for every student but it is also an important way to develop the kinds of skills and strategies students will be able to use throughout their lives allows us to begin to plan how to introduce it into a variety of classroom contexts. The next section details stages that lead to strong creative processes through effective formative assessment.

The Creative Process

While creativity is not prescriptive and can be unpredictable, there are four main stages students move through as they explore creative endeavors while working toward achieving learning goals: (1) exploration, (2) elaboration, (3) expression, and (4) reflection and response. The following subsections (pages 18–19) define and elaborate on each stage. It is important to note up front that while the four stages of the creative process may seem sequential, they are, in fact, flexible. Students may move fluidly back and forth between each, as need dictates. There is no hierarchy, and there is no hard-and-fast rule about how long students should spend in each stage of the process. In fact, it is through the process of assessment that these decisions are made. Assessment reveals degrees of comfort with materials and processes, prior knowledge about the topic or context for the creativity, and learning preferences that may predispose students to certain approaches. Assessment acts as the bridge between one stage and the next. It tells teachers and students when it is time to extend and deepen thinking and focus on new short-term goals. It predicts how much time students might spend in each stage of the creative process.

With regard to timing, it is important to know that creativity can be an extended process that frames an entire unit of study taking several days, or it can move quite quickly, occurring in a single lesson. Students may spend an entire class period generating questions and brainstorming ideas in the exploration stage, or teachers may limit exploration to a five-minute introduction of a single concept that is the focus for one class period. Creativity can occur in many different ways with varying degrees of longevity, scale, and scope. The important thing is to be open to the possibility of inserting the creative stages into daily experiences.

Part of our work in unlocking creativity is exposing our learners to the following four stages in a variety of contexts and inviting them to discover who they are as creative individuals. Some students may find that they need more time in the elaboration stage while others find the expression stage to be the most time consuming. Some learners discover they are able to engage in reflection best when they work with another person, while others prefer to do it alone. Creativity manifests differently for different people, and our students are no exception. We can diligently expose our students to creative processes and ask them to consider which conditions support their creative work and which do not.

Exploration

Exploration is the stage that invites learners into creative processes. This is when students explore materials, questions, and goals and begin to imagine how their creative pursuit might unfold. Elementary students might explore the connection between blocks and LEGO figures, spending time creating stories that involve both. Middle-grades students may choose materials around which to design a lab that answers a critical question. High school students may identify needs within their community that could act as a catalyst for an action plan in physical education. It is at this stage that students first explore goals, derived from standards and learning targets in combination with their own hopes and expectations, as well as criteria that will define their creative decision making.

Elaboration

Elaboration occurs when students settle on a purpose for their creative work. They engage in research and develop the additional skills they might need to expand on their original ideas. This may look like first-grade students exploring butterflies on the internet as part of a science project or middle school students interviewing a community leader to determine important aspects of an advertising campaign. This is the time when learners linger in their questions and refine their goals and criteria for success.

Expression

Expression occurs when students decide how to share their creative work and prepare to do so. This may manifest as a large-scale architecture project that learners in the elementary grades create and share with their peers or a performance that senior students share with the rest of the school, or a small-scale output over a short period of time such as sharing a solution to a mathematics problem with classmates. It is at this point in the creative process that students refine their work and prepare to engage with an audience (big or small), seeking feedback both before and after sharing. At this stage, students may rehearse in front of a smaller group before a larger performance, or they may share a prototype with a critical friend before creating the final, polished version. This stage is about preparation and expression of creative work.

Reflection and Response

Lastly, reflection and response occurs when learners consider their creative efforts and make decisions moving forward. At this stage, they set goals that bridge past creative efforts to future ones. They determine which of their decisions are most successful and which need adjusting. In many cases, this stage is also the final opportunity for students to refine creative products before submitting them for summative assessment. Students focus on celebrating successes and setting goals for future learning.

Figure 1.1 (page 20) illustrates the connection between these four stages and the role that assessment plays in unlocking creativity, connecting and driving creative work from one stage to the next. Also see the reproducible "Applying Assessment Within the Stages of the Creative Process" (pages 45–46) for information on how different types of assessment apply within each stage of the creative process, and guiding questions for assessment work in each stage.

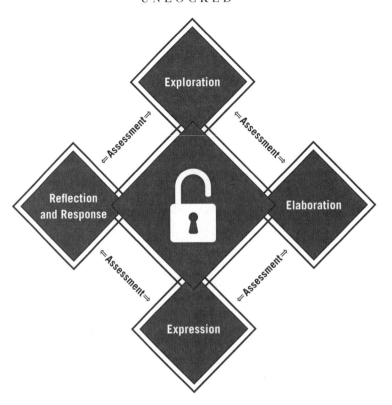

Figure 1.1: *Assessment and the creative process.*

Creativity in a Classroom Context

Reading research about creativity is fascinating. The topic, even in its most general sense, could keep a person exploring for quite some time. Added to that is all the research on creativity in an educational context, which is equally informative. In the interest of providing a succinct and practical book about how to use assessment processes to unlock creativity, I will spend just a little time sharing some of the keys to understanding creativity in a classroom context, acknowledging the immense volume of work that precedes and informs this one, followed by a discussion of embedding opportunities for creativity in the different content-area classrooms.

Big C and Little c Creativity

Understanding *creativity* as I am using the term in this book means understanding the difference between those highly creative, almost magical moments inventors and artists experience during their life's work (what some call *big C creativity*) and those day-to-day creative moments every human being can experience as part of existing in a complex world (*little c creativity*). Sawyer (2006) explains the difference between big C creativity and little c creativity—which we can think of as *everyday creativity*—the kind of creativity we are striving to develop each day in our classrooms:

*In contrast to big C Creativity, [there is] "little c" creativity. Little c creativity
includes activities that people engage in every day: modifying a recipe when
you don't have all the ingredients called for; avoiding a traffic jam by finding
a new way through side streets; figuring out how to apologize to a friend for
an unintended insult. A person's dreams or a child's block tower could be
creative under the second definition, but not under the first. (p. 47)*

This distinction is important to establish in order to understand educators' work
inside schools to develop little c creativity so those learners who are interested, someday, in becoming big C creators in any variety of fields have the foundational skills and
dispositions to be able to do so.

Furthermore, little c creativity, on its own, cultivates practical real-world skills students will need for success in various aspects of life after school. Tony Wagner (2008)
refers to these as *survival skills* that students need as they navigate this complex world.
Among the proposed skills Wagner (2008) identifies (based on several hundred inter-
views with business, nonprofit, and educational leaders) are critical thinking, problem
solving, curiosity, imagination, adaptability, and agility. I would argue patience, resilience, and several others belong on that list as well.

Being able to think critically and solve problems in the workplace is highly valuable
to employers who hunger for self-starters who can think on their feet. Curiosity and
imagination are critical for students as they navigate the adult world, searching for ways
to live productive lives in which they are able to relieve stress, maintain fitness, and
nurture friendships, for example. Patience and adaptability become highly important
as our students build their own family systems, which will inevitably be complex and
taxing at times. Resilience and agility are critical for maintaining balance, for seeking
help when needed, and for navigating the difficult journey of human life. Little c creativity can provide a context through which students can develop and hone these skills
in a safe environment, where mistakes are not yet high stakes.

Components of Creativity

Creative Schools (Robinson & Aronica, 2015) and *The Element* (Robinson, 2009) are
two of the most practical discussions of creativity in schools. These books explore some
of the fundamental reasons why creativity is so essential and why it is so elusive at the
same time. We can build our shared understanding on Robinson and Aronica's (2015)
following definition of creativity, which includes three critical components: (1) original
ideas, (2) ideas that have value, and (3) ideas that spring from our imagination—

*Creativity is the process of having original ideas that have value. There
are two other concepts to keep in mind: imagination and innovation.
Imagination is the root of creativity. It is the ability to bring to mind things
that aren't present in our senses. Creativity is putting your imagination to
work. It is applied imagination. (p. 146)*

It is important to start with the component of *original ideas* because one critical misconception students have about their own creativity is that if their ideas resemble those of others or if they build on ideas shared in a collaborative setting, for example, then they aren't truly creative ideas. In fact, some of the most creative acts spring from the work of others, from stimuli quite outside our minds. Robinson and Aronica (2015) clarify this when they explain, "Creativity is about fresh thinking. It doesn't have to be new to the whole of humanity—though that's always a bonus—but certainly to the person whose work it is" (p. 139). Original ideas don't always mean original to the whole world. *Original* can be very personal. I have observed students arriving at solutions to problems or creating artistic effects that people before them discovered or created, but the idea was original *to them*. These acts were no less creative simply because someone else in the world experienced them, too. These students arrived at their results on their own, in a highly creative manner. Therefore, the idea of *original* is contextual and personal.

Deciding when ideas have *value* is a highly personal decision as well. The creator determines something's value first and foremost, and then others determine its value when the work is shared. However, this determination may not be as straightforward as it sounds. There are times when the value of an idea is obvious to a learner because it fits with a clearly defined goal, need, or desire. Other times, students may question whether an idea has value because of a lack of clarity about the purpose of the idea generation or lack of self-confidence, or because they may not be used to acknowledging their own strengths. In these cases, instead of stepping in to assert the value of an idea, we might instead refer students back to their goals, materials, or criteria. Helping students make decisions about the value of their own ideas is part of our role as teachers and is a teachable skill in and of itself. The critical factor in determining whether something holds value is whether it meets a desired outcome or need. Robinson and Aronica (2015) clarify the personal nature of assigning value when they say, "It's also about judging critically whether the work in process is taking the right shape and is worthwhile, at least for the person producing it" (p. 147). As a result, students have to assess their creative acts in order to determine their value, which brings us right back to the integrated nature of creativity and assessment.

The last component of Robinson and Aronica's (2015) definition that needs consideration is their assertion that during creative processes, ideas have to spring from our *imaginations*. Educator and artist Robert Kelly (2012) agrees with this need when he explains:

> *Creativity involves bringing ideas or thoughts into forms, ultimately making something out of ideas that can be shared in the currency or medium of the discipline or field where the creative practice is occurring. This involves imagination. Imagination is the breeding ground for ideas that fuel creative practice. (p. 6)*

This means students will have to visualize and dream, wonder and think while engaging in learning experiences. They will need to have strong catalysts to encourage this imagination and receive time to spend in this state, thinking about possibilities instead of certainties. In a classroom setting, the need to nurture imagination and the conditions required for doing so may feel like quite a shift.

As we work toward creative classrooms that invite imagination and original thought, it is helpful for identifying everyday creativity to open up our understanding of how these components manifest in a variety of contexts. Creative acts can fall into three categories, according to Kelly (2012): (1) inventive, (2) innovative, and (3) interpretive. First, there are creative practices that are *inventive* in nature, involving the creation of original work across disciplines. This may mean creating works of art, narrative texts, experiments, block towers, or construction projects, for example. Next, there are creative practices that are *innovative* in nature, which means students may grapple with redesigning or modifying an existing form, product, or system. One might find this creativity in health classes when students gather information and construct an informative publication to assist families in seeking health supports in the community. We may also see this creative practice in an early year's physical education class when students create their own games while exploring the concept of strategic play. Lastly, there are creative acts that are *interpretive* in nature. This may occur when students engage in redesigning, modifying, evolving, or interpreting existing ideas. We may see this type of creativity in mathematics classrooms as students create complex, multistep problems and performance tasks based on skills they have already explored. We may also develop it in a science class when students create their own classification system for a set of organisms or in an accounting or business setting, when students develop a business plan, given a set of requirements and variables. When we unlock the ways students can explore creativity by expanding our conceptualization of what is creative, we open up the times and places for us to develop it in a variety of subject areas.

Creative Feelings

Another critical aspect of understanding creativity is considering how it *feels* to be creative, to be truly engaged in the creative experience. When describing the optimal state of creative expression, we could refer to this state as *flow*. Psychologist Mihaly Csikszentmihalyi coined this term in 1975 and describes the state of flow as follows:

> *Flow is a subjective state that people report when they are completely involved in something to the point of forgetting time, fatigue, and everything else but the activity itself. It is what we feel when we read a well-crafted novel or play a good game of squash, or take part in a stimulating conversation. The defining feature of flow is intense experiential involvement in moment-to-moment activity. Attention is fully invested in the task at hand, and the person*

functions at his or her fullest capacity. (Csikszentmihalyi, Abuhamdeh, &
Nakamura, 2005, p. 600)

Flow connects to creativity in classrooms because when students are fully immersed in creative pursuits, their investment is tangible—they groan when the recess bell rings; they continue to glue, tape, and fold even after being asked to place their creations on the back counter; they rush from friend to friend, excitedly explaining how they are making decisions. This bodes well for all kinds of deep learning. Erkens et al. (2017) explain the importance of the kind of student investment in a flow state: "When people invest in something, they typically devote resources (time, talent, energy, and so on); persist through challenging problems that arise; seek help when needed; and develop confidence in what they are doing, learning, or investing in" (p. 113). The flow state invites authentic self-assessment and peer assessment and serves as a natural platform for seeking and giving feedback at times that matter to our students. They quite naturally move through creative processes, trying out ideas, seeking others' advice, and reflecting on successes and challenges. In the state of flow, creativity, investment, and formative assessment are almost inseparable.

The line between process and product blends during creative flow. Students seek processes that get them to the products they are trying to create. Assessment and feedback from both teachers and their peers lead them in new directions or reinforce the choices they are making. The road of creativity is never straight. As Sawyer (2006) explains, "Creativity occurs while we're doing a task, and as we're performing the task we have to improvise through it, responding movement by movement to the changing needs of the situation. Everyday creativity is improvisational" (p. 445). Students imagine products, and we work alongside them to discover the processes that will get them to those products in meaningful and enriching ways.

Creative Qualities

When a process is not yet successful in approaching the goal, students refine and adjust; they revise and revisit. In the end, we help them decide when to stop and begin a new task. Anyone who creates something knows that the creative process could go on infinitely. Often, bringing closure to a creative effort means accepting that the process has run its course for the time being.

Regardless of whether we are working to enhance creativity through our attention to processes within our classroom or striving to provide catalysts to creativity through unique products, we are primarily working to develop or enhance specific personal qualities that are closely associated with creative people, which include the following (Dacey & Conklin, 2004; Renzulli, 2000; Sawyer, 2006; Wagner, 2012). (For a more in-depth list of the qualities of people in tune with their creativity process, please refer to table A.1 on pages 201–202 in appendix A.)

◇ Curious   ◇ Flexible

◇ Integrative thinker   ◇ Fluent

◇ Persistent   ◇ Divergent thinker

◇ Collaborative   ◇ Convergent thinker

◇ Imaginative   ◇ Courageous

◇ Critical thinker   ◇ Reflective

◇ Risk taker   ◇ Intuitive

◇ Tolerant   ◇ Observant

Developing these qualities is part of the most important work we (as teachers) do with our students because it influences who they become as learners and creators in the long term. Being aware of these qualities allows us to support students' whole development as they grow and learn.

Through creative processes in our classrooms, we can build curious, imaginative learners. Very young students, such as those in preK through fourth grade, often enter our schools filled with wonder and possibility. Through creativity, we can sustain those qualities. By providing time for students to ask their own questions and imagine their own products, stories, and solutions, we communicate the importance of these qualities in a variety of learning contexts.

Creativity also provides the perfect fertilizer to grow the qualities of risk taking, critical thinking, and persistence. When elementary-grades students work with unfamiliar materials or create their first stories in writing, we can take the opportunity to invite them to try things in new ways, seek new ideas, and persist through immediate challenges. As students advance through the grades, we can continue to invite them to solve problems in unique ways and try different approaches on for size. By withholding summative assessment in favor of formative assessment in the early stages of the creative process, we explicitly show students that the creative journey is equally as important as a right answer. We give students time to persist through wrong answers and solutions that do not yield desired results. We allow them time to fix mistakes and try new approaches when necessary.

By structuring conditions in which students can develop and use these qualities, we are supporting the move toward an increasingly creative classroom. When we understand the qualities that underlie creative processes, we can explicitly encourage students to strengthen them in their everyday experiences. We can share these qualities with students, assess their development, and celebrate them when they are visible.

Instruction and Assessment Processes

It is important that we have clarity about *when* it makes sense to insert the opportunity to develop these qualities and the creativity they support into our learning plans. Sometimes the creativity will lie in the *products and performances* that students create, and sometimes the creativity will rest in the *processes* we use to get to very specific products. We may look to our learning goals (standards, outcomes) to guide this decision.

When a goal asks students to focus on developing a specific product (informational writing, a map, a short narrative paragraph, a formula, an accounting spreadsheet, a dramatic play), then allowing students to determine the form their product will take and determine their own success criteria may not be an option. In these cases, we may choose, instead, to use creative processes to get to that single end product. We may invite students to explore how to best work through the writing process and design a plan that is personally relevant. Or we may allow students to engage in research in ways that encourage personal decision making, source curation, and data collection. We may ask them to imagine a plan for rehearsal that will give them the best results possible. By employing creative decision making within the process of learning, even when the product is non-negotiable, our students have a strong hand in creating the learning design and, as a result, practicing many skills they need to become creative individuals.

Other learning goals may require students to engage in very specific processes (collaborative thinking, data analysis, lab safety, ball throwing). In cases like these, predetermined criteria guide and develop the process, and the creative potential lies in the product. Students may create their own games in which to practice throwing a ball. Or they may be able to engage in data analysis as part of a creative service project. They may employ lab safety in experiments of their own design, or collaborate as part of creating a mural with classmates. The opportunity for lesson design that unlocks creativity is immense, even when certain aspects of our teaching and learning seem non-negotiable.

We can always plan learning experiences that allow students to practice developing qualities of creative people. We may specifically encourage curiosity by introducing unusual or unfamiliar objects to elementary students in a science or a social studies class and ask them to generate questions based on what they see (or smell, or hear). Or we may show students in middle or high school ambiguous images and have them engage in a quick write (writing for two to ten minutes without stopping, editing, or planning ahead) based on all the things they wonder about what they see. If we were trying to nurture risk taking, we may invite students to work in teams to solve unfamiliar mathematics problems, promising only feedback and discussion (no grades) as a result of their efforts. Or we might invite students to engage in new cardiovascular fitness activities, even though they may not feel completely comfortable with them, and then praise them for trying something new, followed by a reflection on the results in order to improve their performance. Fostering creativity means attending to not only *what* students do but also *how* they do it in our classrooms. Understanding the qualities of creativity supports our work toward developing these qualities in our learners.

Creativity Across Contexts

For the sake of practicality, teachers may find it helpful to explore the nature of creativity within various content areas. Teachers can develop creativity in every subject area at every grade level—they just have to imagine new ways for learning to emerge. Table 1.1 explores ways to develop creativity within and across content areas.

Table 1.1: *Accessing Creativity in Various Content Areas*

Content Area	Ways Teachers Can Develop Student Creativity
English Language Arts	• Allow students voice and choice in their work. • Use leading questions to help students identify the purpose for and meaning within their work. • Have students revise and review their work to enhance, elaborate, refine, and focus. • Combine ideas across texts. • Let students use varied modalities to enhance their message (for example, images, video, digital tools, sound effects, maps, voice-overs). • Invite students to respond to texts in ways that matter to them (for example, choose a song to go with the text, write a letter to a friend, design a commercial).
Mathematics	• Engage learners in open-ended, interdisciplinary, and real-world processes. • Create problems where the steps are not formulaic and the solutions are not predetermined; reinforce original and flexible approaches. • Provide open-ended materials and loose parts (for example, materials like buttons, beads, nuts and bolts). • Connect mathematics to real-life applications. • Invite students to create problems. • Provide mathematics artifacts and invite students to form questions. • Engage in complex *mathematics talks* (exchanges of mathematical ideas and problem-solving strategies).
Science	• Engage in experimentation. • Seek connections. • Invite students into real-life problems and challenges. • Generate questions and identify potential errors. • Allow students to choose materials, methods for sharing research, and audiences for their work.

continued ⇒

Content Area	Ways Teachers Can Develop Student Creativity
Social Studies or History	• Challenge students to propose solutions to world challenges. • Prompt students to imagine social or political structures under a variety of conditions or variables. • Design tools or resources to enhance a need (for example, build a tool to drain a playground puddle or create a resource to support students new to the school). • Have students relate personal identity with social realities. • Connect the present to the past. • Allow students to engage in a variety of artifacts (for example, maps, data) and invite questions.
Health Education	• Ask students to craft supports and plans to address health-related challenges. • Have students examine relationships (between factors, structures, organizations, and emotions). • Explore issues from individual and societal perspectives. • Challenge students to propose impacts, solutions, and future concerns.
Physical Education	• Encourage students to design new activities, games, or events. • Have students craft a plan to achieve a desired outcome. • Ask students to propose solutions to fitness-related challenges. • Challenge students to invent and organize drills and activities that enhance performance and precision.
Arts Education	• Encourage students to express a unique vision or message through artwork. • Challenge students to improvise and elaborate. • Have students combine elements (notes, tone, line, shape, movement, voice) in personally meaningful ways (a score, a play, a painting, an installation, a dance). • Ask students to select or curate components and items. • Allow students to engage in a performance as a performer or a viewer.
Practical and Applied Arts	• Have students use practical skills to imagine new products, new applications, and new designs. • Ask students to apply resources (ingredients, materials) in new and unique ways. • Encourage students to curate and make decisions; consider many variables when designing.
Foreign Languages	• Ask students to imagine multiple ways to communicate meaning. • Instruct students to craft personal messages. • Guide students in synthesizing isolated information to generate new meaning. • Synthesize a variety of strategies to comprehend meaning.

Business and Career Education	• Challenge students to build on the ideas of existing businesses. • Have students identify societal needs for development of products. • Ask students to collaborate in teams to design business plans. • Prompt students to imagine a variety of career options and the requirements for them. • Encourage students to invent new careers.

Source: Sawyer, 2006; Smutny & von Fremd, 2009.

For more in-depth examples of how students might practice creativity in mathematics and English language arts, see figure B.1 (pages 204–208) and figure B.2 (pages 208–212) in appendix B.

Threats to Creativity

In order to develop this kind of organic creativity in our classrooms, teachers need to be aware of those factors that may reduce or even inhibit its development. Table 1.2 captures some of these potential threats to creativity.

Table 1.2: *Detailing Threats to Creativity*

Threat	Explanation
Right Answers	When the goal is arriving at the correct solution, product, or understanding, the divergent thinking required during creative processes is limited. There is a time for right answers but not when creativity is the goal.
Teacher Control	When teachers control the brainstorming, drafting, or revision stages, it stops learner creativity in its tracks. Help-seeking behavior is critical for the teacher-student relationship during times of creativity, but control over the creative process must rest with the learner. Hovering can also inhibit freedom to explore because students may feel overly monitored.
Lack of Purpose	When our efforts hold meaning, our motivation and investment are authentic and personal. Tasks that hold little purpose or relevance for students make creative work within those tasks a tremendous challenge for even the most compliant student.
High Stakes	When learners believe their teacher will judge or value (including grade) processes and products too early and without time for revision, risk taking and creative approaches might disappear, and the quest for compliance may take over. Premature grading and a focus on competition or comparison can threaten the creative process.
External Rewards	Studies demonstrate the devastating effect of external rewards on creative outcomes (Amabile, 1996; Torrance, 1965). The desirable state of flow depends on intrinsic motivation. Even praise can shift the learning away from exploration, toward the search for even more praise.

continued ⇒

Threat	Explanation
Negative Self-Talk	Student and teacher beliefs about their creative abilities can determine whether students develop creative qualities. Negative self-talk and a belief that only a few possess creativity reflect a *fixed mindset* (the assumption that abilities are static and cannot be changed in any meaningful way; Dweck, 2006) that yields little creative output. This kind of thinking can also lead to learned helplessness in students, which is not productive.
Limited Understanding or Skill	Creativity emerges from skill and understanding. In order to manipulate, imagine, and create, students must first have understanding and skill with which to do so. It is very difficult for students to be creative when they know too little about the realm in which they are working.
Tight Timelines	To engage fully in creative processes, students need time to generate ideas, experiment, ask questions, set goals, reflect, revise, and assess their progress. Short timelines can limit both creativity and assessment and can result in products that are less than satisfactory to the learners.
Overstimulating Environments	Creative people often need a balance between time to engage with others and seek stimulation and time to reflect. An environment that is overstimulating can overwhelm students and reduce the productivity during stages of the creative process.
Silence	If creativity is going to flourish, there needs to be conferring, discussion, debate, research, sharing, and collaboration. All these activities require two-way communication, which will result in an environment that strays from silence.
Prescriptive Steps	Formulaic steps can certainly lead to consistency, and when products and processes that yield similar results each time are the goal, formulae work. However, true creativity is much messier than this. The organic nature of creativity lends itself to students leading the way more often than not, with each student engaging in a slightly different journey. Therefore, student choice is intimately tied to creativity.

It is important to acknowledge that learning is complex, and the various ways learners engage in the experiences we design for them are multifaceted. This book does not assert that students need to engage in creative pursuits all the time, every day in our classrooms. Indeed, there are times when listening to others is critical. There are moments when exploring patterns and algorithms is highly advisable. There are times when direct instruction is the most effective way to explain concepts and skills and guided practice is the most efficient way to build confidence. Creativity is a highly desirable and important aspect of human learning, but it is not the only one. Therefore, there are times when the threats in table 1.2 emerge as the most effective approaches in certain contexts. However, when creative processes are always on the back burner in favor of more expedient approaches, then the scales have tipped too far in the other direction. Teaching is about finding a balance and developing a vast skill set that readies learners for the life in front of them.

It is also important to note that embedded *within* the creative process, there will be moments of direct instruction. If a student is struggling to organize his or her thinking, the teacher may need to offer directed guidance. Similarly, when a student is preparing to express his or her creativity, a teacher may offer a systematic guide for effective speaking. Creativity in classrooms is not without teacher intervention and support. There are times when the most direct route to the solution to a smaller problem can open up creative growth in other areas. We do not have to choose between creativity and instruction. Both live in partnership within the creative process. Paul A. Kirschner, John Sweller, and Richard E. Clark (2006) assert the importance of teacher guidance during creative learning: "In so far as there is any evidence from controlled studies, it almost uniformly supports direct, strong instructional guidance . . . during the instruction of novice to intermediate learners" (p. 83). Understanding the important role of the teacher in creative work is critical. The interplay between student decision making and exploration and assessment to guide targeted instruction and support is vital for ensuring that students gain the maximum benefits of creative work.

Assessment Processes That Unlock Creativity

When we imagine new ways of designing our assessment and instruction to support creativity, it is not so much about throwing everything out and starting again. We aren't going to stop using summative assessment, nor are we going to suddenly change every aspect of our learning environment. Like much of the growing we do in our lives, the shift is more about looking at existing practices in new ways. It is using the skills and processes we already possess, but using them differently. Accomplishing this change might involve exploring our existing practices with a different lens. In creative classrooms, teachers still preassess to determine students' needs and strengths. They invite goal setting and reflection from the learners in the room. They continue to utilize formative assessment to guide instruction and support feedback and self-assessment processes. And they still make time to verify learning through summative assessment. These types of assessment processes are critical in any kind of learning environment because they support long-term learning. However, how they unfold or manifest may be a little different from what we usually practice, especially with regard to teachers' and students' roles in the assessment process. This book will focus on three of these assessment practices, which constitute the heart of assessment to support creativity: (1) formative assessment (information gathering), (2) feedback (dialogue with others), and (3) self-assessment (dialogue with self). See the reproducible "Applying Assessment Within the Stages of the Creative Process" (pages 45–46) for information on how these types of assessment apply within each stage of the creative process, and guiding questions

for assessment work in each stage. The following sections will explore the shift in classroom roles as we use assessment to promote creativity; note the ways in which teachers
may apply formative assessment, provide feedback, and facilitate self-assessment; and
examine the need for explicit instruction for supporting feedback and self-assessment
among students.

Assessment Roles for Teachers and Students

In classrooms where teachers work to develop creativity, assessment processes most
often rest in the hands of learners, as opposed to remaining solely the responsibility
of teachers. Teachers still play a part, of course, but their role shifts to facilitator and
co-constructor as opposed to director and owner. Readers may wonder if elementary-
age students are capable of assessing. It has been my experience that even students in
the earliest schooling years are indeed able to assess and apply impressive insights as
they reflect on their and their classmates' work.

Teachers may choose the direction of the creative process based on learning goals,
but they shift decision making to the students at critical times. The majority of this
process involves teachers observing and engaging in conversations, collecting formative
assessment information, and responding through feedback, conferring, and guiding
students' self- and peer assessment, goal setting, and questioning processes.

When teachers use summative assessment, they have likely witnessed student problem solving, brainstorming, questioning, and experimenting after a highly organic
learning process. In many ways, these teachers are *more* equipped to reflect on the
learning of students because the creative processes that led to the products and artifacts
they are examining are so rich. Creative processes build deep relationships between
learners and the teacher guiding and supporting them. Furthermore, teachers who
work to develop student creativity get even more insight into learners' progress on
learning goals because they bear witness to students forming learning relationships
with themselves. As students increase the control they have over their learning contexts,
previously unseen qualities may become evident. For example, we may see students
relish the opportunity to ask their own questions. We may see them hesitate as they
wonder how to approach a challenge. We might witness their frustration and then
pride as problems emerge and they overcome them, and observe them taking risks and
collaborating with others. Students may also document many of these processes in
creative portfolios. This kind of learning and the documentation that can accompany
it nurtures a deep knowledge of our learners, so when the time comes to verify learning
goals, teachers can make a professional judgment with confidence. With these criteria
in front of them and the knowledge of their learners in hand, educators can engage in
summative assessment that truly reflects the learning they want to see from students.

Formative Assessment (Information Gathering)

While summative assessment is a critical aspect of our work as teaching professionals, formative assessment is truly the bread and butter of developing creativity. During the creative process, formative assessment serves to propel the growth and development of ideas. At every stage of the creative process, from exploration to elaboration and expression, formative assessment serves as the basis for decision making and refinement because it connects what is happening in the moment to a desired future state.

During the creative process, formative assessment will occur in a variety of ways. Teachers may choose to use more traditional assessment methods like quizzes and student practice work to determine student needs. Alternately, they may choose to use organic methods, like observation or questioning, to collect assessment information. The power of formative assessment rests in the quality of information gathered and the alignment to goals and success criteria. The use of portfolios can support decision making by both teachers and students by making the various iterations of creative thinking visible. A purposeful collection of artifacts that represent the various creative stages can support reflection at all stages and, most significantly, in the final stage of reflection and response.

Both students and teachers craft goals and engage in exploration that serves the key questions guiding the learning. Through embedded reflection, self-assessment, and engagement with criteria for success, students journey through the creative process in personally meaningful ways. Feedback sessions, during which students and teachers analyze efforts in relation to goals, ensure that students feel their efforts are heading in a desired direction. Indeed, without this continuous formative assessment built into the creative classroom, imagination would suffer, risk taking would lack purpose, and products students produce would be meaningless. Formative assessment is the oil in the creative engine, and it is a primary way we can ensure that students develop the ability to sit in the driver's seat. Administrator, teacher, and author Myron Dueck (2014) explains further, "Learning is greatly enhanced through individual creativity, ownership, and empowerment. When learners are given the opportunity to explain and reason using their own creative skills, they are better able to demonstrate evidence of learning" (p. 121). The importance of student engagement in the formative assessment process and the creativity it supports cannot be overstated.

Formative assessment is critical for the growth of creativity, and teachers will certainly play a pivotal role in gathering formative data and making sure students progress in the development of essential skills and understanding. Perhaps a quick exit ticket at the end of class might let us know which students are effectively moving toward intended outcomes and which have hit a roadblock. There may come a time during creative learning when we educators give a quiz to determine whether our learners are developing a critical understanding necessary for deepening their creative efforts.

Perhaps a teacher spends time observing students so she can follow up with a targeted conversation that both identifies a student need and provides the instruction required to address the need. Formative assessment is one way to ensure students' creative efforts yield the intended learning. See the reproducible "Applying Assessment Within the Stages of the Creative Process" (pages 45–46) for information on how formative assessment and other types of assessment apply within each stage of the creative process. Important by-products of formative assessment during the creative process are the feedback relationships we establish with our students and the relationships learners develop with themselves through self-assessment. The processes of feedback and self-assessment that emerge from formative assessment are critical to creativity, and we want to be sure we utilize them to maximum impact.

Feedback (Dialogue With Others)

Effective feedback translates formative assessment information into a dialogue for growth and learning. Feedback within a creative experience often emerges organically from a mutual quest to solve a problem or express an idea. In a classroom, the learner is striving to make sense of something personally meaningful, and the teacher or a peer may act as a mirror, reflecting experiences back to the learner to help the learner truly see what is in front of him or her. This is important in a creative endeavor because at times creativity can feel all-consuming and the creator may hunger for a way to step back from his or her efforts for a while and see them with fresh eyes. Therefore, effective feedback should include describing what is happening, noticing processes and decisions before making a judgment about their effectiveness. Feedback slows down creativity just a little, so students can explore things from various viewpoints, allowing powerful conversations between a creator and a trusted friend or advisor. A conferring session with a teacher or a conversation with a peer can be the very thing students need to move into the next stage of creative thinking.

Feedback may also emerge from a shared exploration of criteria for success. A learner might ask, "Does what I am creating accomplish my desired outcomes? Am I sharing my ideas in a way that makes sense? Have I overlooked some aspect of the problem I am trying to solve?" In this way, feedback may sound a great deal like a conversation, where both parties are alternating between asking questions and expressing ideas. (For more information on assessment through conversation, see chapters 3 and 4, pages 67 and 103.) The key is to return consistently to the goals that drive the creative process. Feedback conversations are a chance to remind students of what they were setting out to do and to review their criteria for success. *How will you know when your efforts have been successful? What will a quality result look like and sound like to you? How will you know when you are finished?* Questions like these allow students to take stock of where they are in this moment and plan next steps.

Feedback can exist in service of a current creative effort and serve future creative efforts. Teachers might ask a question that invites students to think about their creative processes, instead of saying to learners, "Here is how I suggest you fix this [current, specific challenge]." Potential questions to ask include, "Why did you make this choice? How did you decide? What was effective or ineffective in your approach? How might you approach this differently next time?" Questions like these invite students to focus not only on their current efforts but also on their strategic approaches to creative work. Open-ended questions ensure the decision making rests with the learner, and they are a way for teachers (and peers) to develop processes that lead to refined results on future creative efforts. See the reproducible "Applying Assessment Within the Stages of the Creative Process" (pages 45–46) for information on how feedback and other forms of assessment apply within each stage of the creative process.

Self-Assessment (Dialogue With Self)

Focusing on self-assessment to drive both personal reflection and feedback is one way we can be sure creativity stays in our students' hands. Withholding feedback until our students have done some personal reflection can inform what we say and how we respond to their needs. For example, we can then structure our feedback around the student's reflection if a student examines her work and says, "I like what I have done on this half but the last half still doesn't say what I want it to say." We may follow up with, "What do you think needs to be in your second half in order for it to have the impact you are hoping for?" Alternatively, we may ask, "Why do you think you were able to get the results you hoped for in your first half? How did you approach it? Was your approach different from the one you used later?" These kinds of questions lead students back to their goals and the criteria they use to define those goals. We are simply helping them solve their own problems. We can give suggestions (resources and strategies), but students remain in control of the creative endeavor.

In this way, self-assessment is not about assigning the product a value. Nor is it about sitting with a checklist in hand, sorting the list into *present in my work* or *absent from my work*. Self-assessment is about reflecting on the degree to which students are solving their own problems and answering their own questions creatively. It is about taking personal responsibility for their outcomes, and connecting their thinking, planning, and exploration to their goals. Self-assessment is about making decisions and taking action, and without it, the students' efforts and the ensuing results will be less creative and, likely, less satisfactory to the students themselves. See the reproducible "Applying Assessment Within the Stages of the Creative Process" (pages 45–46) for information on how self-assessment and other types of assessment apply within each stage of the creative process.

Explicit Instruction for Developing Feedback and Self-Assessment

In order for students to be strong self-assessors and engage in effective feedback processes, they will need us to teach them how to engage in these processes. John A. Ross (2006) echoes this need: "There is persuasive evidence, across several grades and subjects, that self-assessment contributes to student learning and that the effects grow larger with direct instruction on self-assessment procedures" (p. 9). Self-assessment and feedback do not come naturally to many learners. Without explicit teaching, these assessment processes can end up with students who focus on stagnant practices of looking to the teacher to identify their mistakes and tell them how to correct those mistakes to get a higher grade. Students need to develop trust in the true benefits of these practices, and they need explicit instruction about how self-assessment and feedback should look and sound while they are in the midst of innovating, imagining, and creating. Table 1.3 and table 1.4 (pages 38–39) offer critical components of feedback and self-assessment, respectively, and explore examples for ways to approach feedback and self-assessment during a creative endeavor.

Table 1.3: *Identifying Components of Feedback Within the Classroom*

Critical Components of Feedback	Teacher Implementation and Examples in the Classroom
Schedule regular time for feedback and response.	• Assign a day of the week or a specific time during the creative process as *feedback day*, when students will engage in feedback and have time to respond. • Teach and invite feedback in many ways: teacher-student feedback, peer feedback, digital feedback, expert feedback, oral feedback, written feedback. • Make sure feedback sessions occur while work is in progress, so students aren't in too deep.
Ask questions whenever possible instead of giving answers.	• Ask questions like, "How do you feel about your work today? What do you feel still needs attention?" • Invite students to pose their own questions about their work, such as, "What am I still curious about? What questions come to mind as I look at my work?" • Teach students to ask each other questions during the creative process, such as, "How are you getting started?" and "What might you try next time?" Use scripts to help students see how feedback conversations flow.

Pair feedback with goals and criteria.	• Ensure that goals and criteria are readily available (in a journal or on the wall, for example). • Explicitly ask, "Which criteria do you feel you accomplished? Which do you feel might need more attention? How do you know?" • Have students explicitly connect criteria to their product, performance, or service. Text markups, text boxes, or reflection sheets can facilitate this.
Be cautious with praise.	• Ask questions about creative efforts, such as, "What did you do to arrive at this answer (or product)?" Resist statements of value or worth (for example, "This is great!"). • Invite students to tell you more about their decisions. • Invite students to identify their own strengths. Draw their attention to their criteria and goals.
Work from strengths.	• Use strengths to help determine where the work will begin. • Use strengths to identify skills and knowledge that will support future challenges. • List students' strengths on a *Need Help?* list. Invite students to access each other for support.
Help students identify both what and how.	• After leaving a feedback-based interaction, ensure students have a clear understanding of not only what they are going to focus on but also how they might do so. • Invite students to examine approaches that others take. • Provide students a menu of possible strategies they might use next. • Encourage learners to experiment with new ways to think strategically (for example, concretely or symbolically).
Consider readiness and preference.	• When students are struggling, give feedback that is immediate, limited, and specific or guided. • When students are deeply immersed in their creative process, delay the feedback or make it more open ended. • Seek student feedback about the option that works best for them (for example, face-to-face or digital).
Encourage curiosity and experimentation.	• Post questions in a public place to honor them. • Provide a menu of options for learners. • Have students track their approaches and assess the degree of success or challenge.

Table 1.4: *Identifying Components of Self-Assessment Within the Classroom*

Critical Components of Self-Assessment	Teacher Implementation and Examples in the Classroom
Develop the subskills of self-assessment (White, 2017).	• Give students the opportunity to practice some of the individual skills that support the complex skill of self-assessment. These subskills include noticing, remembering, and describing; relating, comparing, analyzing, and connecting; predicting, visualizing, and imagining; empathizing and forgiving; decision making and self-regulating; and organizing, revising, and revisiting. • Offer prompts that address these subskills.
Ensure a strong purpose.	• Make sure students are clear about the purpose for engaging in creative processes and the purpose for engaging in self-assessment. • Make the purpose visible by clarifying essential questions, a defined audience, and a tangible outcome (product, performance, or service).
Set both short-term and longer-term goals.	• Invite students to set goals that relate to the very next action they will take (short-term goals). • Celebrate and acknowledge the accomplishment of short-term goals at regular intervals. • Invite students to set longer-term or "end" goals that articulate the final destination (broader, larger goals that define success in a more holistic sense). • Make sure students understand the role of both short-term and long-term goals.
Ensure a strong cognitive foundation (Hattie, 2009).	• Help students identify what they don't know and what skills they are lacking that may be preventing next steps. • Work with students to build the cognitive foundation they need to be successful in their chosen creative pursuits. • Utilize small-group instruction and whole-group minilessons to target needs.
Create a safe environment.	• Keep the stakes low for as long as possible (for example, no summative assessment in the early part of the process). • Ensure student-led goal setting determines the focus of the work.
Embed within the learning.	• Ensure self-assessment happens during the creative process. • Structure time for students to consider, continuously, how what they are doing is connecting to their goals and criteria for success.

Reflect on both products and processes.	• Ask students to examine the products they are creating (paintings, stories, solutions, informational texts, experiments, and so on) and the processes (brainstorming, question generation, trial and error, concept mapping, and so on) that are leading them to these products. • Provide time for students to reflect on what they need to do in order to foster the conditions necessary to maximize their creativity.
Document learning as it is happening as a catalyst for self-assessment.	• Find ways to capture learning *as it is happening* (for example, photographs, video, and anecdotal comments). • Slow down decision making long enough to reflect on the options. • Invite students to stop and notice their status. Have them pair up and describe exactly where they are in the creative process before moving forward.
Make time to respond to decisions students make.	• Give learners the opportunity to learn from their decisions, good or bad. • Provide time for students to respond to self-assessment. Set aside time each day to reflect and design a response (five to ten minutes of focused reflection may be enough).
Use self-assessment to connect the present task to the next one.	• Ban the phrase "I'm done"—it reduces the connection making that is so important to deep learning. • Explicitly connect ongoing processes to future ones to help students see that all learning connects. Use journals, documentation, and discussion to fuel connection making. • Use reflection to fuel goal and criteria setting on the next task.

Myths and Misconceptions About Assessment

After all these years immersed in both assessment and creativity, I still have moments of panic. I worry that if I let students (or teachers, in the case of adult learning) direct the learning experiences too much, I won't be able to make sure they have the understanding and skills that the learning goals prescribe. I move back and forth between knowing that creativity is essential for deep learning and meaningful expression, and believing that I need to "get done" what I think I am supposed to do every day. I think this is a normal internal conversation for many teachers, and I think it originates in a desire to be the best teacher we can be, no matter the context. We want to do what is right, but sometimes we aren't sure what that means.

Addressing some misconceptions or myths that surround assessment and the learning it serves can help us respond to our internal dialogue. Following are seven pervasive myths and misconceptions teachers should be aware of. Addressing these items can assist teachers in responding to their internal dialogue and settling conflicting feelings about the assessment work they are doing.

1. **Teachers should own all assessment:** While teachers are certainly responsible for owning the verification of proficiency in order to report to stakeholders (summative assessment), they certainly do not need to own all aspects of assessment. In fact, sharing this ownership with the learners is incredibly empowering for everyone involved in the learning context. Kathleen Gregory, Caren Cameron, and Anne Davies (2011) confirm—

   > *Providing time for students to pause and think, to look for proof and connect to criteria allows teachers to slow down the pace of their teaching to match the speed of student learning. Students have to think about and consolidate their learning. (p. 21)*

   Teachers can share responsibility for decision making with students and students can develop the independence and autonomy critical for lifelong learning.

2. **Assessment is one-dimensional:** When we view assessment as an object instead of as a multidimensional process, we limit its capacity to unlock creativity. Assessment is not simply about generating a grade in a gradebook or on a report card. In fact, prioritizing grades stifles creativity. Pink (2009) shares this viewpoint when he says, "In environments where extrinsic rewards are most salient, many people work only to the point that triggers the reward—and not further" (p. 56). In order to avoid this outcome, it may be helpful to think of assessment as a process through which we set goals, explore criteria, take actions, give feedback, ask questions, and craft products. When we open up what assessment is and what it can accomplish, we unlock its potential to support creativity in our classrooms.

3. **Assessment happens after learning:** To build on the second myth, when we open up our understanding of the potential of assessment to unlock creativity, we can begin to imagine how it might live inside the learning journey instead of outside it. Dylan Wiliam (2018) explains, "The regular use of minute-by-minute and day-by-day classroom formative assessment can substantially improve student achievement" (p. 56). He goes on to say, "We cannot predict what students will learn as the result of any particular sequence of instruction" (p. 56). Accepting this reality necessitates the use of assessment throughout the creative learning process. Assessment can happen before learning begins, through a preassessment. We may check ahead of time to see how comfortable students are with generating questions, taking risks, and using the tools necessary for their creative process. Perhaps we engage in assessment following the first attempt learners make at creating a product that expresses their ideas, so the students can seek feedback and decide where revisions and refinement may need to occur. Assessment supports all stages of creativity.

4. **Assessment should only measure written products:** Requiring students to put their thoughts to paper makes sense. It is a great way to document thinking so future actions can be taken. However, teachers don't have to limit assessment evidence to written form, and it does not have to be product based. Davies (2011) reminds us, "When evidence is collected from three different sources [observation, conversation, and products] over time, trends and patterns become apparent, and the reliability and validity of our classroom assessment is increased" (p. 46). In order to support students as they engage in creative thinking during exploration and elaboration and product generation during expression, we may need to assess their processes. For example, we may want to watch them as they generate questions, to see which learners are struggling to connect with the topic. Alternatively, we may assess students' current strengths in using technology or other tools that will support their exploration. We may want to check in on their collaborative processes and their ability to give and receive feedback. This type of assessment might happen through video or audio capture, through journaling, or through anecdotal observations, for example. However, assessment processes like these are as important as any other because they help us make decisions about how to challenge students just enough and how to support them when necessary. These types of assessment processes ensure that we are capturing accurate indicators of learning for every student. Some tasks do not lend themselves to written products and some learners struggle to communicate in written form, despite proficiency in other critical areas. For this reason, using a variety of assessment processes to document and reflect on creative learning is important.

5. **Assessment is objective, and creativity is subjective:** There is a belief that assessment cannot be objective unless students are providing us with answers that are either right or wrong. People may be uncomfortable with assessing creative processes or products because they believe creativity is subjective. They may question whether they have the right to offer an opinion about another person's creative efforts, when those efforts are so personal. Certainly, creativity holds deep meaning for the person who is creating. Furthermore, beauty can, indeed, be in the eye of the beholder. That said, the kind of creativity this book advocates is not about beauty nor is it about opinion. Rather, it is about problem solving, imaging, predicting, experimenting, and inventing; and students can develop their ability to engage in these processes through attention to specific criteria that lead to successful action. Drapeau (2014) explains the connection between assessment and reflecting on the processes that drive creativity—

Assessment is needed to promote students' metacognition, or thinking about thinking. When students are able to tell us what strategy they used to help them think of many different ideas, or why they chose the solution they did, they are using metacognition. (pp. 143–144)

Assessing during creative processes isn't about whether we like something; it is about determining whether that something and the processes used to create that something achieve a goal. It is about the degree to which they meet very specific needs.

6. **Students do not accurately self-assess:** There are certainly instances when students' self-assessment paints a different picture from the one that teachers see. This might happen for a number of reasons. For one, they may not be clear about criteria for successful processes and products. When students don't set their own goals or make decisions, they may not be clear about what we are hoping they achieve. On the other hand, students are far more confident in what success looks and feels like when they are responsible for their own goals and for co-constructing success criteria. This kind of clarity indicates a truly authentic creative experience. Furthermore, it leads to the development of skills that serve students in the long term. Davies (2011) explains, "Students who self-monitor are developing and practicing the skills needed to be lifelong, independent learners" (p. 57).

Even after we determine criteria, students may still over- or underestimate their proficiency. They may perceive greater success than we perceive because we have not found time to share mentor texts (texts that model the effective application of criteria) or sample products. These kinds of items can help students connect criteria to an actual product and invite them to reach further than they originally intended. Samples are great to introduce after students make an initial attempt so they move into reflection and response with clarity about how to enhance their creative efforts. Timing does matter—introducing these things too early might encourage imitation. Students may also inflate their self-assessment if they perceive the stakes are high. If inflation is happening, reflection and then purposeful action on our part can reduce the likelihood of it occurring again.

Students may underestimate their success because they are lacking confidence, or they may feel like they are bragging if they acknowledge their strength. Whatever the reason, this habit indicates a need to build in self-assessment processes that require analysis based on clear criteria and support for self-assessment decisions based on evidence.

7. **Feedback should be immediate:** While research establishes the importance of feedback in advancing learning (Black & Wiliam, 1998; Hattie, 2009),

how and when feedback should occur is less clear. Certainly, feedback that is immediate and precise will help with the majority of learning outcomes. Immediate and clear correction can be very helpful when misconceptions interrupt student learning, for example. However, the path is less clear when feedback occurs during creative processes. Misconceptions are not always the reason why students find that their movement through creative processes becomes challenging. Instead, they may find themselves lacking commitment to the original problem or they may be unsure whether the results they achieve through their experimentation are what they hoped to experience. In these cases, feedback that is immediate and prescriptive may over-scaffold the learning, when what students really need is the opportunity to figure out, on their own, where they need to go (Wiliam, 2018). Further experimentation, as opposed to the answers, is what will drive the creativity forward (Hattie & Timperley, 2007; Shute, 2007).

When we begin to challenge our assumptions and preconceptions about assessment and its relationship to creativity, we can carefully design assessment processes that support creativity in our classrooms.

Assessment as the Key to Unlocking Creativity

When teachers and students use assessment to advance the creative process, students learn deeply, create meaningful products, and engage in classroom experiences with purpose. Now that we have explored some critical aspects of both creativity and assessment, we can explore how they look when assessment moves creativity forward. Understanding how they are deeply connected helps us navigate their use inside our classroom spaces.

Embedding assessment within the four stages of creativity propels the acts of thinking, problem solving, imagining, experimenting, and decision making. Formative assessment, self-assessment, and feedback invite our students to dive back into the creative process again and again, and explore deeply. Consider Drapeau's (2014) quote about creativity: "When students are thinking creatively, they are applying known or learned content and extending their knowledge by considering possibilities, options, and solutions" (p. 147). Assessment invites both teachers and learners to analyze what students are creating in relation to the success criteria that connect to goals so they may determine next steps. This is one way that assessment moves creativity forward.

Creativity unlocked through assessment can nurture empathy and build self-confidence. It can invite students to examine personal truths and maintain a primary position within their own learning journey. During creative processes, assessment helps students develop reflection and self-regulation skills (an ongoing process whereby learners set goals for learning and monitor, regulate, and control their cognition, motivation, and behavior, guided and limited by their goals and their environment [Pintrich, 2000]) and increase their independence as they engage in unfamiliar contexts. Students learn to manage their time and efforts as well as learn to work collaboratively with others. Effective feedback during creative processes enhances ownership over decision making and supports students to actively seek assistance and develop a greater understanding of their goals and the specific needs they are trying to meet through their creative outputs (Hattie & Donoghue, 2016). Lastly, self-assessment during creativity honors diversity, meeting students where they are, based on what they believe and what they need. These assessment processes, during creativity, invite students to make meaning in ways that are culturally respectful and personally relevant.

Final Thoughts

Assessment is the key to moving students through the stages of creativity because it:

◇   Invites students to ask questions about their work and consider the decisions they make in relation to personally meaningful goals

◇   Acts as a catalyst for reflection and meaning making

◇   Slows learners down enough to develop their thinking and adjust as necessary

◇   Allows us, as teachers, to build knowledge and skill when it is required, to encourage risk taking when it is essential, and to celebrate successful choices the moment they occur

◇   Provides us teachers the opportunity to discuss failure and help students see their way through it

Before assessment can move creativity in these ways, teachers must establish a classroom climate and culture that supports this kind of learning. The next chapter explores ways to unlock creative spaces so the right kinds of assessment can flourish.

Applying Assessment Within the Stages of the Creative Process

Stage of the Creative Process	Applicable Assessment Forms and Concepts	Guiding Questions
Exploration	Formative assessment (information gathering), which includes: • Preassessment • Observation Feedback (dialogue with others), which includes: • Conferring with teacher or adult • Peer assessment Self-assessment (dialogue with self), which includes: • Goal setting • Criteria setting • Reflection	• What do I already know about this topic? How can I access my own creativity? • What matters to me in this creative work? What do I want to achieve? Do I have ideas about how I will recognize success? • What am I going to try to create? • What will my creativity look like as I explore? Who should I talk to about my work and getting started? • When does it make sense to stop and check my progress? How will I know when I am ready to go on to the next stage? • Who might I ask to offer me feedback?
Elaboration	Formative assessment (information gathering), which includes: • Observation • Artifact analysis Feedback (dialogue with others), which includes: • Conferring with teacher or adult • Peer assessment Self-assessment (dialogue with self), which includes: • Goal refining • Criteria refining • Reflection	• Have my goals changed at all as I have worked? How will I know I am having success? • What will my creativity look like as I elaborate? Who should I talk to about adding to my ideas? • When does it make sense to stop and check my progress? How will I know when I am ready to share with others? • Who could help me with my decision making?

Stage of the Creative Process	Applicable Assessment Forms and Concepts	Guiding Questions
Expression	Formative assessment (information gathering), which includes: • Observation • Artifact analysis Feedback (dialogue with others), which includes: • Conferring with teacher or adult • Peer assessment Self-assessment (dialogue with self), which includes: • Goal refining • Criteria refining • Reflection	• How am I doing on my goals? Do I need additional criteria to help me express my creative ideas well? • What will my creativity look like as I prepare to share? Who should I show my work to or rehearse with to collect feedback? • When does it make sense to stop and check my progress? How will I know when I am ready to share with others? • Do I need to prepare my audience? • Who will give me good feedback before I share? After I share? • How will I check my success and reflect on my work? • Do I understand how I will be assessed?
Reflection and Response	Formative assessment (information gathering), which includes: • Observation • Artifact analysis Feedback (dialogue with others), which includes: • Conferring with teacher or adult • Peer assessment Self-assessment (dialogue with self), which includes: • Goal refining for current project and setting for next project • Criteria refining for current project and setting for next project • Reflection Summative assessment (verification)	• Are there things I need to do before sharing this with my teacher (if I haven't already)? • What have I learned that I want to remember for next time? • Will it help me to reflect with another person or a group? • What does strong reflection look and sound like? • Do I need some support with my reflections? • Who can offer me some feedback about my creative work and my reflections? • What criteria do I need to focus on while reflecting? • Do I understand how I will be assessed? Am I ready?

page 2 of 2

Unlocking the Creative Space

I head in to the classroom a little early, knowing I want to have all the materials out before the first student arrives. I stack the magazines, black ink pens and markers, and glue on the side cupboard in neat rows. On the other side, I pile up large white paper and colored construction paper. I head over to the bookshelf to make sure I have all the found poetry books and samples from previous students ready to be used as mentor texts if needed.

Next, I head to the whiteboard to write the statement, "Everywhere I look, I see poetry." I stick a single newspaper page beside the statement, ready to use during my think-aloud. I scan the room, making sure the desks are grouped together and the table at the back of the room is clear and ready for collaboration and conferencing. I place my laptop on the end of the table and open my conferencing and goal-setting files. I am ready to enter today's student goals and my observations of their process when the time comes.

Lastly, I head to my phone to select my music for the morning. I choose something soothing to signal a calm and thoughtful environment. My students know that the music selection always tells them something about the day. When the music stops, we will begin the lesson. I can hardly wait to see what students do today.

As we construct and nurture creative spaces in our classrooms, we will engage our learners in formative assessment, self-assessment, and feedback opportunities so we can learn more about their strengths and challenges and help them advocate for their creative needs. Furthermore, we can invite our learners into conversations about the criteria for effective creative spaces. This will help them discover who they are as creative learners and the conditions they need to construct to continue to grow in this area.

The classroom spaces in which we find ourselves when we agree to teach groups of learners are as varied as one could imagine. Some classrooms exist in buildings that are brand new and designed with learner needs in mind while others reflect school designs from long ago. We often do not have control over the physical spaces of our schools, but we can control the degree to which students feel emotionally and socially ready to create when our classroom doors close at the beginning of the day. When we consider the conditions that support student thinking, we may find the need to move away from the locked spaces of desks in rows, perpetual silence, and materials hidden from view. Unlocking creative spaces for our students establishes the groundwork for creative processes. When we attend to the intellectual, emotional, and physical needs of our learners from the outset, we begin to lay the groundwork for a classroom climate and culture that supports innovative, imaginative thinking. By sustaining these spaces over time, we ensure learners understand that creativity is what we do in our classrooms; we take risks, ask questions, and support each other as we solve problems. The more flexible we can be in how we support learning, the more we invite our students to think deeply about the conditions that best support their own creativity. The more accessible creative materials are for our students, the more independence they can practice as they learn.

Indeed, how students interact with their environment and the objects within it can influence their creative processes. The creative space can support the intellectual, emotional, and physical needs of creative learners, so making sure that these ends receive support through the spaces we establish is an essential first step to unlocking creativity in our classrooms. In this chapter, we will explore the critical actions for constructing intellectual, emotional, and physical spaces that are essential for creativity to flourish and using the language that communicates our creative intent, and the teacher's role in constructing for students spaces that facilitate creative work.

Critical Actions for Teachers and Students When Unlocking the Creative Space

There are four critical items to remember when setting out to unlock creative spaces in our classrooms and schools.

1. Constructing an intellectual space
2. Constructing an emotional space
3. Constructing a physical space
4. Considering language

The environments we design can make or break creativity. However, we also have to prepare ourselves for the implications of changing things up—we have to be ready for things to look different in our schools and classrooms, and this takes a measure of fortitude and determination. After reviewing these critical actions, see the reproducible "Unlocking the Creative Space: Observation and Self-Assessment" (pages 62–64) for guidance in navigating self-assessment and observation related to these critical components. Additionally, see the reproducible "Suggestions When Designing Creative Spaces" (pages 65–66) for helpful suggestions for teachers as they work to design spaces that help students unlock creativity in our classrooms.

Constructing an Intellectual Space

No one would question that the purpose of schools is to nurture intellectual development in some form or another. Educators devote most of their day-to-day work to constructing and sustaining environments in which students can exercise their intellects; this exercise calls students to listen to new ideas, read about and explore unknown concepts, make connections between what they know and what they are learning, and practice critical skills all the way through to retention. Even when our aim is to develop the creative processes students use in their quest for connection and meaning, we are still engaging in many of the same strategies we use for all sorts of learning. Students still listen and read; they make connections and practice. So how is constructing an intellectual space that unlocks creativity different? The difference can be subtle sometimes, but it often comes down to how much autonomy students retain over either the ways they think about what they are learning or the products they produce as a by-product of the learning. Two key aspects of intellectual spaces to consider are developing domain knowledge and discovering problems and posing questions.

Developing Domain Knowledge

As we prepare our classrooms to engage in creative work, we should understand the importance of domain knowledge in fostering creativity. Technologist John Spacey (2016) explains, "Domain knowledge is understanding, ability and information that applies to a specific topic, profession or activity. The term is commonly used to describe the knowledge of experts in a particular area." In our classrooms, this refers to the knowledge contained within our subject area. Each domain has its own set of rules, its own language, and its own conceptual framework. For example, in a mathematics classroom, the concepts of reduction, division, and expression hold a nuanced meaning, slightly different from the same concepts in an English language arts classroom. Sharing this information is part of the work teachers do every day.

When we introduce creativity into our classrooms, this domain knowledge remains important. Certainly, creativity is about pushing boundaries, flexing assumptions, and manipulating ideas. However, creativity cannot exist in the absence of domain knowledge. This knowledge serves as the foundational tool of creative pursuit. Sawyer (2006) explains, "Creativity is always specific to a domain. No one can be creative until they internalize the symbols, conventions, and languages of a creative domain" (p. 117). In other words, knowing what the box is helps us think outside of it. This means that a large part of the teacher's role is to build this domain knowledge both before and during creative work. Domain knowledge gives students the foundation needed to move into innovation, exploration, and invention. Conversely, creativity gives our students a unique process for engaging in domain knowledge. Kelly (2012) expresses the importance of this relationship:

> *What is the sense of accumulating masses of information and discipline content if we are not equipped with a creative disposition to utilize this information to deal with the challenges of everyday life and those that future generations will face? (p. 5)*

Creativity provides the means to invite our learners into a more complex relationship with the domain knowledge we are trying to impart. Through assessment, we can help our students in their interactions with domain knowledge to ensure it supports not just the recall of important information, but deep engagement in the concepts and ideas of our subject areas.

Discovering Problems and Posing Questions

If we can frame creative endeavors as problems seeking a solution, as this book suggests, then the quest for information, resources, and experimental approaches all serves the desire to find an answer to an important question. Creativity rests in how our students tackle the problem and the degree of latitude we give them to do so on their own terms.

However, our environment has to be conducive to identifying problems to address before students can begin to explore their own solutions to any number of problems. For example, a social studies unit may begin with a compelling video about the mistreatment of a minority group, followed by a classroom discussion about the problems identified in the video for both the minority group and society as a whole. The video and discussion open up the opportunity for students to ask questions and consider challenges that need to be addressed. This is perhaps the most important step in nurturing creativity—making sure our students have a compelling reason to be creative. This reason lies largely in the kinds of problems we invite students to solve, and this is why creating a space that nurtures both student and teacher questions is so critical. Wall displays, notebooks, journals, and portfolios are all places where students might post their questions about identified problems. Questions precede creativity but they also rest within the creative cycle, driving it forward. Questions connect our learners directly to the assessment processes that are also part of creative endeavors, because they emerge out of reflection and analysis of a current context against a desired outcome.

As students work through a creative process, they are faced with challenges or unexpected outcomes. Perhaps a prototype they are working on does not perform in the way they hoped, or perhaps the response to an advertisement they created was not what they desired. This prompts them to ask new questions about domain knowledge, the product they are attempting to create, and their approaches to their exploration. Establishing an intellectual space where we not only tolerate but also encourage the creation of questions that address problems will go a long way in unlocking creativity.

Making time for collaboration can assist this quest for problems that prompt creativity. Together, students with diverse perspectives and worldviews are able to search for a wide variety of problems and generate questions within a single context. This helps individual students expand their creative or innovative output.

The problems students identify may produce many desirable outcomes when we encourage creative approaches. Batchelor and Bintz (2013) agree:

> *Creativity today is viewed as individuals involved in a creative process—the process of taking an existing idea or problem, seeing the idea or problem in multiple ways with multiple solutions, and solving or transforming it into something new and worthwhile. (p. 3)*

Making space in our classrooms to identify problems that could serve a creative endeavor is a great way to start.

Documenting problems and subsequent questions as they emerge and keeping them easily accessible helps students generate creative ideas and approaches as they move through the creative process. Instead of devoting wall space to polished, finished products, we might consider creating a space to post messy problems and questions. Perhaps, as an anchor to our class time, we might invite teams of students to post "problems we are working on right now" and "problems we want to work on someday." Alternately, maybe learners work in pairs to explore each other's work in progress, making time to add sticky note questions that identify new areas. These approaches place student wonder in front of all learning. A single compelling problem can inspire more creativity than all the paper and paint in the world.

When students select a problem they wish to work through creatively, they activate assessment within the creative process. Their chosen problem will serve as the foundation of a learning goal and subsequent criteria by which success toward reaching that goal will be determined. This is why problems are so critical to both the creative process and the assessment that supports it. Figure 2.1 (page 52) offers a list of questions to support students when working in the intellectual space you have created for them.

Questions to support students when working in the intellectual space:

- What am I trying to find out?
- Did I choose the most important thing to focus on right now? How do I know?
- How am I expanding my understanding of my challenge? Where am I going for help?
- Which question or problem am I most interested in exploring? Why?
- What knowledge do I need to reach my goals? Where do I have to do some more learning before starting?
- What helps me get new ideas?
- How does what I know affect what I am planning to do?
- Why do problems matter?
- Do I feel ready to create? How might I feel more ready?
- When do I think it might be helpful to share my ideas with someone else?

Figure 2.1: *Select and reflect—Questions to support students when working in the intellectual space.*

*Visit **go.SolutionTree.com/assessment** for a free reproducible version of this figure.*

Constructing an Emotional Space

Unlocking a creative space means we also need to attend to the emotional needs of our learners as they work through what can sometimes be a tremendously challenging process. When we consider the kinds of activities that invite students into the realm of creativity—asking questions, debating, analyzing, defending, imagining alternatives, reflecting, wondering, reworking—we can see that many of these behaviors carry an element of emotional risk. Creativity involves risk, so in order to unlock creative spaces, we have to start with supporting emotional safety in the midst of risk.

Perhaps one of the most difficult aspects of a creative space is the notion that not all problems have a specific answer or solution. In fact, many of the world's most compelling problems have many possible solutions or no solutions at all. This paradigm is quite contrary to the way many students perceive the experience of education—to them, school is about answers. Even more specifically, it is about figuring out what answer the teacher wants, right or wrong, because that is where the points come from.

With this mindset, students can begin to reference their peers and their teacher (other people outside themselves) as sources of affirmation or contradiction. Such aspects of the traditional schooling paradigm serve to lock students' creativity. Wiggins (2017) explains, "If you mandate form, content, and process and ignore the impact, you inhibit creativity and reward safe, uncreative work." Pink (2009) explores these ideas of motivation and the drawbacks of rewards, including grades, stating, "Rewarded subjects often have trouble seeing the periphery and crafting original solutions" (p. 44). He also reminds us, "[Rewards] can transform an interesting task into a drudge. They can turn play into work. And by diminishing intrinsic motivation, they can send performance, creativity, and even upstanding behavior toppling like dominoes" (Pink, 2009, p. 35). In this rewards-focused (grades-focused) paradigm, students begin to think, "Does my work look like her work? Is he solving this problem the same way I am?" We may underestimate the degree to which students rely on social cues and others' work to reduce their own feelings of vulnerability and failure. They may think, "If my work looks like their work, I know that even if I am wrong, I am wrong with other people." This feeds a cycle of compliance and sameness over innovation and imagination. Our students may end up shutting down their own creative thoughts in favor of belonging and safety. They may resort to putting down the creative work of others for the same reasons.

If we are going to shift our classrooms to creative spaces in which students pursue questions that may have no answers or multiple answers, we are going to have to help students learn a different way of doing business. Because this will make many students who have become accustomed to their existing system very uncomfortable at first, we must show them that we will support them every step of the way. This does not mean helping them get to a specific product, but it does mean walking alongside them as they wrestle with ideas and materials, explore options, and make decisions. Most important, we will:

◇ Help students reflect as they go, so they can engage in processes and arrive at products (in other words, work with their problems) that are personally meaningful and satisfying

◇ Facilitate the setting of goals

◇ Make time for students to self-assess and engage in feedback when it makes the most sense

◇ Step back and let students struggle and take steps, even when the outcome is uncertain

◇ Help them discover what it feels like to be creative

◇ Help them develop their confidence in the midst of ambiguity

As Tom Schimmer (2014) notes, "There is nothing more important to a student than confidence—with it, students can learn anything; without it, they'll learn nothing" (p. 16). We must teach our students that confidence doesn't just arise from success; it arises from failure, too. Students maintain confidence and even hope in the middle of failure when they remain optimistic that they can work through it and emerge out the other side with something better than they had before. This kind of confidence and hope builds creative products over the short term and resilience over the long term.

However, if we are going to nurture confidence, hope, and resilience, we have to make sure that our learning environment allows students the time and space to address their misconceptions, misguided decisions, and changing goals. This time and space offers students the opportunity to recover from the decisions that did not serve their creative intent. Jacie Maslyk (2016) refers to this time and space as the *recovery phase*, and explains the importance of this attention to time for recovery:

> *The recovery phase is an integral part. Failure makes people feel helpless and reluctant to engage in risky tasks where failure can occur again. As educators, we need to reengage our students in these tasks and refocus them on their successes. (p. 48)*

We have to engage in processes that allow students to revisit, revise, recover, and reinvest if we are going to unlock emotionally safe spaces.

This is where assessment and creativity link inextricably. Formative assessment offers students the information they need at important times so they can examine and reflect on their work as it happens and adjust where they need to. The results from a daily quick formative assessment can allow us to work with students to plan next steps. A quick video conference, an exit ticket, a journal entry, or a sticky note comparison to criteria might be all we need to pause for a moment and determine the focus for the next day. A feedback conversation that we schedule every couple of days might be enough to address student needs. It is during these kinds of formative assessment that we can determine how the creative process is proceeding, but we can also determine when an environment has become emotionally unsafe for learners. We can make sure that students are not feeling like their ideas are being shut down by their peers or even by themselves. We can listen to be sure student collaboration is positive and productive—that no put-downs are emerging in our classroom spaces. Human beings are vulnerable in the middle of a creative process, so using assessment to determine emotional needs is vital. Figure 2.2 offers a list of questions to support students when working in the emotional space you create for them.

Questions to support students when working in the emotional space:
- When do I feel most discouraged? How do I move past it?
- What does taking a risk feel like?
- How do I feel taking risks at school? How could I feel even more comfortable with it?
- How can I work with other people and share my ideas about their work without hurting their feelings?
- How do I build my confidence?
- When is being different a good thing? How can I avoid judging my thinking and work by what others are doing?
- What matters to me in my work?

Figure 2.2: *Select and reflect—Questions to support students when working in the emotional space.*

*Visit **go.SolutionTree.com/assessment** for a free reproducible version of this figure.*

Constructing a Physical Space

The physical environment in which we create can be as important as any other variable in our creative space. Most people can likely recall a time when they walked into a room and felt a certain energy that affected their mood and productivity. Many people also prefer specific environmental conditions in which to engage in a creative pursuit. For example, I need to be in a room with a window and natural light when I write. Breaking to look outside helps me gain a wider perspective every now and then before I dive back into my words. Other people need muted lighting and cozy spaces to experience creative energy. Still others thrive on an open space filled with stimulating materials to choose and manipulate. Creativity is a very personal experience, and our physical environment can influence our ability to achieve and sustain flow.

Living With a Mess

The reality of creative processes is they are messy. This mess originates in our thoughts as we begin creating, but it often overflows into our physical spaces. This does not mean we should expect our classroom to look like it has been turned upside down all the time, but there will likely be physical evidence of searching, trying new approaches and materials, changing direction, and abandoning ideas. Often, when people are in the middle of problem solving, they cannot imagine stopping halfway through to clean up an area before moving on to the next thing.

However, there is a time to tidy—both mentally and physically—and this often happens when we purposefully invite our students to pause, step back, and reflect on their progress in relation to their goals. As students take this breather, their teachers may invite them to make decisions and put away any items that no longer serve their quest. These decisions are, in fact, reflective of a self-assessment process. Students make decisions about where they are headed and then make decisions about how their physical space might support their next steps. Morgan (2015) reminds us, "Slowing down a bit helps minimize the risk that the significant effort of trying to convert or invent is misspent fixing the wrong problem" (p. 42). Taking time to tidy, both physically and mentally, invites progress in intentional directions. Teachers can ensure students have time to tidy their physical and mental space by building this time into their lessons (such as regular check-in times at the end of a class period or at a natural break when the students are collectively moving to a new stage of the creative process). They can also support this work by being mindful of individual students' needs and prompting individuals to take these breaks as necessary as they navigate their own creative processes.

It is important for students to develop a familiarity with the idea that creativity happens over time and over multiple attempts. Douglas Reeves (2015) explains the importance of embracing assessment processes that support this idea when he says:

Assessments that require a beautiful product, but do not also expect to see several less beautiful products along the way, give students the false impression that creativity is born of one-shot efforts by clever students who are bright enough to get it right the first time. (p. 39)

Physically stimulating environments combined with time for reflection and curation support the notion that the first attempt in a creative endeavor will most certainly be followed by revision. Such environments may include readily available raw materials like paper, markers, scissors, and loose parts; spaces for conferring with others; whiteboards, chart paper stands, or chalkboards; accessible technology; or flexible seating. As students access materials that could potentially serve their creative work, they unlock new possibilities and make their thinking visible. This leads to reflection and decision making as exploration and elaboration progress.

It is important to note that many schools do not have the funding or resources to equip classrooms with pristine and plentiful supplies. I have often found the greatest treasures at garage sales and in secondhand stores. Unused balls of yarn, old greeting cards, dried beans, and discarded fabric can be just as inviting as art and craft supplies purchased in a department store. These items also help create a stimulating environment for creative thinking at minimal cost.

Designing our classroom spaces to support creativity by both filling them with a stimulating mess and giving students the ability to contain the mess when needed is important. Making sure that materials are available but they have homes within our classrooms can help our students develop independence and help establish clarity and calm when it is time to do so. No longer do we always have to hand students what they need—instead, they can gather needed supplies because they know where they are. They can also tidy during a self-assessment period, because they know where everything goes. They can place those items they no longer need in their designated spots so others may use them.

Using Space Flexibly

The most ideal creative environments are those over which we have total control. Imagine a student who is designing a prototype for a car that protects its contents when it crashes. The student drafts ideas on paper and looks for a partner to help her see things she may have missed. The student moves from her independent work surface to a larger table, where two people can sit side-by-side and look at a large drawing. Across the classroom, a learner is designing a lab for testing acids and bases. The student is working with liquids and a hot plate. He has a flat surface on which to set his laptop away from the lab materials. He also has access to a whiteboard, where he tracks measurements in a large table. Another set of students is working in a smaller room, recording a video about a flight simulator. This room is soundproof and away from the clamor of the set's classmates. In this classroom space, students move fluidly from one area to the next as their needs dictate. This is a truly flexible, student-centric space. It is also a dream for many of us who teach in areas with tight funding.

However, students are very adaptable; see the amount of time they spend in uncomfortable desks and plastic chairs that challenge their physical needs as evidence. When they need to work together, they slide desks side-by-side, ignoring the differences in height. They move to the floor to paint on a larger surface and lean up against walls to read and talk together. Our students have found flexible spaces in coatrooms, cubby areas, hallways, and storage areas when necessary. Many of us did the same when we were students. However, where possible, the more we can facilitate flexibility and comfort, the better for our learners. Good lighting and work surfaces yield creative output. Storage containers that move and chairs that turn can help students determine their creative needs and act on them. Whiteboards and access to technology can further support creative work.

Furthermore, when physical space is limited, we may need to be creative in how we approach flexible spaces. I once bought very inexpensive mats at a bargain store to create miniature zones in my first-grade classroom. Students knew what zone each mat represented (a research zone, a coloring zone, a talking zone, for example), and we used very little physical space in our already tiny classroom. Teachers are infinitely resourceful as they create flexible spaces with the room and items they have at their disposal. Figure 2.3 offers a list of questions to support students when working in the physical space you create for them.

Questions to support students when working in the physical space:

- Which materials do I wish I had to get me started?
- Which materials and resources make me want to create?
- Which materials make me ask questions? What kinds of questions?
- Am I using my materials the way I imagined?
- What kind of room helps me think and create?
- How do I feel about levels of noise when I am creating? How about lighting?
- Does moving to different kinds of spaces affect how creative I can be? How so?
- Which materials are no longer serving me and why? How do I know?
- How do I know when my environment is helping me create?

Figure 2.3: *Select and reflect—Questions to support students when working in the physical space.*

*Visit **go.SolutionTree.com/assessment** for a free reproducible version of this figure.*

Considering Language

The language we use in our classrooms communicates what we value. Drapeau (2014) explains, "Establishing meaningful definitions and creating shared language surrounding innovation will help students understand the process as well as the importance of innovation and innovative thinking" (p. 99). When we carefully consider the words and phrases we use in our learning environments, we can create spaces that unlock creativity. The following phrases are examples of the type of language we want to use in creative spaces. The words in italics emphasize concepts that connect directly to creative thinking. Using these words regularly when speaking with students signals their importance.

◇ Share your *wonders*.

◇ Tell us how you would *approach* that.

◇ Look for a *creative* solution.

◇ *Imagine* a new way of doing that.

◇ Let's look for the *stretch* in our *thinking*.

◇ Let's talk through how you made that *decision*.

◇ That was very *brave*.

◇ Take a *risk*.

◇ Great *out-of-the-box* thinking!

◇ Try to find an *original* solution.

◇ You offered an *innovative* approach.

◇ Explain the *problem* you are trying to work out.

◇ Share where you are *stuck* right now.

Perhaps the greatest indicator that our language has had an impact on creative thinking in our classrooms is when we hear our students using the same words and phrases we have used, when they reference their own or others' work. We want to encourage our students to use the language of creativity on their own, when they are immersed in thinking and problem solving. When we hear them use phrases that illustrate an understanding and acceptance of the critical components of creativity, we know learners are becoming comfortable with creativity. This transference of creative language is just one aspect of the role of the teacher in creative work. The next section explores this role in more depth.

The Role of the Teacher

The teacher plays a critical role in establishing and maintaining a creative space. Through our actions and words, decisions and responses, we nurture intellectually, emotionally, and physically safe spaces in which our learners innovate, wonder, imagine, and explore.

Following are some important roles for teachers to be aware of as they unlock creative spaces for learners and construct a classroom climate and culture conducive to creativity.

⬦ **Nurturer of safe spaces:** During creative work, there may be times when teachers and students disagree, and times when students experience disappointment or failure. How a teacher responds to this reality will define the climate and culture of the learning space; teachers must nurture a safe space to support students' creativity.

⬦ **Catalyst for student thought:** Teachers should act as a catalyst to provoke thinking and deep exploration of a wide variety of topics in a myriad of ways, which could include providing stimulating materials, asking guiding questions, sharing multiple perspectives, or structuring collaborative time. Students are accustomed to looking to teachers for both the questions and the answers. When teachers act as catalysts for creativity, they can instead continuously shift learning toward student ownership.

⬦ **Creative learner and mentor:** Teachers need to model creativity by accessing their own creative selves. Students are often flooded with the voices of adults who assert their own lack of creativity, such as teachers apologizing for the drawings or diagrams they create to illustrate a point while claiming a lack of artistic ability, or parents asserting that they "don't have a creative bone in their body." They are often taught that creativity is either something you have or something you don't have. By being creative learners ourselves, we can act as mentors and show our students what it means to be a creative learner.

Table 2.1 (page 60) suggests specific actions that a teacher can take as he or she attempts to fulfill these roles.

Table 2.1: *The Role of the Teacher and Key Actions in Unlocking the Creative Space*

Role of the Teacher	Key Teacher Actions
Nurturer of Safe Spaces	• Help students develop strong self-assessment skills so they address their own goals. • Develop processes that honor disagreement in a safe and respectful environment. • Place the final decision in the hands of the students when possible. • Ensure criteria rest with the learner or within a negotiation between the learner (apprentice) and the teacher (expert). • Embrace the tension between the teacher's expectations and the student's expectations as a learning opportunity. • Address defiance when it emerges, and talk honestly with students about the difference between creative license and a refusal to follow guidelines, directions, or feedback. • Build a culture of risk taking. • Allow decisions that may not bear fruit. • Withhold feedback until students have the chance to think things through and solve their own challenges. • When students appear unduly discouraged or stuck, step in and offer support. • Use formative assessment to inform decisions.
Catalyst for Student Thought	• Stimulate thinking and imagination through open-ended materials, prompts, and activities. • Provoke new questions. • Work with students to determine their compelling reasons for exploring an idea or creating a message. • Tune in to student interests. • Facilitate self-assessment and self-regulation, critical to focusing imagination and ideas into processes and products.
Creative Learner and Mentor	• List student questions about a topic, and offer personal stories of creativity, including the strategies that led to success and those that led to challenge. • Build things, make things, draw things, write things, solve things, and share things with learners. • Model personal creative processes from start to finish as a guide for students who are just beginning to flex their creative muscles. • Share real-life examples (such as home décor, gardening, planning, and cooking).

Final Thoughts

Establishing a creative space provides the intellectual, emotional, and physical foundation necessary for creativity and the assessment that supports it. We know we have created classrooms that will support creativity in its many forms when our students feel safe to take risks, choose materials, ask questions, and set their own goals. Whether we are working with young or adolescent learners, securing their intellectual, emotional, and physical safety is paramount. Using our own creativity, we can create flexible classroom spaces, select stimulating materials, and provide healthy places of problem solving and wonder.

The next chapter unpacks the important first stage in the creative process: exploration. It is during this initial stage that we can leverage the classroom spaces we have so carefully constructed to springboard our learners into truly creative thinking. Using the classroom environment and culture as fertile soil for creative learning is one of the great joys of teaching.

Unlocking the Creative Space:
Observation and Self-Assessment

As we construct and sustain creative spaces, we will use observation to support instructional agility and respond to student needs. When we observe, we use learning targets (actionable statements that describe critical steps in developing skills or understanding) to ascertain degrees of proficiency within creative contexts.

Teachers can use this tool to monitor the strengths and challenges of the creative space through observation (an important assessment method in creative spaces). This tool contains criteria for successful creative spaces (which emerge from the critical actions [see pages 48–58]), how these criteria look when lived out day-to-day, and how educators can nurture these criteria within their instructional and assessment plans. The final column offers suggestions for how to respond when criteria are absent or need additional support.

Creative Space Targets	What the Teacher Sees	Teacher Facilitation Techniques	Teacher Response
I can explore materials and choose those I want or need to try using in a way that is appropriate for the content area.	• Students who actively engage in materials—exploring them, testing them, sorting them • Students who respectfully lay claim to the items they want to use • Students who connect material selection to the context (domain)	• Have many options available for students so they can curate their own materials. • Give learners time to explore the choices. • Ask them to capture ideas as they develop, while exploring materials.	• Model how materials can lead to creative ideas. • Create guidelines for students who are overwhelmed (say, for example, "Take three minutes to choose five materials to start with"). • Use a framework to help students see the connection between materials and ideas or subject matter.
I can create or choose an environment that helps me learn and use space flexibly.	• Students who can describe conditions that help them learn • Students who make environmental choices and then demonstrate productivity • Students who self-regulate and adjust environments as they need to	• Invite students to make choices and then reflect on the impact (for example, with music, without music). • Explain how needs impact decisions (for example, flat surfaces if gluing). • Offer options.	• Require quick reflections each day (for example, Was my learning space good for my creativity today?). • Limit options for students who are overwhelmed by choice. • Pause frequently and facilitate self-regulation checks (for example, Am I being productive here?).

page 1 of 3

Creative Space Targets	What the Teacher Sees	Teacher Facilitation Techniques	Teacher Response
I can be respectful to myself and others while creating (no shutdowns or put-downs).	• Students who change their materials and environments when they are not working • Students who encourage their peers when they make decisions • Students who show interest in what others are doing • Students who share their own thinking with others • Students who use positive, risk-supporting language	• Explicitly teach respectful and supportive language. • Discuss the effect of words on our emotional safety. • Share conversation or feedback guides. • Facilitate empathy talks (ask, for example, "How does it feel when someone grabs a material you want to use? How might we resolve this?").	• Redirect when students are not working well together. • Model supportive language and actions. • Explicitly teach skills for respectful creation. • Revise working areas if they are not supporting respectful interaction. • Examine the creative work to determine if students are sufficiently engaged.
I can identify topics of interest and generate problems.	• Students who can generate ideas, topics, and problems • Students who move beyond first ideas • Students who can explain why an idea matters to them	• Have a space in the room to generate ideas as a class. • Have a journal, where students can openly brainstorm. • Model the connection between materials and ideas. • Discuss how we know when ideas are truly interesting to us.	• Do not allow students to choose topics to please someone else. • Expand the materials and catalysts available for learners. • Offer guidelines for narrowing down options (for example, List as many ideas as you can, choose your five best, and talk with a partner and focus).
I can approach creativity with confidence and live with a mess for a while.	• Students who show interest in approaching creative pursuits • Students who solve their own challenges and resist support when they don't need it • Students who can describe their creative processes, preferences, and choices • Students who tolerate a mess for a while	• Explicitly teach what the classroom looks and sounds like when learners are confidently creative. • Invite students to discuss their ideas with someone else (to build confidence). • Explore what "ready to be creative" means.	• Confer with students when they are lacking confidence. Identify the root cause and address it. • Avoid taking charge (for example, saying, "Here is what you need to do"). • Avoid empty praise (for example, saying, "Your idea is great!"). • Teach students how to take risks and work through discomfort.

Creative Space Targets	What the Teacher Sees	Teacher Facilitation Techniques	Teacher Response
I can use the language of creativity.	• Students who talk about their creative process • Students whose language illustrates an acceptance of risk and ambiguity • Students whose language shows a focus on personal goals	• Post some phrases that can be part of a creative classroom. • Model the use of language that shows acceptance for risk taking and ambiguity. • Model goal-focused language. • Reinforce the use of creative language.	• Notice language that seems to indicate limits, self-criticism, comparison, and binary ways of thinking. • Use creative language, and preteach key words related to creativity. • Gently replace harmful language with language that supports the creative process.

Suggestions When Designing Creative Spaces

Places to meet and places to reflect:

◇ Students need a spot to collaborate and, when possible, furniture to support this effort. A vertical writing surface (such as chalkboards, whiteboards, paper on a wall or an easel) can help students document ideas as they work together. Tables and chairs that easily move can help students maintain eye contact and give them a surface on which to write.

◇ Students may need a quieter area during some stages of their creative process. For those students who are really working through an idea, soft seating in a private area can be helpful.

Adequate materials:

◇ Loose parts and open-ended materials can stimulate creativity. Storing these items in baskets and easily accessible containers is helpful in building independence during creative times.

◇ Books and resource materials related to domain-specific understanding can help students when questions emerge.

◇ Templates and graphic organizers support students in their quest to organize their thinking. Allowing choice ensures they are thinking about the versions that best suit their creative style.

◇ Technology is often essential during all aspects of the creative process. It can be a tool for research, a tool to generate thoughts, a tool to organize ideas, or a tool to create a meaningful product. The more students can choose technology, the more control they can maintain during their creative process.

◇ Visual materials are highly engaging for some students. Access to images and mentor products can serve as strong catalysts for creative thinking.

◇ Tools for the creative process are important to have easily available. Scissors, paints, lab equipment, wood, cloth, glue, string, paper, hammers and nails . . . you name it, if students need them to create, making materials like these available can ensure the creative process runs smoothly. For example, it is amazing how powerful a special piece of paper and nice writing utensils are to inspire creative thinking. Tools matter.

◇ Protective clothing is an often overlooked item to have, especially in classrooms with older students. Old shirts, lab coats, gloves, and eye protectors may be important items to have available. Creativity can be messy.

◇ Protective furniture coverings may also be important during creative processes, and can save everyone time during cleanup. Plastic table covers go a long way in protecting furniture from creative mess. Also, cleaning materials are handy to have during some creative work.

page 1 of 2

A spot to honor questions:

◇ Questions are the fertilizer for creative thinking. Having a special bulletin board, a wall, or a creative journal to hold these questions is important. It is helpful for students to see the questions and problems that are guiding their creative work in the beginning, middle, and end of their creative processes.

◇ Keep track of great questions, discuss the qualities of good questions, and use questions to guide the daily work of learners.

A spot to celebrate drafts:

◇ Creative processes are as important as the products they produce. Making space available to celebrate drafts in their various forms shows students that all thinking is important thinking. A special spot on the wall or a special binder labeled "Our Work in Progress" can do this for students.

◇ Invite families to explore drafts as evidence of learning. Share the importance of drafts in getting to quality creative work. Ask parents and trusted friends to offer feedback, celebrate strengths, and encourage risk taking.

Unlocking Exploration

I am half an hour into class time and the students are moving around the giant sheet of brown butcher paper on the floor. They are talking in small groups, pointing to the images drawn onto the paper.

We are working on a class project related to a social studies learning goal. The students will need to develop an understanding of how settlement patterns have been impacted by the location of natural resources, as well as geographical features. We are going to design our own village and trading post, but I have given them the challenge of working within preset geography. I have asked them to look at the river's, the trees', and the hills' location, so they can begin to plan where they might place their village and then design their own houses in relation to their chosen surroundings.

When students entered my class this morning, they immediately noticed a change in their environment. Their desks had been moved to the side, to make room for the very large and mostly empty map drawn on the butcher paper. I handed each student an envelope containing a description of a role (farmer, schoolteacher, trading post owner, or trapper) that he or she would be adopting as part of this creative exploration.

I am also working on developing collaborative and decision-making skills in my students. I have noticed that I have some students whose voices are often not heard in group work, and I am using this experience to invite more sharing in a greater variety of ways. I also want to slow down my learners' decision making long enough to consider all relevant information. I have created this experience with the intention of introducing new questions and challenges at various points in the process.

I first task the students with deciding where to place their village. We have already listed each role on butcher paper and, in groups of three, have listed the aspects of their roles they thought would be important in deciding where to place the village and trading post. Every now and then, a student proposes a location and a classmate offers feedback about that suggestion. The engagement level is high, and I am able to step back and jot down observations I am making about engagement, productive contribution to the collaborative effort, and gaps in understanding I will need to address. Every now and then, I step back into the conversation and invite a reluctant student to explain his or her role or offer suggestions.

Following this collaborative effort, the students will need to choose a location for their home and place of work, when applicable. I will then invite them to spend time designing their house based on both their roles and the natural resources available in the area. Students will eventually submit a design, complete with a materials list and rationale. For now, though, it is all about idea generation and decision making.

Exploration is the stage of creativity during which students engage in or initiate creative thinking and planning. Our job as educators is to create interest, open the learning space, and help students begin to imagine possibilities in their quest to answer questions, solve problems, or create innovative products. While this exploration can occur in a completely open-ended context, we will most often initiate the creative process as a way to serve specific learning goals. It is important to remember that creativity can serve a wide variety of needs. It may be how we explore a learning goal in its entirety or it may be how students explore smaller targets within that larger goal. Creativity and learning goals can very much live in harmony if we are clear about the reason why students are engaging in creative processes and if we employ very specific strategies to invite exploration and other creative skills in ways that work alongside our learning goals.

In order to ensure creative processes work in conjunction with learning goals, we may introduce specific materials, share a focused problem, or present an important controversial topic to begin exploration. We may also invite students to ask and then refine their own questions. We might use the creative process to introduce learning goal content or to refine knowledge and skills our students already possess. Exploration is about investigating and connecting topics and concepts; about generating ideas and possibilities; about visualizing potential outcomes; and about curating materials and resources. Exploration occurs when teachers' plans for creativity, in service of the learning goals, begin to unfold in the hands of our students.

In this chapter, we will explore the critical actions for unlocking exploration, the teacher's role in this stage of students' creativity journey, and how creative exploration and assessment intersect.

Critical Actions for Teachers and Students When Unlocking Exploration

The expectations in today's classrooms can feel overwhelming to teachers and students. With numerous learning goals, it may feel like the pressure is always on to move quickly, covering topic after topic. This perception of the need to speed along at the fastest rate possible has resulted in class periods that move right into direct instruction, followed by independent work. In my years working as an instructional coach, I often witnessed the understandable tension of limited time coupled with too many learning goals, and the resulting pull toward class periods that move right into direct instruction followed by independent work. In our planning discussions, I heard again and again that teachers seemed to feel that this was simply the most expedient way to get through the required content. When this happens, opportunities to explore materials, ask questions, and make decisions at the beginning of learning are locked up because there just doesn't seem to be time for this kind of exploration. However, unlocking opportunities for exploration and wonder is a powerful gift for both learners and teachers. When teachers structure these opportunities into learning plans, creativity can enter the learning space and allow student understanding and engagement in important skills to deepen. In order to unlock exploration, we have to support our students in attending to eight critical actions.

1. Engaging with catalysts

2. Asking questions and generating ideas

3. Practicing patience and taking incubation time

4. Collaborating, trusting, and playing

5. Suspending judgment and accepting ambiguity, failure, and chaos

6. Making connections

7. Having choice and making decisions

8. Setting effective goals and success criteria

These critical actions, discussed in the following sections, support creative exploration and the assessment needed to advance it. After reviewing these critical actions, see the reproducible "Unlocking Exploration: Observation and Self-Assessment" (pages 95–98) for guidance in navigating self-assessment and observation related to these critical components.

Engaging With Catalysts

I like things—old greeting cards, colored spools of yarn, swatches of fabric, stickers, buttons, ceramic tiles, old wooden frames, pieces of interesting paper, popsicle sticks, shells, pine cones—you name it. Things. I have filled my classrooms with items like these, and now a room in my home stores them for the art classes I teach. I see these things as catalysts for creativity. Students dig through my boxes for items that catch their interest, and pluck shiny buttons out of my jars as they explore their ideas and create images in their heads of the art they are readying themselves to create. When I taught science, I filled my room with news articles that my students and I could use to explore everyday science as it was happening and stuck photos of animals to the walls to practice classification. Students then examined each other's classifications and offered feedback. When I taught mathematics, I saved containers of beads so students could make various quantities and construct an abacus so we could make sense of place value. When I taught English and French, I saved magazines and posters, photographs and calendars that might act as an invitation to write, represent, or communicate in some way. I think all these things have served as essential tools in unlocking creativity for students. They spark curiosity and wonder. They help students imagine possibilities and practice the very important skill of assessment right from the very beginning of the creative process.

As students sift through all these items, manipulating them, curating them, placing them side-by-side, they are already making decisions based on goals that are forming. The items help the goals evolve, and the goals help the selection of items become meaningful. The materials and the methods teachers use to introduce a challenge can provide students a catalyst for engaging in the creative process. These catalysts then serve as a compelling reason for students to engage in criteria setting and peer feedback as part of their exploration. For example, I recall bringing four boxes of materials I had picked up at a garage sale into my English language arts classroom. Inside the boxes were things like lace ribbon, miniature cloth flowers, small figurines, old brooches, toy cars, shells, and clip-on earrings, to name a few. I gave every student an inexpensive, unfinished shadow box (a deep frame with a back, into which objects are placed—a shoe box or an empty cereal box would suffice) and I invited students to brainstorm what they thought the project might be about. I then invited them to explore the raw materials and choose three things that appealed to them for some reason. The students chattered excitedly with each other, the idea of making a choice motivating them to really dig into the materials. Students picked items and tried them out in their shadow box, discarding them because of size or effect or keeping them because they held promise. They asked each other for opinions, engaging in authentic peer feedback as part of their decision making.

Self-assessment naturally kicked in as they explored the items. The act of curation invited students to choose objects based on internal criteria and a developing goal. In effect, the materials shaped the decisions and the goals, and the goals shaped the choice of materials. The two processes worked symbiotically. As we continued to explore their visual messages, their criteria setting became more rigorous. They became clearer about what they were trying to say, connecting their shadow box assemblages to themes we were working on in English language arts. It was a beautiful thing.

A strong catalyst can set the stage for student investment and for personal goal setting, even when the area of focus is related to a specific learning goal. Catalysts such as engaging materials, a chance to ask questions, a room arrangement that is out of the ordinary, a compelling video or photograph, or a challenging task are ways teachers can capture the attention of their students and propel them into the creative process.

John Dacey and Wendy Conklin (2004) explain how creativity can begin: "The creative act often starts with a spontaneous thought followed by reflection on the implications of the idea" (p. 25). Building creative classrooms means inviting students into interesting materials, ideas, or problems so our learners can engage in new learning experiences that stimulate personal connections to the things we are sharing. As part of this introduction, we can build in processes (for example, the creation of concept maps, journal entries, or flowcharts) that allow students to take their initial impressions and ideas and develop them in ways that lead them toward creativity. Students may benefit from time spent generating initial ideas and then connecting them to personal experiences, familiar materials, or planning tools that will advance their creative work. Pairing a strong catalyst with strong question-generation processes or open-ended brainstorming can serve as a strong foundation for creative output. For example, in the English language arts example I described earlier in this section, when students were directed to choose three items that appealed to them, it signaled the beginning of the brainstorming process in the creation of shadow boxes. Pairing this selection of materials with a brief journaling activity in which students explained their reasoning for choosing their three items would further advance their commitment to the creative process. Furthermore, inviting students to reflect on their object choices opened up the opportunity for a connection to the themes we were discussing. It all started with catalysts, but carefully designed processes led students to products that were far more than simply a grouping of random objects. Figure 3.1 offers a list of questions to support students engaging with catalysts.

Questions to support students engaging with catalysts:

- What materials am I most curious about?
- What am I wondering?
- Were there any materials, images, questions, or problems that got me thinking right away? What does this tell me?
- Which topics are most interesting to me? Why? Do I have other questions about that topic?
- Can I imagine a different possibility?
- Which question, statement, video, image, or problem seems most interesting to me? Why?
- How do I know when something captures my attention?
- How do I imagine I might use these materials?
- Are there any other materials I wish to have?
- How might I change what is already here (materials, audience, setting, genre, function, perspective, values, variables) to get something new?
- How could looking at things from another perspective change what I might do and how I might respond?

Figure 3.1: *Select and reflect—Questions to support students engaging with catalysts.*

*Visit **go.SolutionTree.com/assessment** for a free reproducible version of this figure.*

Asking Questions and Generating Ideas

Following the introduction of a strong catalyst, unlocking creativity even more will mean building in processes, within exploration, that invite students to begin to make sense of the catalysts on their own terms. Educator and author Mark Gura (2016) explains, "The resource itself won't make creativity happen. . . . The resource merely enables and facilitates an artist's creation" (p. 187). It follows that our work as teachers in a creative classroom is to help our students move from inspiration to creation through the purposeful generation of questions or ideas. When we don't take this next step, our efforts to nurture creativity can quickly become chaotic and directionless for both ourselves and our students. Questions serve to anchor exploration. However, this is not a one-and-done activity. Rather, questions continue to be critical during every stage of the creative process. Questions move creativity forward and go hand-in-hand with idea generation. Questions can lead to students' identification of learning goals in their creative work, or they can move students from a learning goal (where many lessons originate) into creativity. It flows both ways. It is through reflection during the creative processes that our students begin to narrow their focus by asking more and more questions. Over time, their queries become more refined and precise. For example, instead of asking, "How do birds stay warm in the winter?" they may ask, "Do the feathers of arctic birds vary from those of tropical birds?" Later, they may ask, "How can I find more information about feather structure so I can draw it?" and then, "How can I mimic the structure of arctic bird feathers in warm clothing I am designing?" Each stage in the creative process yields new questions, but they start during exploration. Without questions to drive students' creative exploration, creativity can lose momentum quickly. Learners may simply play with the materials and quickly lose interest, without any growth or depth of thinking. Questions give our learners a reason to search, to experiment, to explore. Questions are the foundation upon which creativity is built. This is why they are so critical during exploration.

Question generation is also tied very closely to criteria setting, self-assessment, and feedback. Questions related to what students are learning (content, topics, or ideas) emerge out of a gap between what students currently know and what they seek to understand or do, and this gap is determined through assessment processes. For example, middle school science students may ask, "How do I make my roller coaster work so the cars make it up the hill at the end?" When they ask this question, they are identifying where they are (I have created a roller coaster that doesn't gain enough speed for my cars to make it up the hill) in comparison to where they want to be (I want my car to be able to make it up the hill). In essence, the question emerges from a self-assessment of the current state of affairs relative to the desired state of affairs. As they continue their pursuit of creative solutions, their self-assessment (and the associated questions) may become more sophisticated. They may ask, "How does the slope of my track impact the speed of my cars?" or "How much more track will I need to have to increase the rise and, therefore, the speed?" Students are still identifying where they are (I do not yet have a roller coaster that accomplishes what I want it to accomplish) and how to get to where they want to be (I am going to need to think about slope and track length in order to resolve this problem). These kinds of questions are the sweet spot between creativity and self-assessment.

It is important to note that students do not always naturally identify increasingly sophisticated questions all on their own. When teachers ask students questions about their work in progress, they should model how questions become more complex as one develops understanding, and advance students' creative exploration by inviting them into ideas they hadn't considered. However, instead of feeding students questions throughout the creative process, it may be helpful to simply ask, "What are you wondering now?" or "What does this make you think of?" as a way of assessing understanding. As we observe and listen to our learners, it will become clear who needs our support and prompting and who is ready to ask the next question on their own.

It's important for unlocking creativity that students ask questions about not only *what* they learn but also *how* they learn. Questions such as, What conditions support my learning? and Why are my creative efforts not bringing success as I imagined they would? advance not only students' skills and understanding within the context of their creative work but also their creative capacities. These kinds of questions bridge creative output with creative skills and invite students to think about their own creative preferences and decisions. They can consider what they are trying to learn and create as well as how they are going to do so.

Whether students are asking questions about what they are learning or how they learn, their questions help them identify criteria for success. Whatever the question (How do I make my bridge structure stop falling down? or How do I make my car look good without affecting how the wheels roll?), the question itself signals an act of self-assessment. A desire to prevent a bridge from falling down means that a successful bridge structure stays upright (criterion). A resolve to create a car that both looks good and moves well identifies two criteria—(1) aesthetics and (2) function. The criteria setting then merges with the goal setting and subsequent planning present in strong self-assessment. (My goal is to create a bridge that stays upright. My goal is to design a car that looks good and moves well.)

When our students seek clarification and conversation with others about their creative efforts, their questions drive feedback. For example, when a student asks a question about supporting the span of her bridge, she may turn to classmates and observe the decisions they are making with their own bridges to seek answers. Alternately, she may ask a friend for suggestions about how to support her bridge. This might result in a give-and-take conversation, where the friend offers suggestions and the student accepts or dismisses them, based on her own vision for the project. Perhaps the student tries a few alternatives and, when the teacher checks in with her, he or she invites the student to think more deeply about solutions that do not affect the width of the bridge. This process illustrates what Robinson (2009) describes when he says, "Creativity involves several different processes that wind through each other. The first is generating new ideas, imagining different possibilities, considering alternative options" (p. 66). Teachers' feedback conversations with students, including the use of questions, move them to pursue alternate creative ideas, and the ebb and flow of the creative process continues with the help of strong questions and assessment.

As we begin creative processes with students, we can establish and nurture a class-room culture that encourages student questions. The act of honoring questions communicates the importance of adopting a stance of inquiry when learning. It also increases the chances that students will invest in any process that emerges from self-generated questions, which bodes well for deep learning. Dacey and Conklin (2004) assert, "Students who develop this sensitivity to quandaries tend to become eager learn-ers, and thus are much more likely to remember what they have learned" (p. 29). It is for this reason that we need to support students in becoming strong questioners. We need to encourage them to explore their natural curiosities and think about topics from many different angles and perspectives.

Asking questions is a skill in and of itself, and it doesn't always come naturally to every student in every instance. Some topics are more engaging than others and, there-fore, more easily facilitate questions. Some students have more background knowledge on specific topics, and so questions emerge more quickly. Sometimes we have to work with our learners to help them develop good questioning skills. Jenny Frost (1997) points out the importance of focusing on this skill when she says:

> It seems important to get away from the notion that questions come bubbling out of children in a form that is easy to use and that children will automati-cally ask questions about all the things teachers want them to learn. (p. 176)

Co-directors of the Right Question Institute Dan Rothstein and Luz Santana (2014) echo the importance of developing this skill in students:

> As students learn to produce their own questions, they are thinking diver-gently—that is more broadly and creatively. When they focus on the kinds of questions they are asking and choose their priority questions, they are thinking convergently—narrowing down, analyzing, assessing, comparing, and synthesizing. And when they reflect on what they have learned through the process, students are engaged in metacognition—they are thinking about their thinking. Students who learn to use all three of these thinking abilities become more sophisticated questioners, thinkers, and problem-solvers.

When we work with learners in exploration to develop their skill in asking questions, we will advance creativity and learning at the same time.

Question formulation technique (QFT) is a useful technique that moves students through a process for generating, refining, and prioritizing questions. The Right Question Institute (n.d.) designed this technique and clarifies its importance, stating, "By deliberately teaching questioning skills, we will be facilitating a process that will help students develop a mental muscle necessary for deeper learning, creativity and innovation, analysis, and problem solving." The QFT can guide any creative pursuit. The process begins with a *QFocus*, the question focus, which is a stimulus for deep thinking and wonder. This focus might be a provocative statement, a compelling photograph, or an object—anything that invites curiosity and opinion. Students engage in this QFocus and begin to generate questions. The QFT then moves students through expansion, clarification, and modification of questions. Visit the Right Question Institute (http://rightquestion.org) for more information on this technique. (Visit **go.SolutionTree.com/assessment** to access live links to the websites mentioned in this book.)

After posing many questions, students will begin to generate ideas. Asking questions and proposing ideas often go hand-in-hand. In fact, one aspect of the QFT is to invite participants to turn ideas or statements into questions. The most important thing is to allow students to be as expansive as possible in their questions and ideas, because this is how students move past their inside-the-box thinking to unlock true creativity. Renzulli (2000) explains the value of asking a large volume of questions:

> *Research has shown that individuals who produce a large number of ideas are more likely to produce ideas that are more original. . . . The best way to promote free-wheeling and offbeat thinking is to value quantity and withhold criticism and evaluation until students have exhausted their total supply of ideas related to a given problem. (p. 8)*

The freedom to explore through questions and ideas can be very freeing for students. As these processes intertwine with assessment and response, creativity is further unlocked. Teachers use observation, conversation, and question analysis to formatively assess whether learners' exploration questions are guiding inquiry. Using what they learn, teachers may then encourage students to dig deeper and ask additional or richer questions by offering students additional catalysts or opportunities for collaboration with peers or personal reflection. In addition to using the QFT, figure 3.2 (page 76) offers a list of questions to support students asking questions and generating ideas.

Questions to support students asking questions and generating ideas:

- What do I wonder?
- What am I trying to figure out? What problem do I need to resolve?
- What do I already know?
- What does this make me think about?
- What might I ask someone about this topic if I could?
- What things about this topic, these materials, or this process are important to me?
- What processes might work for me, based on my initial idea?
- What do I know for sure?
- What is my main challenge right now?
- What are the ways I might solve this problem?
- How else can I think about this?
- How could I illustrate my message visually? How do I know which pieces are important to represent visually?
- What might be an unusual way to approach this task, question, problem, or product?
- What do I not know? What do I think I know? What do I definitely know?
- Did I list all the things I am trying to figure out?

Figure 3.2: *Select and reflect—Questions to support students asking questions and generating ideas.*

Visit go.SolutionTree.com/assessment for a free reproducible version of this figure.

Practicing Patience and Taking Incubation Time

As a creative person, I can assert with confidence that I sometimes drive my colleagues crazy. We can plan a group facilitation or work through ways to share our ideas with an audience, but often on the morning of the planned event, I get an insight that ultimately changes plans. I will incubate ideas for days, rolling them around in my head, weighing them against goals. I cannot speed up this process, and I will only reach insight when my brain is ready to do so. However, what it means for my colleagues is that I often change direction at the last minute. This is the nature of my creative process and, fortunately for me, the people I work with have come to expect it. I must have incubation time. I need the space to wrestle with a creative idea until I know it is right.

Sawyer (2006) explains incubation this way: "The incubation stage is often below the surface of consciousness. It's the least understood stage in the creative process. In incubation, mental elements combine, and insight occurs when certain combinations emerge into consciousness" (p. 96). This definition definitely describes my own creative process, and I have witnessed it in students as well when they return to a creative product they are working on after some time away from it, and change directions, possessed by newfound clarity. They can hardly wait to step back into the creative process because they have thought of a way to refine their work to better reflect their vision.

Neuroscience researchers Simone M. Ritter and Ap Dijksterhuis (2014) explore the role of incubation in creativity and conclude, "During an incubation period, unconscious processes contribute to creative thinking." The mechanisms behind incubation continue to hold some mystery but the positive impacts have been well documented. Offering time to briefly leave a creative effort and then return to it can advance the work in the long term.

Unfortunately, more often than not, it is difficult to get students to linger on ideas long enough to reach insight. Incubation runs contrary to a belief many students have about school—that the faster they get it done, the smarter they are, and the better it is for everyone. Teachers play into this myth when they set deadlines that are too short and emphasize speed over quality (for example, by telling students to just hand in what they have done, or hurry and finish it). However, investing time in exploration to incubate ideas is worth it. This gives students the chance to think and explore without committing to action. Examples of ways to provide this time include the following.

◇ Introduce a task one day and revisit it the next, with other things occupying the time in between.

◇ Generate questions together, asking students to choose one to drive their creative pursuit, but offering them a day to make a change if they want.

◇ Involve students in completing a creative project and then returning to it months later, applying new skills and understanding to refine their original efforts.

Devoting time to assess the ideas students generate and expand their initial questions is also important. We teach students to think flexibly when we invite them to abandon old ways of thinking, to develop ideas beyond their initial understanding, and to adapt to new information. This may mean we simply shift our practice from giving students the answers, and instead ask them to decide which answer has the most promise. It may also mean that instead of telling students how to proceed with a task, we ask them for ideas about what each of them needs to do to become successful at a goal. This shift makes space for creative ideas. When we invite students to be the decision makers through self-assessment, it changes their role in classroom experiences from passive to active. Davies (2011) states it this way: "The research is clear. When students are involved in classroom assessment processes, they become more engaged in learning" (p. 55). And Wiliam (2018) concludes, "Activating students as owners of their own learning can produce extraordinary improvements in their achievement" (p. 169). There is little doubt that this is a strength of the creative process and the self-assessment that accompanies it.

During exploration, students will need time to prepare for their creative processes. This may mean gathering materials, searching for resources, collaborating in groups, designing and mapping structures and processes, and preparing their physical space. As students settle on the questions or problems that will drive their creative process, it is helpful to ask them what they will need to begin. These decisions are important for students to make because they assist learners in achieving greater clarity about goals, action plans, and criteria for success. Simply put, when students are asked what they need to begin, they have to have a sense of their goals in order to answer. Their attention to what they need to be successful promotes thinking about what *successful* means to them. English professor and Pulitzer Prize winner Donald M. Murray (1981) describes this in relation to creative writing, stating, "When editors or teachers kidnap the first draft, they also remove responsibility for meaning making from the writer" (p. 34). Exercising patience and letting students take the lead during this initial decision making are critical for independent creativity.

Incubation may lead to insight at the most unexpected moments, and teachers need to allow this to happen. For example, in the middle of a science lesson, a student may suddenly make a connection that had eluded him previously, and ask to try something with an ongoing project. The incubation-insight relationship can be unpredictable. Sometimes, it is only when we are immersed in something new that we see the old with fresh eyes.

Figure 3.3 offers a list of questions to support students developing patience and taking incubation time.

Questions to support students developing patience and taking incubation time:

- What do I need right now?
- What do I need to focus on first?
- How do I know when to leave an idea alone for a while?
- What does insight feel like?
- What might I do when I am stuck?
- Do I have enough time to accomplish my vision?
- How might I use my time differently?
- When I take a break, what might I do to keep thinking about my problem or product?
- Have I given this enough time?
- Is there a place where I can think more clearly and creatively?
- How do effort and learning connect?
- What makes me want to create?

Figure 3.3: *Select and reflect—Questions to support students developing patience and taking incubation time.*

*Visit **go.SolutionTree.com/assessment** for a free reproducible version of this figure.*

Collaborating, Trusting, and Playing

Collaboration in the classroom supports both creativity and the assessment it depends on. Collaboration is different from the traditional group work many students have come to expect (and in many cases come to resent) in classrooms. While students might perceive *group work* as a forced relationship between learners where some do the thinking and others do their best to fade into the background, in contrast, *collaboration* depends on a shared purpose and investment on behalf of all parties involved. Instead of coming together to lobby for their own ideas or to capitulate to the ideas of their peers, when students truly collaborate, they engage with each other in mutually beneficial ways. Robert Marzano (2007) asserts that collaboration is one of the most powerful instructional decisions a teacher can make in the classroom. Wendy L. Ostroff (2016), a developmental and cognitive psychologist and a professor at the Hutchins School of Liberal Studies at Sonoma State University, expands on this idea, noting, "Students take turns being managers of conversations, thereby learning to be good coaches, empowering others, and expressing personal interest in team members. Working together, students begin to help their team achieve well-being and successes" (p. 42). This is the kind of relationship that supports engagement in the creative process.

It is helpful to show students how they already possess the skills for collaboration. Many of our learners use collaboration every day to achieve personally meaningful goals, but often, students do not transfer these skills into classroom contexts because they don't see how their daily lives and the world of school relate. It is useful to help students see that collaboration in school should feel just like the collaboration they experience when they play sports, when they make music, when they play games, or when they engage in imaginary play. If a student has ever prepared a meal with family members, or decorated a room, or cleaned the house, he or she knows how collaboration works. If a student has ever worked with a friend to build a toy house, or acted in a play, he or she understands how collaboration leads to a greater product. These comparisons help students see how true collaboration feels different from group work, where the goal is uncertain or imposed, where roles are not equitable, and where time to practice and learn is denied. Collaboration is different.

When collaboration works well in a classroom setting, students offer each other expertise and ideas, advancing both their own creative efforts and those of their classmates. Collaboration during the exploration stage allows students to bounce their ideas off other people. This can assist them in refining their focus and making decisions about next steps. Reeves (2015) advocates for a flow between individual idea generation and collaborative sharing as a way to advance creativity, asserting that there is a time and a place for both individual creative exploration and collaborative processes.

Student collaboration during exploration also benefits teachers, who no longer have to assume sole responsibility for listening to ideas and questions as they emerge.

Students can work alongside their peers, posing questions, offering advice, and acting as critical friends. This frees the teacher to attend to emergent needs of students who are experiencing more difficulty, who need additional resources, or who would benefit from adult guidance.

When we teach students how to collaborate, our first order of business is to be clear about the role collaboration will serve within exploration. If we are asking students to collaborate in order to generate ideas, we can use processes like Chalk Talk (Ritchhart, Church, & Morrison, 2011) or Make and Pass. During Chalk Talk, students work as a group to write or draw ideas about a topic without speaking. They can share their own thoughts or they can build on the ideas of others, but they have to do so in written or illustrated form. All students engage in building a shared understanding. During Make and Pass, students write or draw ideas for a limited time and then, when signaled to do so, pass their work on to the next person, who builds on it. Students can pursue several topics or questions at once, with each student contributing to the overall understanding.

In both processes, the collaborative effort continues through debriefing and refinement of the ideas or images shared. These processes can occur through the use of graphic organizers, through structured conversations, and through reflective practices like journaling, blogging, or vlogging. Students reflect on their initial collaborative efforts to determine which parts are worth expanding on and which do not advance the creative cause.

If the purpose of collaboration is to offer feedback to fellow classmates, teachers can engage students in activities such as Carousel and modified fishbowl. Carousel, in which students rotate through several centers that each explore a different question or topic, is a great way to invite students to move through the ideas of others and offer feedback, or ask additional questions on sticky notes. A modified fishbowl, during which a group of students sit on chairs in the middle of the classroom (like fish in a bowl) and respectfully discuss the ideas of students sitting around them in the shape of a circle (the bowl itself), is another way to encourage collaborative feedback. In contrast to a traditional fishbowl, where the outside "bowl" of students are simply observing the discussion of the "fish," this version has the outside students receiving feedback for their work from the students on the inside. Processes like these give students a method for learning to collaborate and a means to develop creativity.

Regardless of the purpose that collaboration will serve, students need to learn effective communication skills like listening well and taking turns. They may need to learn how to phrase feedback or ask additional questions in respectful ways. They need contexts in which they can practice showing interest, summarizing what they have heard, signaling encouragement, observing nonverbal cues, clarifying, and staying open-minded. Collaboration is a skill in and of itself, and like any skill, teachers may need to teach it explicitly through modeling and supporting students as they practice these skills.

Nurturing classrooms where collaboration is done well and in the service of creativity means teachers also have to attend to trust. Students have to be vulnerable to be creative, which can put emotional safety at risk when they are collaborating. Students need to feel sure that their peers will respect their ideas and that they have value in their group. Building this trust means allowing students to be vulnerable in our classrooms. Teachers need to model vulnerability, acknowledge and support it when they see it, and teach students how to do the same. For example, a teacher may share a piece of his or her own creative work and ask students to offer feedback. He or she may then lead a discussion on how feedback was both given and received, and the class may generate ideas for effective feedback sessions. In a physical education class, the teacher may participate in a game invented by students, modeling what it means to try something new. He or she may then work with students to generate questions about a strategy that arose during the first run-through. Together, the players could work with the inventors to modify the game or add a rule. Both examples offer the opportunity for vulnerability to live within a classroom space and for teachers to teach students how to respond compassionately and constructively in a vulnerable context. Lauren Porosoff and Jonathan Weinstein (2018) say it so well when they state, "Your best shot [at creating trust] is to be as present, attentive, compassionate, and flexible as your beautifully imperfect self can muster" (p. 10). When we work hard to build trusting communities in our classrooms, creativity can grow.

Once trust is secure and collaboration is in full swing, exploration can invite students to play. This means they have freedom to make sense of the things in front of them—to manipulate objects, craft language, imagine possibilities, and simply explore and enjoy themselves. Exploration can feel just like play when time is given to just exploring ideas. Perhaps students are invited to interact with mathematics materials in any way that makes sense to them before mathematics concepts are explored in detail. Teachers may allow students to experiment with safe science materials in a playful manner, or they may invite them to add colored paint to water to play around with the idea of color mixing. Working with materials, in these examples, is playful, but the teacher can then use the play as a catalyst for deeper exploration. Students can allow themselves to interact, exchange ideas, and wonder together without the burden of needing immediate answers or finding the "right" way and teachers can sit back, observe, document, and plan for the next step in learning.

Figure 3.4 (page 82) offers a list of questions to support students collaborating, trusting, and playing.

Questions to support students collaborating, trusting, and playing:

- How would I describe what is going on with me and my group members?
- What are we trying to do together?
- How might each of us do something to achieve our goal?
- What am I looking for feedback on?
- Who might I ask for help or ideas?
- What do I think other group members are thinking, feeling, or wanting?
- How might I check my assumptions about group members in a respectful way?
- How is collaboration frustrating? How might we overcome that?
- Am I clear about my role?
- Do I know how to offer respectful feedback?
- How might I relate differently with my partner?
- What do I want for myself and others in this moment?
- How can we reach agreement about our goal in working together today?
- How might each of us feel great about what we are offering to the group?

Figure 3.4: *Select and reflect—Questions to support students collaborating, trusting, and playing.*

*Visit **go.SolutionTree.com/assessment** for a free reproducible version of this figure.*

Suspending Judgment and Accepting Ambiguity, Failure, and Chaos

One reason many teachers and students are uncomfortable with creativity is because it is a process filled with ambiguity and even chaos. Certainly, there are times when next steps are unclear; when products are unformed; and when the room is filled with the buzz of productivity, conversation, frustration, and failure. Creativity doesn't always feel good for both the creator and the person facilitating the process. Furthermore, the results of assessment during the creative process may well signal a lack of success. However, without these experiences, creativity cannot flourish. Creativity depends on failure and uncertainty. This means that teachers and learners in creative classrooms have to become accustomed to a climate and culture that accepts challenge, that gives time for reflection, and that allows for revision and changes in direction.

It also means that learners have to accept creative learning as a series of decisions that may or may not yield immediate success. Robinson (2009) reminds us, "Doing the thing you love to do is no guarantee that you'll be in the zone every time. Sometimes the mood isn't right, the time is wrong, and the ideas just don't flow" (p. 80). When students generate questions, they have to develop tolerance for a lack of immediate answers. When they brainstorm ideas, they have to learn to accept ambiguity and initial ideas that never take shape. They have to suspend judgment of their own efforts until they have exhausted all possibilities. While this tolerance is important in the process of creativity in schools, Tony Wagner (2012) notes it is just as important for students' lives beyond school when he states, "The most innovative companies celebrate failure" (p. 174). The ability to stay calm in the midst of failure and continue to persevere despite challenges has long-term benefits. Creativity builds confidence and resilience in learners and this is worth unlocking as soon as we can. Figure 3.5 offers suggestions to help students who are wrestling with ambiguity work through their discomfort.

When I feel uncertain, I can:

- Sit still and think about what is making me uncomfortable
- Talk with a trusted friend or elder
- List possible next steps
- Try a new approach or material
- Revisit my goal, my purpose, and my success criteria
- Write in a journal about how I am feeling
- Breathe and remove myself from my work for a while until I can regroup
- Work on something else and wait for clarity

Figure 3.5: *Working through ambiguity.*

*Visit **go.SolutionTree.com/assessment** for a free reproducible version of this figure.*

Figure 3.6 offers a list of questions to support students suspending judgment and accepting ambiguity, failure, and chaos.

Questions to support students suspending judgment and accepting ambiguity, failure, and chaos:

- What can I do when I feel overwhelmed?
- Which ideas deserve more thought?
- How can I describe what I see without giving my opinion?
- How might I start to take all these parts and combine them?
- Why is it important to withhold deciding too early?
- How might I think of my problem in a whole bunch of ways? Why might this be important?
- What might I do differently that I have not done before?
- How can I approach this in a new way?
- What can I do if my idea doesn't work?
- How can I prepare myself for failure?
- How do people keep trying when things keep going wrong?
- What do I hate doing and why? How do I work through that?

Figure 3.6: *Select and reflect—Questions to support students suspending judgment and accepting ambiguity, failure, and chaos.*

*Visit **go.SolutionTree.com/assessment** for a free reproducible version of this figure.*

Making Connections

Making connections is part of the creative process. In fact, it is through connection making that student efforts can move from knowledge or skill to creative insight. As students work with new materials, they may connect their current use with a new possibility. Robinson (2009) describes this when he says, "You can think of creativity as a conversation between what we're trying to figure out and the media we are using" (p. 69). Similarly, learners may connect two seemingly disparate ideas in order to generate a creative solution to a problem. For example, in a high school social studies or history class, in an exploration of world conflict and creative solutions, a student may see how two separate world events had similar qualities (economic disparity or conflicting worldviews, for example) and begin to imagine a way to avoid those circumstances. Perhaps students may connect a current experience with a related idea or object, resulting in a metaphor or analogy that leads to deeper understanding and richer products. Making connections can yield creative output.

In exploration, to make connections, learners first must collect data, information, materials, and questions, and search for related ideas. They need the opportunity to share their thoughts with their classmates and listen to suggestions and connections their peers may make, and time to let these connections incubate and grow. As students move from exploration to the elaboration and expression stages, the ability to make connections supports students developing insight (an important aspect of the critical actions in these subsequent stages). Sawyer (2006) describes how in business contexts, creative innovation in collaborative teams emerges and builds incrementally on a long history of prior innovation, multiple discoveries are common, and there is frequent interaction among teams. These kinds of connections in business contexts produce innovative results and echo the importance of making connections in classroom contexts. Throughout exploration, students need the opportunity to connect their initial ideas to those of their peers, to those of experts, and to experiences the students, themselves, have had in order to elevate their creative efforts.

Teachers can use the prompts in figure 3.7 to support students making connections during a brainstorming session (listing of ideas, experiences, or objects in connection to a prompt or topic), when accessing prior knowledge, or during the question-generation process (listing of questions in response to a prompt or topic). We may also access these kinds of prompts as students gather materials and begin to explore their ideas.

Questions to support students making connections:

- How might I use these two objects or materials together to make something new?
- What else does this make me think of?
- What do I already know, and how do I know it?

- How do those two ideas relate to each other? How are they different?
- Can I see how these two materials might work together?
- How do we know when we have enough information? Where else might I look?
- What do these two related ideas make me wonder?
- How do these things connect?
- What do I already know and how do I know it?
- How might I use these two materials together?
- How might this resource help me find other related resources that offer different perspectives?
- When have I seen or done this before? What did I learn that I can apply now?
- Are there other places that can tell me more?
- Are there other ways of approaching a challenge that I can apply here?

Figure 3.7: *Select and reflect—Questions to support students making connections.*

Visit **go.SolutionTree.com/assessment** *for a free reproducible version of this figure.*

Having Choice and Making Decisions

Many qualities of classrooms that nurture creativity are the same qualities that nurture all learning. Giving students choices so they can make decisions is an example of a classroom practice that supports engagement, risk taking, and learning, regardless of the kind of learning we are trying to grow. Ai-Girl Tan (2004) explains, "When learners perceive they have control over and responsibility for the learning process, methods and strategies, they are likely to be committed to the task and thus be motivated to achieve" (p. 103). From question generation to brainstorming, from materials to plans, it is important that teachers offer students choice in both how they will engage in the creative process and the products they will create as a result of it. True creativity is borne out of ownership. Students need to grapple with decisions large and small in order to work through the creative process and emerge with a product that matches their personal vision. Giving students choice offers them a chance at the autonomy Daniel Pink (2009) describes as so critical to motivation and as so natural to all human beings when he says, "Our basic nature is to be curious and self-directed" (p. 87). However, it is important to recognize that *autonomy* is not synonymous with *free-for-all*. Pink (2009) goes on to clarify that offering autonomy through choice does not mean students have no expectations or responsibility: "Encouraging autonomy doesn't mean discouraging accountability. Whatever operating system is in place, people must be accountable for their work" (p. 105). Choice offers students the chance to make meaningful decisions, exercise their voices, and take risks in a supportive environment. Choice also offers us, as teachers, the chance to develop learners who accept responsibility for their own outcomes. This serves our students in the long term as they navigate a complex world filled with many choices and possible outcomes. As they become comfortable with making choices and navigating the consequences of those choices on their own, they build confidence and resilience. Education professor Dana L. Mitra (2004) concludes in her research that offering students a voice in the decision making in classrooms produces:

> *meaningful experiences for youth that help to meet fundamental developmental needs—especially for students who otherwise do not find meaning in their school experiences. Specifically, this research finds a marked consistency in the growth of agency, belonging and competence—three assets that are central to youth development. (p. 651)*

This is the win-win of creativity in the classroom.

Figure 3.8 offers a list of questions to support students making choices and decisions.

Questions to support students making choices and decisions:

- What are some ways I am planning on approaching this? Why am I choosing that approach to begin with?
- What will I do next?
- Am I comfortable with my choice of focus right now? If not, why?
- What other choices are available to me?
- Which materials will I choose to use? Why?
- How will I choose to solve this problem?
- What is within my control? Where am I able to make decisions?
- What parts of this matter most to me? How might I maintain control?
- What helps me focus?

Figure 3.8: *Select and reflect—Questions to support students making choices and decisions.*

*Visit **go.SolutionTree.com/assessment** for a free reproducible version of this figure.*

Setting Effective Goals and Success Criteria

While many teachers understand the importance of establishing goals and success criteria for and with students, the timing of these activities in a creative process may require finesse. When teachers focus on inviting students to openly explore and pose questions, offering explicit goals and criteria at the outset might suppress students' intended progress during exploration.

While teachers may select specific *learning* goals and targets to address through the creative process (for example, solving problems using fractions, or understanding the water cycle, or recognizing and replicating patterns), they can invite students into materials, questions, and contexts that allow them to share in the construction and generation of specific *creative* goals. Even when the content is tied to prescribed learning goals and is non-negotiable, the processes by which students will explore this content will require *process* goals (for example, constructing a model that uses fractions, creating a three-dimensional representation of the water cycle, or engaging in a nature walk and photographing examples of patterns). Teachers and students can co-construct these process-related goals after some exploration has occurred and can later refine and expand on them during elaboration.

In this earliest stage of creativity, it might be beneficial to delay delivering not only creative goals but explicit criteria to students. Instead of handing out a rubric or a checklist immediately to communicate our expectations, we might, instead, engage in exploration for a while before introducing criteria. For our students, perhaps the only criterion that matters at the outset of their creative effort is the freedom to just experiment without restriction. For example, instead of laying out an experiment step-by-step, ask an open-ended question, such as, "How might we discover how the digestive systems of mammals and fish are the same and different?" or "How might we determine how the salinity of water affects corrosion?" Students can then create theories, test prototypes, design experiments, and share ideas for how exploration might occur. Once students have shaped their ideas around an important question, a teacher could then invite students to pause and consider the qualities (criteria) of a strong experiment (goal).

When we embed goal and criteria setting within experiences and thinking during exploration, student responses are often far more insightful and grounded in their actual observations. John A. C. Hattie and Gregory M. Donoghue (2016) explain, "Providing [students] early on with an overview of what successful learning . . . will look like (knowing the success criteria) will help them reduce their anxiety, increase their motivation, and build both surface and deeper understandings" (p. 27). Using open-ended exploration to frame goal and then criteria setting nurtures creativity and innovation, while an experiential context ensures goals and criteria that have the potential to be "lived out" and acted on immediately by both teachers and learners. Robinson and Aronica (2015) describe this relationship between creativity and assessment when they say:

> *Being creative is not about having off the wall ideas and letting your imagination run free. It may involve all of that, but it also involves refining, testing, and focusing what you are doing. It's about original thinking on the part of the individual, and it's also about judging critically whether the work in process is taking the right shape and is worthwhile. (p. 147)*

This kind of delayed timing of prescribed goals and explicit criteria generates stronger products and processes, and positions students as instructional designers alongside their teachers.

To be clear, when we share ownership for goal and criteria setting with students, we are not abdicating control over quality, nor is the destination a shot in the dark. When students determine what they are hoping to achieve and what proficient work looks and sounds like, it does not mean that they will arrive at different conclusions from us. I have found many times in my own classroom that when teachers are curating and sharing specific and purposeful mentor texts and samples after collaboratively settling on goals for the creative work with students, students can then identify the criteria that reflect quality work in the same ways teachers arrive at the criteria. In fact, there is consistency in what indicates quality work. For example, consider the following experience I had teaching first and second graders.

I once heard a well-known presenter tell an audience that engaging students in assessment should be reserved for learners over the age of twelve. I had taught students younger than twelve many times in my career and had witnessed some profound thinking by some amazing little people, so I wanted to test the accuracy of this presenter's statement. I arranged to work in a combined first- and second-grade classroom and test this notion.

On my fourth day in this classroom, I witnessed just the right evidence to contradict the idea that these students cannot assess. The teacher and I were working on fluency in oral reading, and I began the class by handing out a book my own parents had written. It was a lovely, artistic book filled with colorful images and plenty of rhyming words. I asked the learners to follow along as I read aloud. I proceeded to intentionally read the book with terrible fluency. I stopped and started, stumbled over pronunciation, and repeated phrases when I shouldn't have. After a few pages, I stopped and looked up at the class. I asked them what they thought of my oral reading.

With the lack of inhibition that only young children possess, they proceeded to tell me all the things I had done incorrectly. I listened to their concerns and then I asked them to help me get better by giving me advice on how to read more fluently. They provided responses like, "Read at the same speed more often," and "Try practicing before you start so you can try out all the words." I dutifully recorded their responses, and before long, the class collectively generated a list of criteria for fluent oral reading. It was a beautiful thing.

Perhaps the most creative moment in that assessment-driven lesson was when a student in the first- and second-grade classroom compared my first reading to how her father drives their all-terrain vehicle—he stops and starts, stops and starts. The little girl said it made it hard for her to hang on just like my reading made it hard for her to follow the story. Can students younger than twelve years assess? You bet they can. By inviting students at any age into creative processes and asking them to determine criteria for success, we are not allowing a free-for-all in standards of quality. Our assessment processes still need a precision that will inevitably lead to growth for all learners.

It remains vitally important that before we engage students in any creative and assessment processes, we, as teachers, must be crystal clear about what we are asking students to engage in and why, what learning goals we are addressing through creativity, and what quality means within the creative context. Creativity does not absolve us of the responsibility to insist on clarity around quality work. In creative classrooms, learning emerges from the student, but the degree of quality learning should be no less than what we are hoping to achieve using other methods of instruction.

Figure 3.9 offers a list of questions to support students setting goals and criteria.

Questions to support students setting goals and criteria:

- What is beginning to seem important to me? Why?
- What is less important?
- How do I imagine my product might look?
- What are my goals for this work?
- Do I have creative goals that connect to learning goals the teacher has provided me?
- How do I see my work happening? What will tell me my work is good work?
- What are criteria for a good solution to this problem? How do I know?
- How will I know when I have achieved what I hoped to achieve?
- What would signal failure?
- How might this look, sound, or feel when I am done?
- Where might I go to see examples of quality or success?
- What am I trying to do, learn, or achieve?
- What do I need to do to avoid missing my goal?
- How will I know when I am learning? How will I know when I am not learning?
- When I explore mentor texts, what do I notice?

Figure 3.9: *Select and reflect—Questions to support students setting goals and criteria.*

Visit go.SolutionTree.com/assessment for a free reproducible version of this figure.

The Role of the Teacher

The teacher plays a critical role in establishing and maintaining the opportunity for learners to explore, question, and gather ideas and materials. Through our actions and words, decisions and responses, we nurture classroom processes that invite students to wonder, imagine, and explore. In order to unlock exploration for our learners, we need to:

◇ Construct a classroom climate and culture that is conducive to creativity and the kinds of assessment that support it (for example, self-assessment, observation, conversation, and documentation through artifacts)

◇   Invite wonder and risk taking

◇   Nurture collaborative processes that support the sharing of questions, ideas, skills, and interests

◇   Teach students to be comfortable with ambiguity and delayed closure

◇   Support decision making, even when the results are not yet optimal

◇   Facilitate processes, such as brainstorming, question generation, portfolio creation, and collaboration, that invite students fully into the exploration stage of creativity

Following are some important roles for teachers when unlocking exploration that can support some of the challenges students experience in this stage.

◇   **Inviter of wonder and risk:** While it is true that human beings are naturally inquisitive, many students have learned that curiosity wastes time and that questions are not welcome unless they emerge from the teacher. As a result, some students do not know what it means to feel wonder and do not feel safe to take risks.

◇   **Facilitator of collaborative processes:** Students are often unskilled at being part of collaborative teams. They have not learned how to share ideas with others, how to offer feedback, how to co-construct meaning, and how to work with others on a shared goal. Furthermore, their experiences with group work often teach them to hate working with others. They may see it as a waste of time, as humiliating, as frustrating, or as a chance to coast and let others do the thinking.

◇   **Facilitator of creative processes:** The idea of a blank page or a completely open-ended creative project can make some students feel overwhelmed and even threatened. Students who are used to school looking and feeling like compliance and structure can find creative pursuits risky and unsettling.

◇   **Co-generator of learning goals and targets:** Students may find goal setting a difficult practice when first beginning creative learning. Learners have come to expect that goals come from teachers. That being said, teachers hold responsibility for verifying degrees of learning. Finding a balance between student autonomy and teacher responsibility is a key challenge of teaching.

Table 3.1 suggests specific actions that a teacher can take to overcome the challenges of these roles.

Table 3.1: *The Role of the Teacher and Key Actions in the Exploration Stage*

Role of the Teacher	Key Teacher Actions
Inviter of Wonder and Risk	◆ Invite students into ideas and materials that generate wonder. ◆ Provide new information to push thinking. ◆ Teach skills that enable risks with a greater chance of success in the end. ◆ Pass on enthusiasm and excitement about topics and processes.
Facilitator of Collaborative Processes	◆ Explore topics and possibilities from multiple perspectives. ◆ Encourage diverse audiences. ◆ Place a focus on short- and long-term goals to establish a need for shared effort. ◆ Explicitly teach and model collaborative skills (eye contact, active listening, powerful peer feedback, and shared reflection). ◆ Be clear about the purpose of collaboration.
Facilitator of Creative Processes	◆ Guide students through the process. ◆ Use formative assessment to make strong decisions about when students need support and when they need to make their own decisions. ◆ Facilitate brainstorming processes, help learners form questions, and guide students to choose materials and resources that will springboard them into creativity. ◆ Help students manage their time and take risks. ◆ Protect silence and focus when it is needed.
Co-Generator of Learning Goals and Targets	◆ Co-generate learning goals and targets with the students. ◆ Invite learners to make as many decisions as possible and explore their creative learning in personally meaningful ways. ◆ Share knowledge and skills that are essential to developing strong learners. ◆ Help learners craft actions that make sense, given classroom contexts. ◆ Help students imagine possibilities they hadn't considered. ◆ Push students just enough to maximize growth.

Assessment and Exploration

Assessment within exploration helps students make decisions and ready themselves for the next stage of creativity. In turn, it helps us support our students, determining when a learner is having a difficult time choosing an area of focus or is lacking the background knowledge to ask meaningful questions. Through assessment, we can work alongside learners, deepening their understanding of meaningful content while simultaneously developing their skill in engaging in creative thinking. Assessment is the means by which we work with our learners to take risks and persevere in the face of failure. When we use assessment in the service of creativity, we not only build relationships with our students but also help them build relationships with their creative selves.

As mentioned in chapter 1, achieving creative ends in the classroom requires engaging in three assessment practices during exploration: formative assessment (information gathering), which leads to feedback (dialogue with others), and self-assessment (dialogue with self). Prior to engaging in assessment, allow students to set their own goals and make their own decisions whenever possible. This facilitates the critical actions of having choice and making decisions, practicing patience and taking incubation time, and setting effective goals and success criteria. Then, during feedback conversations, use praise sparingly, substituting other affirming statements that more fully encourage creativity. This nurtures the critical actions of asking questions and generating ideas; engaging with catalysts; collaborating, trusting, and playing; and suspending judgment and accepting ambiguity, failure, and chaos. Finally, as part of developing the foundation for strong self-assessment, reframe success as actions and decisions that support a student-directed, as opposed to a teacher-controlled, goal. This supports making connections, setting effective goals and success criteria, and having choice and making decisions.

Additionally, using the reproducible tools at the end of this chapter (pages 95–102) can support teachers in their classrooms to help facilitate assessment that moves creativity forward. "Using Conversation as a Formative Assessment Tool During the Creative Process" (pages 99–100) offers techniques for you to use conversation as a formative assessment approach when you are developing creativity. "Collecting Conversation Data" (page 101) offers teachers a way to capture conversation data so they can use them to advance the creative process. You might use the "Self-Assessment and Goal Setting During Exploration" reproducible (page 102) to facilitate student self-assessment and goal setting during the exploration stage.

Formative Assessment: Allowing Students to Set Goals and Make Decisions

Establishing or articulating goals is the foundation of assessment. Goals are the destination, and formative assessment captures our temporary position in relation to this destination. It is during exploration that students begin to formulate their goals. These goals may shift and adjust during the elaboration stage, but, certainly, decisions about goals begin within exploration. Who owns these goals determines whether they support intrinsic motivation and personal decision making. While teachers set the context and structure environments for creativity, it is important that students have a hand in deciding what they are going to do with these contexts and environments. Teachers can lead learners to content and specific skill development, but students have to own the choices. Drapeau (2014) explains:

> *Let students decide what and how to measure success. For some students, the challenge is working with an idea that causes the greatest positive impact rather than the idea that they like the best. Engage students in determining what is measurable and what results are meaningful. How will they determine to what degree their results are effective? (p. 98)*

This is perhaps the hardest challenge of assessment in today's classrooms. It is difficult to let go of control over every aspect of learning, but without letting go, the learner never owns the creative process and product. Students cannot be intrinsically invested in something over which they have little control. Sawyer (2006) clarifies, "Creativity almost always results from intrinsic motivation; from people who work in an area just because they love the activity itself, not because of eventual payoff" (p. 466). Payoff is a hard thing to avoid in our grades-driven schools, but allowing students to set their own goals and delaying grades until the very end of the creative process can help students lose themselves in the joy of creativity and feel safe to try new things in pursuit of something that is meaningful to them.

Feedback: Using Praise Sparingly

Our use of praise in exploration can make student ownership over their processes and products go sideways. Pink (2009) confirms, "Done wrong, praise can become yet another 'if-then' reward that can squash creativity and stifle intrinsic motivation" (p. 189). Praise can set in motion a student's desire to please teachers as opposed to the desire to please him- or herself. As soon as we say, "I love what you are doing," or "I like how that is turning out," we communicate a recipe for our approval that some students cannot help but choose over their own impressions and opinions. I have witnessed many times students who may be dissatisfied with aspects of a product, but when a teacher praises those very aspects, these students turn away from their own goals and toward what they perceive to be the teacher's goals for them. Education professors Anne M. Orr and Margaret Olson (2007) describe this as "the story that says that fulfilling the teacher's expectations is more important than saying what you really think" (p. 824). This stops creative exploration. This does not mean that we cannot ever communicate pleasure or happiness in relation to our learners. It just means our praise needs to focus on our pleasure in our students as human beings and not on the exploration in which they are engaging. John Hattie (2012) explains, "Praise the students and make them feel welcomed to your class and worthwhile as learners, but if you wish to make a major difference to learning, leave praise out of feedback about learning" (p. 121). An alternative to praise is to use phrases like, "Tell me more about that," or "Show me why you made that decision." These kinds of open-ended affirmations remind students that they are in the driver's seat. We still value student efforts through statements like these, but we do not define success for them.

Self-Assessment: Reframing Success

By allowing our students to articulate and adjust their own goals and by resisting praise as a way to reinforce progress, we can turn to reframing our definitions of successful creative endeavors. It is a tremendous shift to move from saying, "This is exactly how you will know what success looks like," to "How do you think success might look and sound? How might you work toward that?" We can help students move toward independence by persistently asking them whether they are achieving what they set out to do. This helps them develop decision-making skills and the ability to set effective success criteria. We can help them reframe their own ideas of what it means to be successful in school by asking them to explore the relationships between their attempts at new approaches and what they are hoping to achieve. This supports the development of a safe learning environment in which there are multiple solutions to problems, there are diverse perspectives on a variety of issues and approaches, and grades are not the only source of affirmation. Educator Doug Johnson's (2015) assertion that "educators will need to stop looking at student work as right or wrong, but perhaps as effective or ineffective" supports this need for a new definition of success (p. 94). Once teachers stop looking at work as right or wrong, we can begin to show students how to do the same, and education can be less about getting the right answer and more about asking the right questions.

Final Thoughts

Exploration gets creativity moving. It allows teachers to create classroom contexts that light a fire within learners. As a result, students ask questions, explore materials, pose problems, and begin to set personally meaningful goals. We guide them to begin to form their ideas and imagine how they might begin to deepen their work.

The next chapter dives into elaboration—the stage during the creative process when students begin to expand their thinking and enhance their questions. As always, the bridge between exploration and elaboration is assessment. Let's continue onto the next stage of the creative process and learn how we might invite our students to elaborate on their thinking.

Unlocking Exploration: Observation and Self-Assessment

Teachers can use the following tool to self-assess the strengths and challenges of exploration through observation. The following table contains the criteria for successful exploration, how these criteria look when lived out day-to-day, and how educators can nurture these criteria within their instructional and assessment plans. The final column offers suggestions for how to respond when criteria are absent or need additional support.

Critical Action	Exploration Targets	What the Teacher Sees	Teacher Facilitation Techniques	Teacher Response
Engaging With Catalysts	I can engage with catalysts.	• Students who willingly approach resources, materials, questions, and so on • Students who use catalysts to frame their work	• Ensure proper time and processes for students to engage in catalysts.	• Examine the catalyst; determine if it is engaging. • Work with students who are reluctant to engage. Teach them how they might use a catalyst to inspire creativity. • Explicitly connect catalysts to questions.
Asking Questions and Generating Ideas	I can generate questions.	• Students who know how to ask a question • Students who know how to expand on a theme • Students who can explain why questions are important	• Designate a space in the classroom for emergent questions. • Engage in question-generation processes. • Celebrate new questions. • Show the connection between questions and creativity.	• Use a guided process (for example, QFT). • Model the process as a whole group. • Refer to questions often and use them to guide exploration. • Allow students to choose questions from a list to begin with.

Critical Action	Exploration Targets	What the Teacher Sees	Teacher Facilitation Techniques	Teacher Response
Asking Questions and Generating Ideas	I can generate multiple ideas.	• Students who can list, draw, and verbalize ideas and use them to flesh out a creative idea • Students who look at things in more than one way • Students who collaborate with others to build their ideas	• Use templates, journals, and digital tools to web, brainstorm, and craft ideas. Record these ideas in a portfolio. • Encourage the exploration of resources, artifacts, and experts. • Use collaborative processes to help students expand their ideas.	• Invite a guest or expert to help students push their thinking. • Offer a list of ideas and invite students to choose from and expand on these. • Model an idea-generation process.
Practicing Patience and Taking Incubation Time	I can define or describe the problem I am trying to solve and allow the time and patience needed for incubation.	• Students who can express their problem either orally or in writing • Students who clearly show a focus and use the focus to define their actions (material choices, and so on) • Students who engage in actions that allow them to really dwell on the problem and allow it to incubate	• Have students record and post their guiding problem. • Use templates that invite students to identify the problem. • Pair up students to describe their problem of choice. • Have a place where students can track their thinking during incubation. • Provide time and space for problem creation.	• Confer with students. • Show examples and nonexamples where possible. • Return to the catalyst, materials, and questions if necessary. • Give students extra time if they need it.

Critical Action	Exploration Targets	What the Teacher Sees	Teacher Facilitation Techniques	Teacher Response
Collaborating, Trusting, and Playing	I can collaborate, trust, and play with others.	• Students who speak and listen with respect • Students who willingly share and receive ideas • Students who show an awareness of a shared goal • Students who are helpful, curious, and kind • Students who take turns	• Utilize collaborative processes (such as think-pair-share, sharing circles). • Explicitly teach collaboration skills. • Ensure students have a strong purpose for collaborating. • Invite reflection during and after collaboration.	• Reteach skills when necessary. • Set time limits. • Establish smaller, short-term goals to guide collaboration. • Model collaboration. • Offer explicit feedback about collaboration. • Have students observe effective collaborative groups.
Suspending Judgment and Accepting Ambiguity, Failure, and Chaos	I can tolerate ambiguity, suspend judgment, and be OK with chaos.	• Students who remain curious • Students who explore before deciding • Students who seek alternate opinions • Students who persevere	• Prepare students for ambiguity—talk openly about it. • Help students move through ambiguity with reflection and planning.	• Map out possible outcomes and timelines—make the ambiguity finite. • Show students how to manage chaos when it gets too stimulating.
Making Connections	I can connect ideas.	• Students who continue to ask questions and explore • Students who say, "This reminds me of . . ." • Students who access and utilize prior knowledge	• Offer processes that facilitate connection making. • Activate prior knowledge. • Take time to reflect on connections.	• Model connection making. • Make connections explicit; display them (on the wall).

page 3 of 4

Critical Action	Exploration Targets	What the Teacher Sees	Teacher Facilitation Techniques	Teacher Response
Having Choice and Making Decisions	I can take risks and make decisions.	• Students who are willing to try something new • Students who can identify when something is new for them • Students who self-talk in a positive way • Students who choose options in a timely fashion • Students who can adjust when needed • Students who reflect on possible future outcomes (forecast)	• Celebrate risks. • Identify a risk and help students plan for success. • Allow time for students to recover from mistakes as a result of a risk. • Avoid summative assessment. • Use graphic organizers to facilitate decision making. • Have student goals front and center. • Celebrate decisions made and have students elaborate on how they made decisions. • Model decision making through a think-aloud.	• Allow students to revisit something immediately in order to minimize the negative impact of a risk. • Brainstorm factors students can control within a risk. • Ensure some choices have less risk involved for extra-vulnerable learners. • Confer in order to co-construct options. • Spend time explicitly forecasting the impact of decisions. • Create a pros and cons list. • Allow students to recover from poor decisions, and use minilessons, feedback, templates, and so on to guide them explicitly in making changes that lead toward their goals.
Setting Effective Goals and Success Criteria	I can set goals, clarify my focus, and create criteria.	• Students who can identify their goal or goals • Students who use their goals to guide their decisions and actions • Students who can begin to articulate criteria for success after a while	• Utilize a specific process for students to choose goals. • Confer with students to ensure progress. • Work with students to really begin to formulate criteria for success.	• Confer with students who are stuck. • Re-engage students in catalysts and guide them through idea generation and goal setting. • Offer choices to students who need support. • Offer a list of criteria from which to choose.

page 4 of 4

Using Conversation as a Formative Assessment Tool During the Creative Process

This tool offers guiding questions teachers may be asking themselves about student thinking and decision making during creative exploration, and prompts to use as a way of engaging in conversation with students. The student responses will then allow teachers to assess students' skills, knowledge, and deeper understanding. The information teachers gather during these formative conversations will support their instructional planning.

When assessing through conversation, it is critical to be clear about the purpose of your assessment within the creative process. It is also important to determine how best to document what you hear so you can analyze it and respond in ways that advance creativity. The following sentence stems help construct this documentation.

◇ What I heard:

◇ What it told me:

◇ What I am going to do:

The following table lists assessment questions teachers may be trying to answer and conversation starters that will yield some insight into this preassessment information.

Questions Teachers May Be Trying to Answer	Conversation Starters
What skills does this student bring to the learning?	What do you already know about this topic, task, or skill?
What knowledge does this student bring to the learning?	What do you wonder?
What is our first step?	Where have you seen this before?
	What are you trying to figure out?
How do I need to shift the learning space to meet this student's needs?	Are there any materials you wish you had?
How might this student best approach his or her own learning?	What do you do when you feel discouraged? How might I help you with that?
What processes might I use when moving learning forward?	What do you think you might do first?

Possible instructional responses following the conversation (depending on what the conversation reveals) may include the following.

◇ Begin to co-construct criteria for success together.

◇ Structure a strong learning environment.

◇ Gather necessary materials and resources.

◇ Establish routines.

page 1 of 2

◇ Set initial goals and plan for success.

◇ Build additional prior knowledge or skill.

◇ Form groups.

The following table offers assessment questions teachers may be trying to answer to formatively assess students' work and conversation starters that will provide formative assessment information during extended exploration.

Questions Teachers May Be Trying to Answer	Conversation Starters
How is this student progressing in relation to the target, outcome, or goal?	What have you done so far?
	What is working?
Who is helping this learner and how?	What isn't working?
How might I help this learner?	What are you trying to do?
How do I need to respond to what I am seeing and hearing?	What have you noticed?
What do I notice? What do the students need?	Where have you felt challenged? What did you do about it? Did it help?
How might I offer feedback?	Where have you seen growth?
How might we set a goal together?	What do you need now?
How might I help the student understand the criteria for success?	Where are you going next? How might you get there?
How does the learner see his or her own learning unfolding?	What are you still wondering?
	What do you think you are great at?
Which processes will best move this learner forward? Which resources?	How will you know when you are successful?
	How do you imagine this might look when it is finished?

Possible instructional responses following the conversation (depending on what the conversation reveals) may include the following.

◇ Analyze learning in relation to criteria.

◇ Offer feedback.

◇ Structure peer feedback.

◇ Structure self-assessment.

◇ Set goals.

◇ Add resources to the environment.

◇ Seek supports outside the classroom.

◇ Instruct.

◇ Regroup.

◇ Move on.

Collecting Conversation Data

This tool provides a framework for teachers to collect conversation data as part of assessment documentation. Teachers can document the following: the context in which the conversation occurred, a summary of the topic and content of the conversation, what the conversation made them think about, steps they will need to take to offer support, any specific connections to learning goals or targets that emerged as a result of the discussion (for example, targets that reflect specific content or specific skills).

Date:

Subject:

Context (what was happening in the room):

Student's Name	What We Discussed	What It Made Me Wonder or Think About	Steps I Might Need to Take	Criteria and Learning Goal Connections

Self-Assessment and Goal Setting During Exploration

Teachers can provide this tool to students to help them begin to set goals, articulate their success criteria, and plan for the next steps of the creative process. Students can store this tool in a portfolio and use it later in the creative cycle for reflection and planning. Teachers can also use this tool to design supports for students.

Learning goals I am planning on addressing:			
My Goal	**Materials and Resources**	**Prior Knowledge and Skills**	**Action Steps**
I am going to try to . . . because . . .	I think I might need . . . to get started.	I already know . . . I can already do . . .	I am still wondering . . . To get started, I will need to . . .
Criteria for Success			
I will know I am experiencing success when . . .			
I will know I need to rethink my plan if . . .			

Unlocking Elaboration

I think my students are ready for peer critiques. We have been work-ing on our projects for two days, and I have been teaching them how to give effective feedback since the beginning of the year. Today, I want the critique process to springboard us into further engagement and revision of the products my learners have been creating.

As soon as my students settle into their work, I ask them to find their feedback partner. These partners have worked together previously during exploration work and they are familiar with the goals their partners set at the beginning of this learning experience.

I invite the students to start by describing their creative process since the last time they met. I write two prompts on the white-board: (1) What was I trying to do in my work? and (2) How did I approach this work? I then give the partners time to describe their work up to this point. I remind the students of the listening skills we have been practicing and I am happy to see consistent eye contact and nonverbal affirmations around the room.

I then ask the partners to take turns explaining to each other what they think is still unresolved or incomplete in their projects. In the case where students are satisfied with their work, I ask them to describe possible ways they might stretch past where they are right now. I offer all students these prompts to frame their reflection: Imagine that in twenty-four hours we meet again and your projects are even more interesting than they are right this minute. What might change? How will you accomplish this change?

After partners have shared their reflections, I ask all partners to offer one or two suggestions to their classmate about their work. I caution them from using phrases like you should *or* you need to. *Instead, I ask them to begin with* I wonder what would happen if . . . *or* have you thought about . . . . *I ask the students receiv-ing the feedback to record all the suggestions so they can later make decisions about which they will use.*

> *As students begin this discussion, I navigate my way through the class, making sure the discussions are productive. I record evidence of strong reflection and goal setting. I listen for unique ideas so I can share them later when we are exploring how elaboration leads to enhanced creativity. The students know we will discuss this critique later as part of becoming more confident in our creative skills.*

The lessons we learn as teachers come at some of the most unexpected moments, and sometimes a person has to wait a long time before the lessons reveal themselves. One of my greatest lessons emerged from my role as a senior high school visual art teacher a number of years ago. The most challenging students I taught during this teaching assignment were those who already considered themselves artists. Many of these students were academically proficient and had received reinforcement for their artistic attempts throughout their lives. These students also came into my class with a preconceived idea of what they were going to accomplish and why they were there. These impressions were hardest for me to address and help them reform. They firmly knew what art was and how creativity worked. They had developed strategies and approaches that were comfortable and predictable and the results of these strategies were closely tied to their identities as artists. Each time I attempted to have them elaborate their work in new ways, or to introduce them to new genres, subjects, or materials, my efforts were met with resistance. I was "messing with" their understanding of who they were as artists and how they were going to be successful. Nevertheless, I persisted, inviting them into experiences that pushed them and designing art prompts that would cause them to question their current understanding about creativity and how it worked.

I once reconnected with one of these students in a line at a coffee shop. While catching up, she said, "I wanted to thank you. You taught me in a way that was frustrating sometimes, but I see now what you were trying to do. And I wouldn't be making the art I am making if it wasn't for you."

Teachers know these moments don't come very often, so I was truly pleased but also really surprised. I reminded her of the time when I asked her class to work through a project that involved making art with a strong political message, which she had been very resistant to. As we spoke, she conceded that she had learned a great deal about her own beliefs from that assignment. She went on to add that when, in another project, I required her to use acrylic paint instead of the watercolor she was comfortable with, she was angry and she thought she hated it. However, she revealed that she now uses acrylic paint as her chosen medium when she paints at home. She explained, "Without you asking us to do something we weren't comfortable with and without you forcing us to set our own goals, I wouldn't have known how other mediums could help me share my ideas in new ways."

At the time, when I was teaching this student, I questioned my approaches every day. I honestly wasn't sure how far to push my students and when to just accept the art that they were already skilled at creating. I tried to balance time to refine prior skills and time to try new things, in new ways, with new approaches. It was a delicate balance and I often felt like I was losing more than winning with this group of students. While other classes of students relished thinking about art in unique ways, this group did not seem to garner the same joy from the process.

There are many lessons in this single conversation with this one student. She affirms that she learned the most when she was most uncomfortable. I supported her through the development of new skills and understanding, but she most remembers the challenges and her own ability to move through them. She recalled the messiness of the creative process, the difficulty in maintaining her identity as an artist while taking risks when the results were not always perfect or finished or beautiful. She shared the importance of resting in uncomfortable contexts for a while before deciding to leave them. She asserted the important role I played in her personal growth by inviting her into this challenge and then making sure she was able to progress through it. I equipped her with the tools she needed, but I did not accept the challenge as my own. I required students to set their own goals and work through their own ideas. This student's experience in the elaboration stage is just one of many, and different students will require different levels of encouragement to unlock elaboration.

In this chapter, we will explore the critical actions for unlocking elaboration, the teacher's role in this stage of students' creativity journey, and how creative elaboration and assessment intersect.

Critical Actions for Teachers and Students When Unlocking Elaboration

In systems and classrooms where the emphasis is on summative assessment and collecting data for reporting purposes, learning experiences may travel directly from a topic's introduction to a summative assignment. There may be little time to seek a variety of solutions or change directions. In these instances, creativity is firmly locked up, and the focus is on giving the right answers and producing the right work in what is often a limited time frame. If students are going to engage in creative processes, they need permission to seek out possibilities and backtrack or adjust as needed without suffering the penalty of a lower grade and a crunch for time. To unlock elaboration in our learners, there are six critical actions that students must undertake, with our guidance, to build their creative toolkits.

1. Engaging in research and development

2. Building a knowledge base and developing insight

3. Noticing, describing, and analyzing

4. Refining goals and criteria through experimentation and evaluation

5. Experimenting with form

6. Redesigning, revising, and revisiting

Each consideration supports creative elaboration and the assessment that is needed to advance it. After reviewing these critical actions, see the reproducible "Unlocking Elaboration: Observation and Self-Assessment" (pages 133–135) for guidance in navigating self-assessment and observation related to these critical components.

Engaging In Research and Development

The move into authentic creativity means pushing past comfort and competency into uncertainty and risk. In truth, this is the pivot point of creativity, when many people abandon the process because this move is too difficult—too daunting. However, when individuals are on this threshold and feel uncertain, it can be helpful to pause for a while and spend some time thinking about (assessing) the skills and knowledge they possess and those they have yet to build. In truth, the simple act of knowing what we don't know (and owning that we don't know it) is very empowering in the movement toward creative expression.

Helping students take ownership of knowledge they have yet to possess and skills they have yet to learn will propel them into the research and development that underlie much creative output. This may mean they spend time searching books or the internet for images or videos that relate to the topic they are elaborating. Many artists, photographers, designers, and communication media experts draw inspiration from the works of other people in their field. It may mean speaking with an expert in an area of study to gather ideas. Many scientists spend tremendous time investigating current research in order to build their knowledge base prior to engaging in their own creative research. It could mean spending some time with a mentor who can demonstrate and instruct skills students are lacking. The most creative athletes spend hours honing their skills with mentors before their own creative play develops.

Drapeau (2014) explains, "To be able to use flexible thinking, students must know and understand the content beyond a surface level" (p. 20). Research and development allow students to elaborate on their thinking and imagination, to minimize misconceptions and false starts, to maximize prior knowledge and collective experience, and to visualize their own creative possibilities. Robinson (2009) reminds us, "To develop our creative abilities, we also need to develop our practical skills in the media we want to use. It's important to develop these skills in the right way" (p. 70). Reeves (2015) puts it another way: "You can't think outside the box if you don't first understand the box" (p. 4). For example, when beginning a new creative exploration, many artists first spend time learning the medium they will be using, searching for the materials that are associated with, say, a particular kind of paint. They learn techniques and perhaps investigate the work of other artists who use that medium. This research allows them to become familiar with the "box." Later, when they are ready, they may try using a different kind of paper. They may apply the paint in new and creative ways. They may tear up a two-dimensional piece and use it in a different, three-dimensional work. But first, they will research and investigate the known. This concept is the same in a classroom setting. Students may find that they are able to increase their creativity by looking at mentor texts or sample problems. They may seek to learn how certain parts traditionally fit together so they recognize when they are combining them in new ways. They may learn how a game is usually played so, when they create their own version, they know which aspects they might adjust. Research and development help students understand the box and they help them build the necessary *self-efficacy*—confidence or strength of belief that students have in themselves and their ability to make their own creativity happen (Hattie, 2012)—to take the risks involved in creative expression.

When we skip research and development in elaboration, we may position students to *self-handicap*, which will stall creative flow. Hattie (2012) explains that self-handicapping "occurs when students choose impediments or obstacles to performance that enable them to deflect the cause of failure away from their competence towards the acquired impediments" (p. 42). By facilitating research and development, we minimize the possibility that students can opt out of the creative process simply because they lack skills and knowledge. In truth, part of creativity is getting better at the skills students are choosing to use in the creative process. Structuring student self-assessment, as learners transition from exploration to elaboration, helps them identify which skills and knowledge need attention in order to achieve the results they are hoping to achieve.

Once students are clear about what they need to investigate in order to build confidence, we can invite help seeking (when students initiate supports based on self-determined need). For example, a student may be writing and illustrating a story about a family pet. The child has a clear image of her pet in her mind and has spent time describing it in words but has realized, after a few attempts, that she isn't sure what a dog's body looks like. So she approaches her teacher to ask how she can figure out how to draw her dog the way she wants. This student is clear about her goal and simply needs support to research and access resources (a book about dogs with photographs, for example) to advance her creative work. Hattie (2012) asserts the importance of help seeking in advancing learning and building ownership. Facilitating research and development during elaboration ensures that feedback and support emerge from self-assessment, which results in the kinds of help-seeking behaviors that have an impact on learning.

Some students can become immersed in research and development, so it is also important to ensure that this aspect of elaboration does not usurp all other creative choices. Students need time to build their capacities and they also need the encouragement to apply them in the context of their own creative processes. When research and development are simply stalling tactics, or worse, when it becomes clear that the research and development are serving to discourage or overwhelm students, we must intervene and facilitate other processes important to the creative process. This may be as simple as asking one of the questions in figure 4.1 or as complex as returning to a planning document and engaging in a formal review of the creative goals. Figure 4.1 offers a list of questions to support students engaging in research and development.

Questions to support students engaging in research and development:

- What do I already know?
- Where do I need to grow my own knowledge or skills?
- What am I wondering?
- Where might I look for answers and ideas?
- How will I know when I have found the information I am looking for?
- What kinds of activities do professionals in this field do?
- How might I get better at this?
- What mentor texts might help me with this work?
- How might I collect or examine the ideas of others? How does this relate to their work?
- Are there any other materials I wish I had?
- How is this approach like others I have seen?
- Who might I turn to for guidance and support?

Figure 4.1: *Select and reflect—Questions to support students engaging in research and development.*

*Visit **go.SolutionTree.com/assessment** for a free reproducible version of this figure.*

Building a Knowledge Base and Developing Insight

The line between research and development and building a knowledge base and developing insight is often difficult to identify. The two activities may look very similar to an external observer. Students may be asking questions, digging into literature, playing around with materials, mapping ideas, and adjusting goals during both processes. The difference between the two is how students are thinking about what they are learning—whether they are taking what they discover and working through it as part of their own creative engagement. Regarding this move from gathering information to manipulating it for creative reasons, Smutny and von Fremd (2009) explain, "Creating cannot take place unless [students] make what they have learned their own and then take it to the next level—that is, bring out another interpretation, invent a new option, diverge from a convention, and so forth" (p. 9). Creating is more than learning—it is applying learning in new ways, and the beginning stages can happen right inside a student's head.

As students self-assess to identify what they don't know and refine the focus of their own creative goals, they naturally move into building a knowledge base that supports their own work. The stage of research and development is often a process of seeing what information or products already exist or investigating what others have done in a particular area of study. Building a knowledge base occurs when students decide something is worth knowing or doing. This is when they might revisit a picture or a book and make notes, try out new ideas in relation to their research, or investigate an approach more fully and base their future decisions on the results. They may also let new information and ideas simmer, mulling things over for some time, waiting for creative insight. Hattie and Donoghue (2016) explain the complex relationship between what we know, what we are learning, and what creative goals we are trying to reach:

> To consolidate deep understanding calls on the strategy of self-talk, self-evaluation, and self-questioning and seeking help from peers. Such consolidation requires the learner to think aloud, learn the 'language of thinking,' know how to seek help, self-question and work through the consequences of the next steps in learning. To transfer learning to new situations involves knowing how to detect similarities and differences between the old and the new problem or situations. (p. 27)

The organic and complex nature of these processes explains why inviting students to continue investigating the work of others is one of the best methods to move students forward when they struggle. Well-timed questions like, What is this making you think about? or What might you be able to take from this to use in your own work? can help learners access their creative impulse. This means helping students understand that creativity is sometimes simply a way to make personal sense of the ideas of others. Sawyer (2006) explains:

> The sociocultural approach shows that all creativity includes elements of imitation and tradition. There is no such thing as a completely novel work. To explain creativity, we have to examine the balance of imitation and innovation, and the key role played by convention and tradition. (p. 42)

Once students accept that creativity does not happen out of thin air but instead builds on the ideas of others in the world around them, they can settle into developing their own knowledge base and advancing toward insight.

Building this knowledge base is so critical because it is by gaining knowledge and skill that our students will begin to ask more and more questions. Frost (1997) reminds us, "People are more inquisitive about the things they know about than the things they do not" (p. 13). In this way, curiosity leads to building knowledge, which leads to more curiosity. This is the beautiful nature of creativity lived out.

In addition to investigating on their own, another great way for students to build their knowledge base and develop insight is through conversation with others. Conversation or even peer assessment and collaboration at this stage can be a blending between individual and group creativity. Esther Levenson (2011), in her article about mathematical creativity, explains, "Group creativity relates to the generation of creative ideas by groups when the interactions and inputs of several people are considered" (p. 218). Perhaps two students are working on building their knowledge base in the same skills or areas of understanding (for example, applying the Pythagorean theorem to a shed design in a ninth-grade mathematics class, or applying topographical knowledge of a particular region to a hydroelectric dam prototype in a tenth-grade science class). Together, they share what they have learned and work with each other to generate ideas and develop insight, which will lead to the advancement of their creative products.

Another possible approach for helping students who are developing knowledge and working toward insight is to encourage them to *just go*; just create, just write, just begin to assemble. There have been times when I have observed art students staring at a blank sheet of paper, paintbrushes in hand, as if paralyzed. I sit beside these students and encourage them to just choose a color and begin painting. When they tell me they don't know what to paint, I invite them to paint whatever comes out of their mind and into their brush. It doesn't have to be a thing; it can be a feeling. This permission allows students to begin before knowing and it can move them away from a creative paralysis. The editor in the human brain is hard to switch off and, at times, it can halt creative movement. Trying to get things exactly right before even beginning can paralyze even the most experienced creative person. As teachers, we can help our students understand that sometimes we have to just generate ideas before deciding whether they have merit. Giving myself permission to dump out all of my ideas in this way is often the only reason I can move into elaboration. Turning off the judge inside students' heads is a learned skill but an important one because they have to have material to begin with before they can elaborate on it.

Figure 4.2 offers a list of questions to support students building a knowledge base and developing insight.

Questions to support students building a knowledge base and developing insight:

- What am I trying to do, figure out, or solve?
- How will I know when I have enough information?
- What is this making me think about?
- What might I take and use in my own work?
- Which ideas do I want to explore a little more?
- Can I imagine, design, or create different possibilities?
- What are some ways I am planning on approaching this? Why am I choosing those approaches?
- Am I using materials the way I imagined?
- What could happen if I try this?
- What might be an unusual way to approach this task, problem, or challenge?
- Did I experience an aha moment? When? How did I know I had insight?

Figure 4.2: *Select and reflect—Questions to support students building a knowledge base and developing insight.*

Visit **go.SolutionTree.com/assessment** *for a free reproducible version of this figure.*

Noticing, Describing, and Analyzing

There are times when students approach me, armed with their creative work and an air of frustration or resignation to failure that does not lend itself to elaboration. I often approach these moments as an opportunity to reignite the creative passion and revisit goals through what I call *purposeful pausing*. It is a time when I invite students to own their feelings and then step back from them and view their work with fresh eyes by making time to notice, describe, and analyze their work in reference to criteria they have established. Too often, students leap to evaluation and judgment without making time to notice the strengths, the qualities, and the growth. Pausing and noticing, describing, and analyzing are key skills for creativity and also for the self-assessment that should be a major part of students' work during elaboration. Inviting students to look at their work for proof of success or failure is a way to engage students both in their creative decisions and in criteria they are using to determine whether they reach their goals. The only way to ensure students are able to move closer to success is to ensure that what they think is occurring in their work is actually represented in what is before them.

Noticing, describing, and analyzing are skills that serve the integration between gathering ideas and developing them into new creative processes and products. Teaching students how to engage in these skills allows them to make creative decisions based on a fuller understanding of what is currently happening in the creative process. For example, in a photography class, we may ask a student, "What do you notice about the relationship between your object and your background? What do you see?" In a physics class, we may also ask, "Can you describe what you see when you reduce the force you apply to your spring? Does that change the wave distribution?" In English language arts class, we may inquire, "How does your introduction in your story capture our attention? What does it tell us about your main character?" or in an elementary classroom, "How did cleanup go today? What do you notice about how long it took us compared to yesterday?" These kinds of questions slow the learner down long enough to explore what is in front of him or her before comparing it to what he or she is imagining (in other words, preventing the student from deciding that a creative decision is a failure before examining it for all its qualities).

A key requirement to helping students notice, describe, and analyze is to document creativity *as it is happening*. Teachers or students might do this through photographs or video, or we may ask students to reflect on their progress daily in a creativity journal or designate a spot for documentation of progress in their creativity portfolios Students may need to have their thinking made visible before they can truly see what is in front of them. Ron Ritchhart and David Perkins's (2008) research affirms the importance of teaching students to make their thinking visible. They discovered that student understanding increases when they use writing, speaking, drawing, or some other way of visualizing their efforts to document progress. This could include having students illustrate their efforts and label what they see. For example, they could organize a series of photographs taken during an outdoor physical education class and glue them to poster paper, sharing the path they took on their class hike. Then, using markers, they connect the photographs to the hiking route on a map of the area. All these approaches to documenting the work and pausing to notice, describe, and analyze can ensure that the next steps a student makes are well informed and grounded in their actual experiences. Furthermore, all these artifacts of learning represent formative assessment (including self-assessment, peer assessment, and feedback). Using this evidence of student learning can help students avoid statements like, "I can't do anything right!" or "Nothing is working for me." When students get carried away by emotion, slow them down with well-placed questions and invite them back into self-assessment. Figure 4.3 offers a list of questions to support students noticing, describing, and analyzing.

Questions to support students noticing, describing, and analyzing:

- Where am I in my creative process?
- What do I see is happening right now? How does this fit with what I hoped would happen?
- How do I feel about my work so far?

- What have I tried to do?
- What do I notice about my material choices?
- What do I notice about how things are fitting together?
- What kinds of decisions am I making?
- How does what is happening relate to my goals?
- What is my main challenge right now?
- How would I describe what happens with my group members?
- Do I have any bias in my work?
- Can I explain why I am working on the thing I have chosen to work on?

Figure 4.3: *Select and reflect—Questions to support students noticing, describing, and analyzing.*

*Visit **go.SolutionTree.com/assessment** for a free reproducible version of this figure.*

Refining Goals and Criteria Through Experimentation and Evaluation

As students transition to elaboration, they will take goals they began designing during exploration and make them more specific and refined. As students research, build their knowledge and skill, and experiment, they will continue to self-assess regularly and refine their goals and criteria. This may include making decisions about whether their approaches, their actions, and even their goals themselves need to shift, taking into account both their short- and long-term goals to make these decisions during elaboration. These co-constructed criteria guide students in making choices that benefit their creative work.

As teachers, we celebrate self-assessment when it occurs organically as part of the creative process. We also plan specific times when students step back even further and reflect on key questions about their progress. (See figure 4.4, page 114, for possible questions to support students refining goals and criteria.) Both organic and guided self-assessment move creativity forward. They allow students to engage in *forecasting—* the prediction of downstream outcomes of an activity (Mumford, Medeiros, & Partlow, 2012). Forecasting allows students to imagine the future and visualize the kinds of outcomes they are hoping to achieve and the steps that will lead them there. Forecasting then invites learners to try on options before committing to a decision. Sawyer (2006) echoes this idea, stating:

> *Elaboration always goes together with evaluation, because it's often hard to tell if an insight is a good one without elaborating it at least part way. You probably have to work with an idea at least a little bit before you can tell if it's a good one. (p. 111)*

Questions to support students refining goals and criteria:

- ◆ What other ideas could work for developing my product or performance?
- ◆ Could I omit certain parts and get different results?
- ◆ What happens when I try this?
- ◆ How might I record my results? How might I look at my data?
- ◆ Is there more than one solution? How do I know?
- ◆ What happens when I move parts around?
- ◆ What happens when I add colors? Descriptors?
- ◆ What happens when I apply a new process?
- ◆ What other materials might enhance my efforts?
- ◆ Am I satisfied with my results?
- ◆ What am I hoping will happen? When will I know it is time to try something different?
- ◆ What is my main challenge right now?
- ◆ How could I try that a different way?
- ◆ What do I want for both myself and others in this moment?
- ◆ Did my prototype give me the results I was hoping for? Why or why not?
- ◆ Did my new approach give me the results I set out to get? How could I adapt my new approach if I need to?
- ◆ What might cause this outcome?
- ◆ Did I consider multiple possibilities?

Figure 4.4: *Select and reflect—Questions to support students refining goals and criteria.*

*Visit **go.SolutionTree.com/assessment** for a free reproducible version of this figure.*

The integrated nature of expanding on an idea or going in a completely different direction alongside deciding whether those decisions support an end goal is an indication of the existence of creativity in a classroom. When we hear students saying, "No, that didn't work," or "We have to try it another way because this isn't making sense," we know they are deeply immersed in elaboration. They are searching for solutions to problems as they emerge.

Robinson and Aronica (2015) describe this aspect of elaboration within the creative process:

> *Creativity also involves making critical judgments about whether what you're working on is any good, be it a theorem, a design, or a poem. Creative work often passes through typical phases. Sometimes what you end up with is not what you had in mind when you started. (p. 139)*

By allowing students to make their own critical judgments, we are teaching them the power of autonomy and efficacy. Educator Karen Hume (2008) highlights the importance of doing so when she states:

*We must constantly remind ourselves that the ultimate purpose of education is
to have students become self-evaluating. If students graduate from our schools
still dependent on others to tell them when they are adequate, good, or excel-
lent, then we have missed the whole point of what education is about. (p. 254)*

The dynamic nature of creativity makes it rich, complex, and the perfect way to develop
these and many other lifelong skills and competencies. Further, helping students maintain responsibility for their own decisions is important if creative output is going to be
authentic. This is the sweet spot of creativity, when students begin to develop independence and accept responsibility for their creative processes and products because they
are in charge of the decisions along the way.

Equally important in supporting students' responsibility for their own process is
ensuring the work is personally relevant to students. When creative goals are personally
meaningful, students will invest highly in mapping out a process (even if the process is
all about experimentation and risk taking), and frequent reflection will occur naturally.
Erkens et al. (2017) explain:

*Whether they choose to become more independent and take another step
depends on a host of factors, including how relevant, meaningful, or interesting they see the task as being, as well as if they trust the teacher and the
classroom climate. (p. 117)*

When students take risks by experimenting with the ideas they generate during elaboration and reflect on whether those risks brought them closer to their goal, much of
the process boils down to trial and error. Kelly (2012) explains the importance of this
work within the creative process:

*The creative process involves taking ideas that represent possibilities that
are potential resolutions to problems and testing them through experimentation. The greater the number of ideas that are generated, and the greater the
amount of experimentation that occurs to test these ideas out, the greater the
possibilities exist for diverse creative outcomes to emerge. (pp. 12–13)*

Allowing students the time and the means to engage in this idea generation and try
out their ideas is critical. One way teachers can achieve this is to embed an open fifteen
minutes into a lesson or class period for students to experiment and evaluate their results
in relation to their goals. When students are highly engaged and can work in a classroom
climate where they feel safe to take risks and experiment, they do not want to quit before
they have resolution. In this way, self-assessment can relieve some pressure students may
feel about the creative process and the failure that is often part of a creative journey.
Students still feel driven but the drive emerges out of an internal desire for closure.

To further minimize anxiety over failure, it is important that the experimentation
and self-assessment that occur during elaboration are not high stakes. Such summative

assessment is not appropriate at this time because summative assessment best serves a verification of a degree of proficiency, and this runs contrary to the purpose of this stage of the work, when work is still in progress. Even if a student declares completion, making time for the learner to reflect formally on his or her product or performance is critical. Ross (2006) explains the importance of student-driven assessment at this stage: "Goals are more likely to improve student achievement if they are set by students themselves, are specific, attainable with reasonable amounts of effort, focus on near as opposed to distant ends, and link immediate plans to longer term aspirations" (p. 9).

Another way to minimize the pressure students may feel is breaking creative tasks into manageable steps. This supports students in their assessment and goal-setting work and allows them to identify the actions and strategic moves they will need to take to achieve their creative goals. Record keeping and documentation can help students keep track of their decisions as well as the experimentation, evaluation, and self-assessment they do throughout their creative process. Keeping track might occur through photographs, notes, or a simple graphic organizer like the one in figure 4.5.

What am I trying to create, solve, design, or invent?

How will I know I am successful (criteria)?

Date	What did I try today?	What were the results?	Did it get me closer to my goal?

Figure 4.5: Experimenting and evaluating student self-assessment form.

*Visit **go.SolutionTree.com/assessment** for a free reproducible version of this figure.*

After students have spent some time expanding and elaborating on their creative efforts, the possibility remains that they may need to abandon an effort and begin a new one. Not all attempts at elaboration produce the desired outcome, which experimentation and self-assessment will reveal. The purpose of experimenting and evaluating is to make the best decision possible in terms of where to proceed next. In some cases, this may mean acceptance of failure and a return to exploration.

Experimenting With Form

This aspect of creativity might seem self-evident. However, it is important to explore because the form students' creativity takes will vary and depends on the goals both teachers and learners are hoping to achieve. Whatever form creativity takes, it reflects a learner's commitment to creatively explore options and resolve whatever problems the learner sets his or her sights on. This critical action is slightly different from actually determining the final product, which students will do in the expression stage, because it isn't yet about sharing or an audience beyond the self. Instead, it is about taking ideas that the student has been forming, evaluating, and refining and developing a sense of clarity about progress toward an intended outcome.

Dacey and Conklin (2004) describe the journey to deciding what form ideas will take:

> *First, we sense and explore the parameters of a problem through the use of inventive divergent thinking. Then, we narrow down the possibilities by using logical convergent thinking. Once the problem has been clarified, we again use divergent thinking to generate a number of possible solutions. Finally, we evaluate our envisioned solutions by using convergent thinking to select the best solution. (p. 27)*

The interplay between *divergent thinking* (generating several possible solutions to a problem or ways to express an idea) and *convergent thinking* (determining the best solution to a problem or way to express an idea) reflects the interplay between exploration and elaboration. It is about widening possibilities and narrowing a focus, imagining possibilities and selecting the one with the most promise. An insight or idea is like a spark that may or may not light the whole creative fire, depending on the potential of the spark to become something more.

The next chapter on expression explores the stage in the creative process when a commitment most often is made to form and refinement is the focus. However, it is critical to discuss form in elaboration too, because when students play around with possible forms their work could take, it impacts the rest of their elaboration efforts. Experimentation with form dictates the materials they will use, the time they need, the space they require, and the strategies they will employ during elaboration. The relationship between how creative ideas will take shape and the processes students will use to get there is important to make clear to students and nurture by revisiting creative goals and plans to reach those goals, enhancing those plans where needed. If students are going to share their creativity through a mathematical solution, their strategies and supports will look different from those needed when the creative form is a poem or a performance.

There are cases where this critical action takes less of a prominent role. Possessing clarity about what is driving creativity in the classroom is important in connecting creative processes to the form of the creative output and to the decisions teachers make with students about where to focus. In some cases, the form is non-negotiable. In these cases, elaboration is less about experimentation with form and more about an experimentation in ways to arrive at the form. Perhaps students are writing a narrative essay because one standard requires it. In this case, the non-negotiable form will drive a creative process. However, the prewriting can vary for each student. Learners can choose the topics, student goals determine the process for organizing ideas, and revision can result in a collaborative creative effort. There is ample room for creativity in this example, but the form dictates the creative processes. In other cases, the form will most definitely be negotiable. A teacher may ask students to respond to texts in English language arts, but the form these responses take is entirely up to the students. Figure 4.6 offers a list of questions to support students experimenting with form.

Questions to support students experimenting with form:

- What other ideas could work for developing my product, performance, or service?
- Could I omit certain parts and get different results?
- What happens when I try this?
- How might I record my results? How might I look at my data?
- Is there more than one solution? How do I know?
- What happens when I move parts around?
- What happens when I add colors? Descriptors?
- What happens when I apply a new process?
- What other materials might enhance my efforts?
- Am I satisfied with my results?
- What am I hoping will happen? When will I know it is time to try something different?
- What is my main challenge right now?
- How could I try that a different way?
- What do I want for both myself and others in this moment?
- Did my prototype give me the results I was hoping for? Why or why not?
- Did my new approach give me the results I set out to get? How could I adapt my new approach if I need to?
- What might cause this outcome?
- Did I consider multiple possibilities?

Figure 4.6: *Select and reflect—Questions to support students experimenting with form.*

*Visit **go.SolutionTree.com/assessment** for a free reproducible version of this figure.*

Redesigning, Revising, and Revisiting

After having spent ten years immersed in both literacy work and the assessment world, it was not until 2017 that I had my epiphany about self-assessment and revision. The literature on both topics is immense, but rarely are they discussed in relation to each other. Most assessment literature explores self-assessment, and resources and research on literacy explore revision. It is as if the two topics, while critically important, are entirely different. I beg to differ.

When students choose to *redesign* (adjust the original structural plan or prototype), *revisit* (re-engage in a product in order to seek additional information), or *revise* (reconsider or alter something in light of additional evidence) a creative product or performance, they do so as the natural outflow of self-assessment. Students reflect on their work in relation to the success criteria of their goals and make decisions about what they need to adjust, refine, or change in order to get closer to where they want to be. The decision making involved in self-assessment is the exact same kind of decision making used in revision processes.

For example, imagine that a student creates an advertisement as part of an English language arts exploration of persuasive messages. In exploration, the student decides his long-term goal is to create a persuasive message, and during the early stages of elaboration, he decides to use visual images to do so. While he has not settled on the exact form the work will take, he determines the following criteria as important.

◇ The work communicates a clear stand or viewpoint.

◇ The message has emotional impact.

◇ The organization of visual features enhances the message.

◇ The message contains curated details to persuade the viewer.

As this student works through elaboration, trying out different colors, pictures, and organization, he could use a template like the one in figure 4.7 (page 120) to guide his self-assessment.

The revision decisions in this student's chosen form are based on self-assessment relative to the specific criteria the student identifies. Paired with a reflection tool, those criteria invite students to think more deeply about the choices they are making—and revision is all about choices. As Joseph Renzulli (2000) explains:

> *In the real world, people often judge things in terms of self-satisfaction and the degree to which they, as individuals, like or dislike the things they do or the products they produce. The only way that we can teach students to become self-evaluators is to give them numerous opportunities to judge their own work and to modify their work when they are not satisfied with it. (p. 10)*

My goal:

To create an advertisement using only visual images that persuades an audience to a particular viewpoint

Criteria	What I notice in my work right now	Action I plan on taking
The work communicates a clear stand or viewpoint.	I think that my viewpoint is clear because of how I use two groups of people to show two ways of treating each other.	I am going to change some things in the second picture and in the backgrounds to make my message better.
The message has emotional impact.	I think that the first picture of the people is a sad picture. The second picture is maybe not happy enough.	I am going to take another second picture. This time, I will pay more attention to the faces.
The organization of visual features enhances the message.	I think the side-by-side of the two groups is a good idea.	Keep the same.
This message contains curated details to persuade the viewer.	I see that my background is the same for both pictures.	I might try to choose things in the background better to add to my message (for example, clouds on the first picture and a sun in the second or maybe different colors).

Figure 4.7: *Self-assessment guide during elaboration.*

*Visit **go.SolutionTree.com/assessment** for a free reproducible version of this figure.*

During elaboration, self-assessment can transition into peer assessment. It is normal to feel that students lack skills to offer revision and editing advice (types of peer assessment) to their classmates. Indeed, I have often experienced frustration when I see comments like, "Good job, buddy!" or "Great effort," on work that is clearly in need of strong feedback. With that in mind, when we teach students what strong feedback looks and sounds like, we are able to leverage peer interactions to advance creative work. This means we have to be clear, ourselves, about what we are trying to achieve when we ask students to engage in peer feedback. I turn, again, to the work of Erkens et al. (2017), who offer the following five questions to guide strong feedback.

1. Does my feedback elicit a productive response?

2. Does my feedback identify what's next for the learner?

3. Is my feedback targeted to each learner's level?

4. Is my feedback strength based? (Does it point out both strengths and information to guide improvement?)

5. Does my feedback provoke thinking? (Does the feedback offer cues to focus the learner's attention without telling him or her the solution?)

Students can use these questions as a guide to developing feedback skills as they work with their peers during elaboration. Students can also use a feedback frame like the one in figure 4.8 (page 122) when they are working with a partner and beginning to learn strong feedback skills.

Once students are familiar with how to offer strong feedback, invite them to seek feedback from more than one person. When students have multiple people engage in their creative efforts by offering multiple sorts of feedback, learners remain in the driver's seat because they have to make choices; they have to select which feedback (if any) they will apply. This strongly reinforces the development of student autonomy and cognitive flexibility. Educational consultant Andrew K. Miller (2015) notes these benefits: "Developing cognitive flexibility is particularly important when it comes to positive failure, as it enables us to consider multiple points of view and to approach challenges in different ways" (p. 4). Feedback from multiple sources offers students multiple perspectives and the power to make decisions based on their own goals and vision.

A strong precursor for developing redesigning, revising, and revisiting skills is accepting the idea that mistakes are not only probable but also essential to the creative process. Often, getting the best results possible means—as noted in the critical action on refining goals and criteria through experimentation and evaluation—moving in the direction of wrong results for a while, as Robinson and Aronica (2015) remind us when they explain, "Effective learning in any field is often a process of trial and error, of breakthroughs punctuated by failed attempts to find a solution" (p. 174). Dacey and Conklin (2004) say it this way: "Creative people don't effortlessly think of great ideas; they also produce a lot of junk that has to be evaluated to see if it is any good" (p. 79). As an artist myself sometimes, I can attest to the piles of junk sitting in my portfolio in a storage room compared to the two or three works of art that hang on my wall.

Helping students recognize the importance of failure is essential for getting at the root of revision. Instead of thinking of this process of re-engaging in a creative effort as a cumbersome obligation, we can teach students to view it as an opportunity. This means there can be absolutely no summative assessment (grading) penalty for creating things that do not reach the goal the first or even second time. It also means that teachers can facilitate processes whereby we rework various failed attempts into something new. For example, I

Ask your partner	Ask the following questions. • "What do you like best about what you did in this project?" • "Which aspects do you think you really aced?"
(Partner responds)	
Respond to your partner	Describe strengths related to success criteria using the following sentence starter. "Here is what I thought went well . . ."
Ask your partner	Ask the following questions. • "What are some aspects of your learning that you find challenging?" • "What would you like to change or improve?"
(Partner responds)	
Respond to your partner	Choose some of the following sentence starters as appropriate to offer feedback about possible challenges. • "I noticed . . ." • "I wonder . . ." • "I see . . ." • "This criterion or target . . ." • "I wonder if you might . . ." • "Perhaps consider . . ."
Ask your partner	Ask the following questions. • "If we had another half hour to work on this, what would you add or do differently?" • "How would you approach this next time?"
(Partner responds)	
Respond to your partner	Choose some of the following sentence starters as appropriate to offer additional supportive feedback as to how your partner could approach the chosen goals. • "I wonder if you could try . . ." • "Maybe spend more time . . ." • "Before you start, consider . . ." • "Try looking for ideas . . ." • "Something to consider is . . ." • "Perhaps a different way to approach that is . . ." • "Sometimes, I . . ." • "What if . . ."

Figure 4.8: *Feedback frame to guide feedback conversations.*

*Visit **go.SolutionTree.com/assessment** for a free reproducible version of this figure.*

have had students tear up old works of art and combine them to create new art. Likewise, students could separate sections of effective writing from sections that show less strength and combine the chosen pieces in a new creative attempt. Students might take the results of a failed experiment and use them to design the next investigation.

Embracing lack of success is an important part of developing resilience when students can use it as an opportunity to revise and create a better product or performance in the end. This nurtures the belief that in spite of difficulties in life, we can remain committed to our goals and resolve challenges over time. Maslyk (2016) discusses the importance of managing students' experiences with failure to ensure hope. She explains that there is an:

> *Importance of exposing students (and teachers) to failure, but the recovery phase is an integral part. Failure makes people feel helpless and reluctant to engage in risky tasks where failure can occur again. As educators, we need to reengage our students in these tasks and refocus them on their successes. (Maslyk, 2016, p. 48)*

This speaks to the importance of redesigning, revising, and revisiting in elaboration. It is a chance to ensure we build confidence in the creative process. In the end, our willingness to help students engage in revision in a meaningful way allows us to reframe failure as iterations of an idea—a spiraling of innovation, with assessment sending us off in a new round of risk taking and imagining. Figure 4.9 offers a list of questions to support students redesigning, revising, or revisiting a creative product or performance.

Questions to support students redesigning, revising, or revisiting a creative product or performance:

- What could I add? What could I take out?
- Do I want to work on this some more?
- Did I fulfill my criteria? Did I reach my goal?
- How might I get closer to my goal? What needs to shift or change?
- What would make this more valuable to others? To me?
- Could I make a substitution and enhance my message, solution, product, or performance?
- Did I give this enough time?
- How can I achieve even more emotional impact?
- How can I vary this? Extend it?
- Is there anything in my work that might offend others? How do I feel about this?
- What do I need to celebrate?
- What aspects of my work represent the heart of my message?
- What is the most emotional aspect of this work, performance, or solution? Why?

Figure 4.9: *Select and reflect—Questions to support students redesigning, revising, or revisiting a creative product or performance.*

Visit go.SolutionTree.com/assessment for a free reproducible version of this figure.

The Role of the Teacher

As with unlocking the creative space and unlocking exploration, unlocking elaboration depends on the decisions a teacher makes within the context of the creative process. One of the most difficult moments for teachers who are working hard to nurture creativity and autonomy for learners is when a student brings a creative product to his or her teacher and asks the all-too-familiar question, "Am I done?" As an educator for most of my life, I know with certainty that this question—the learner's quest for closure—is a pivotal moment in the teacher-student relationship. More important, it is also a pivotal moment for the student, with his or her investment in the task at hand and the student's own creative process. An important point to remember is that creativity is not about the kind of product we create (not all art is creative, for example), but rather it depends on the development of new skills, new ideas, and new connections. Students have the capacity to develop these skills by continuing to elaborate on their work.

Marnie Thompson and Dylan Wiliam (2007) remind us:

> *Teachers cannot create learning—only learners can do that. What teachers can do is create the situations in which students learn. The teacher's task, therefore, moves away from "delivering" learning to the student and towards the creation of situations in which students learn. (pp. 5–6)*

It is with this idea in mind that teachers play an integral role in ensuring learners are developing the kinds of skills and knowledge important both to their creative efforts and to the intended learning within learning goals. This kind of focus within an atmosphere of uncertainty requires an agility that indicates a deep understanding of how creativity works and how learning develops in a variety of contexts. Erkens et al. (2017) describe this kind of teacher:

> *Instructionally agile teachers operate on a continuum of dichotomies; they are precise yet flexible; they operate individually and collectively to ensure accuracy; they employ research-based practices yet conduct their own research regarding the effectiveness of those same practices in context; and they create instructional opportunities that turn students into teachers so they become learners in the classroom. (p. 109)*

This is precisely the kind of agility teachers who are unlocking creative classrooms require. The role of teachers works in tandem with the role of creative individuals. Despite what some of us may fear, we are not reducing the creative efforts of students by interacting with their work—all works of art are the result of small decisions along the way, many of which are influenced by people other than the artist. Following are some important roles for teachers during elaboration that can support the challenges students experience in this stage.

◇ **Listener, observer, and feedback agent:** When students are working independently, it is tempting to sit back and take pleasure in their autonomy. We might view the quiet hum of activity to be a sign that our work is done—the students are engaged and creating, just as we'd hoped. However, it is during elaboration that our ability to observe, document, and respond to student needs is paramount. This aspect of the creative process can be the most exciting and the most difficult.

◇ **Facilitator of reflective processes:** As with all parts of the creative process, elaboration depends on student reflection. Creativity halts without reflection. In creative classrooms, we are not only unlocking creativity in our students but also unlocking the ability to self-assess and self-regulate through reflection.

◇ **Knowledge enhancer:** Students often do not know what they don't know. Knowledge guides experimentation. When students struggle with creativity, it may signal a lack of knowledge in a critical area. Discovering areas where students need to develop knowledge is part of the creative process. Teachers are lead facilitators of this discovery.

◇ **Skill enhancer:** Contrary to popular belief, creativity takes hard-won skill. Whether students are painting, writing, speaking, computing, imagining, experimenting, designing, inventing, or performing, the success of their creative efforts is largely dependent on specific skills. Often these skills require explicit instruction, modeling, and feedback after practice. Responsibility for this can come from fellow students but most often will need to come from the teacher.

Table 4.1 (page 126) suggests specific actions that a teacher can take to overcome the challenges of these roles.

Assessment and Elaboration

The role that assessment plays in elaboration is immense. Indeed, how we engage in assessment and use the knowledge we gain can effectively make or break creativity in our classrooms. The degree to which investment, skill and knowledge development, self-regulation, risk taking, and reflection occur is, in large part, the result of how we choose to utilize assessment in the service of developing creative individuals. As was the case for exploration, ensuring students engage in effective elaboration requires attention to formative assessment (information gathering), feedback (dialogue with others), and self-assessment (dialogue with self). During elaboration, these three aspects of assessment decision making affect how we gather formative assessment information and how we invite our learners into dialogue with themselves and others. In order to facilitate

Table 4.1: *The Role of the Teacher and Key Actions in the Elaboration Stage*

Role of the Teacher	Key Teacher Actions
Listener, Observer, and Feedback Agent	• Monitor engagement by checking if students seem to be committed to their chosen questions, problems, and goals. Are they clear about the need to experiment, research, collaborate, investigate, and revise? • Monitor confidence by seeking assessment information as to whether learners have the necessary strategies, skills, and knowledge. • Monitor commitment by checking if students persevere through difficulties. Are they able to imagine alternate possibilities? • Monitor self-regulation by noticing whether students are able to seek appropriate environments, materials, relationships, and approaches that will allow them to work effectively. • Observe and make in-the-moment decisions about how to redirect learners if necessary, how to teach when required, and how to encourage when necessary. • Engage in feedback conversations in order to encourage or support students in the moment they need it. • Leave the decision making in learners' hands.
Facilitator of Reflective Processes	• Develop, reinforce, and practice the skill of reflection with learners. • Make adequate time for reflection within the creative process; design intentional opportunities for students to engage in it. • Explicitly model the skills related to reflection and self-assessment when necessary. • Use well-considered prompts, choose a method for reflection (journal, peer conversation, feedback session, blog, portfolio reflection, and so on), and ensure goals are refined and targeted.
Knowledge Enhancer	• Share wisdom, domain knowledge, and pedagogical understanding to make sure that creative elaboration connects to prior knowledge. • Interact with students as they create, and connect what they are learning to what they have learned in the past and what they will learn in the future. • Help students see the end goal through purposeful documentation, through focused conversation, through targeted lessons, and through critical resource selection.
Skill Enhancer	• Help students hone the specific skills they need for creativity (communicative, artistic, mathematical, scientific, kinesthetic, play-based, design, technological, collaborative, and so on). • Help students hone the specific skills they need for assessment that support the creative process (noticing, describing, analyzing, comparing, proposing, forecasting, goal setting, revising, sharing, reflecting, and so on).

the effective use of each of these three components, it is critical that students and teachers work together to establish clarity of purpose and that teachers use noninvasive assessment methods and encourage student decision making.

Additionally, using the reproducible tools at the end of this chapter (pages 133–141) can support teachers and students in navigating this complex stage of creativity. Students can use the reproducible "Elaboration Self-Assessment and Goal Setting" (page 136) to self-assess and set goals during elaboration. "Ingredients for Creativity" (page 137) offers a tool for students to check to see if creativity is moving forward by comparing their current situation with the ingredients for creativity. The "Seeking Feedback" reproducible (page 138) offers learners suggestions for how they might seek feedback. You might use the "Creative Focus Tracker" (page 139) as students make decisions during elaboration. It allows teachers to identify steps we might need to take in order to continue to build creative momentum. "Observations by Target" (page 140) and "Observation and Action" (page 141) are tools teachers can use to track their observations during the creative process.

Establishing Clarity of Purpose

All assessment processes should start with establishing clarity of purpose. Why are we assessing students? What do we hope to learn, and what will we do with the information we gain? These decisions are especially challenging during elaboration because students will have individual needs and approaches as they expand on ideas, try new strategies, and seek answers to the creative problems they are individually exploring. During elaboration, we may decide we are assessing in order to determine whether students are creating work that is meaningful to them. Or we may feel the need to determine whether students possess the necessary skills and knowledge to expand on creative products. Perhaps we are trying to decide whether students are ready to engage in collaborative learning on their own or whether they need support. It is equally possible we are hoping to determine who can independently engage in elaborating on creative thinking and who is less confident. The purpose of our assessment then drives the method.

Establishing clarity of purpose for our assessment decisions ensures that the formative evidence we gather during research and development tells us where students need support. It allows us to guide our learners to build knowledge and develop insight. Through effective formative assessment, we can help them notice, describe, and analyze their creative efforts and refine their goals and success criteria.

Using Noninvasive Assessment Methods

One of the most important outcomes of creative classrooms is the teacher's ability to leverage creativity to develop learner independence. With this end in mind, as teachers, we should be sure that our methods for assessing students during elaboration honor students' right to make their own creative choices. As students experiment with the form their creative efforts will take, we can choose noninvasive assessment approaches that leave autonomy in the hands of our learners. Assessment methods like documentation, observation, and conversation (Davies, 2011) can meet this need. These methods are all types of formative assessment, and we can leverage them to advance the creative process. Using these methods to assess students as they elaborate their creative efforts allows us to witness a myriad of learning behaviors and work with students to enhance their creative experiences. Hattie (2015) explains the importance of gathering this kind of information:

> *We have many achievement measures. We would do well to augment this arsenal with more measures of learning, such as the extent to which students can engage in collaborative problem-solving, deliberate practice, interleaved and distributed practice, elaboration strategies, planning and monitoring, effort management and self-talk, rehearsal and organisation, evaluation and elaboration and the various motivational strategies—the "how to" aspects of learning. (p. 13)*

Documentation, observation, and conversation are assessment methods that lend themselves to addressing students' creative learning needs without interrupting their creative flow. Maxine Greene (1995) explains, "One must see from the point of view of the participant in the midst of what is happening if one is to be privy to the plans people make, the initiatives they take, the uncertainties they face" (p. 10). During creative processes, we depend on assessment methods that allow insight into the minds of learners *while they are learning*. By watching and listening, we can gather information about those behaviors and qualities that affect creativity and plan a response. We can also develop assessment tools that assist both our learners and ourselves in advancing the revision or redesign process.

This noninvasive assessment and the decisions we make as a result of assessment information we gather advance the relationships we know are so essential to work in classrooms. For example, perhaps a teacher observes a student is struggling to locate information she has decided she needs. This learner pulls many books from a shelf but seems to be unable to find what she is looking for. She asks to use the computer but, again, spends far too much time searching for what she needs. The teacher knows she is only at the beginning stages of elaboration, and calls her over for a conversation. Together, they review the student's goal and the steps she feels she wants to take to create her product. The teacher can then lead her to resources that will help her; they decide on a method for recording the information quickly, so she can move on. Collaborating with students and using assessment to help them make their own decisions nurtures the kind of relationship that supports long-term growth. Erkens et al. (2017) explain:

This symbiotic relationship between assessment and self-regulation is like a
dance. As students and the teacher begin to understand each other and learn
about their individual motivational processes, they use assessment infor-
mation to form the sequence of steps that will lead to creating something
beautiful, like a dance, in which both partners feel confident and successful;
both teacher and student achieve more. (p. 118)

This is, without a doubt, one of the mutually beneficial results of assessment during
elaboration. While it, of course, translates to the assessment processes we employ
during all other stages, elaboration is a great time to help our learners see the purposes
that assessment serves.

Observation during creative processes means watching students as they engage in
any of the essential components of creative work. It also means listening carefully as
they voice their questions and frustrations and celebrate their achievements. It means
making space for learning to unfold and documenting what we see. We then analyze
this documentation later in order to make instructional decisions. This requires a high
level of inferencing from teachers. By ensuring we have clarity about not only what we
are actually seeing (through what students share in their words, actions, and nonverbal
cues) but what we need to see when things are going well (success criteria), we can offer
specific and targeted feedback.

Further to observation, we may assist students in capturing their learning as it
unfolds. We may take photographs or video while they make decisions, choose the
form their creativity will take, and later revise their efforts. Dueck (2014) explains, "By
measuring the extent to which students engage in trial and error, inquiry, or research,
we can help guide their creative processes" (p. 132). Documentation of the process of
learning, at its various stages, helps both us and our learners see pivotal decision-making
moments and slow down next steps until we have considered possible outcomes.

Observation and documentation of learning may lead to conversations with students. Sharing documentation with learners can lead to soliciting their impressions and
having them identify their needs. Inviting students to store this documentation in a
creative portfolio can support these conversations at several points during the creative
process. We may ask students questions and seek more information about challenges
and strengths and invite them to refine their goals or move on to new horizons. These
kinds of conversations further enhance the climate essential for creative classrooms.

Encouraging Student Decision Making

Ensuring noninvasive approaches is critical because students should sustain ownership for decision making during elaboration as much as possible, which means that our
assessment approaches will be most effective when they do not interrupt our students'
creative process.

When students ask that all-too-familiar question—"Am I done?"—teachers have an opportunity to use assessment processes to support students' making their own decisions in response to this question. I know for sure that creativity rests in decision making. Without the ability to make choices, students cannot find their creative selves. So how do we respond? Often, my go-to response has been, "What do *you* think?" I will admit, I consistently avoid any kind of answer that insinuates I am in the driver's seat of decision making. I steadfastly refuse to usurp the creative process from students. I honestly believe that in most cases, if we choose to answer, "Yes," we will stagnate the creative process and the resilience, risk taking, self-determination, and struggle that serve as true benefits of seeing creativity through. Instead, we should facilitate students' own assessment of their project.

We can start by imagining possible reasons that students might ask this question of us. Are they asking because they are unsure of criteria for success? This means we need to revisit criteria, mentor texts, and examples, because when they know these criteria fully, they won't need a yes-or-no response from the teacher. Are they asking because they are searching for praise and affirmation? We know this is a slippery slope (as discussed in previous chapters), because when students depend on external praise and affirmation, creative output hinges on teacher approval and student compliance. Are they asking because they feel they have done a competent job or truly feel they have done all they can do? Either may be true (which should be determined by a self-assessment and feedback conversation, with criteria in hand), but it may also mean the students produced something comfortable and predictably good because that was the easiest thing to do. Are they asking because they just want to finish so they can get their grade and move on to the next thing? Perhaps the work in question was either not challenging enough or too challenging or perhaps investment remains elusive for these learners. In this case, we may invite learners to stop and describe their decision making and reflect on whether what they create meets their own personal goals.

The key is to bring assessment into the conversation in the most natural way possible. I may say, "You know in this class, we believe that creativity rests in the hands of the creator (or writer, artist, scientist, mathematician, athlete, and so on). You also know that we have decided that *you* will make decisions about when a work is done. However, if you feel like you need help deciding, we can choose some ways to make the decision easier for you." We can then decide together which method of help the student will seek.

We may discuss whether a peer feedback session is the best bet. In my art classes, for example, I often employ a quick critique process whereby the artist asks for feedback on specific criteria and peers offer thoughts, ideas, and opinions. It is not enough for students to ask, "Am I done?" Instead, they have to ask questions pertaining to these criteria. They may pose, "Is my painting balanced?" or "Have I thought of every possibility in this solution?" or "Am I missing any key arguments?" One of my favorite things is to watch classmates naturally offer feedback in the gentlest and most thoughtful way.

We may also decide together that the student is ready for some self-assessment and then pointed questions and feedback. The student may sit with his or her criteria and reflect on the degree to which his or her product reflects his or her goals. The student may then choose a particular criterion that is giving him or her difficulty and ask how he or she might proceed. This is the moment when I am willing to step in because the student is no longer asking for evaluation or praise. Instead, he or she is asking for help with elaboration. This moment holds rich learning potential.

Another response, particularly for students who are asking the question because they are simply tired of a creative project, is to give them permission to set their work aside and look at what their peers are engaged in, read a resource about the topic at hand, or even begin a brand-new project. The advantage of this approach is space and time, which sometimes brings clarity and inspiration. In most cases, students eventually return to the work and re-engage later when they use this method. The advantage, in this scenario, is that the re-engagement is on their own terms. They retain ownership for decision making and the creativity it produces.

We may even find moments within the creative process when we do not agree with the decisions learners are making. What do we do when there is a tension between our expectations and our students' own standards of quality? It is important to remember that this is the beauty of self-assessment and goal setting. Using assessment and response processes, we can navigate this conflict and help students navigate it, too. For example, if a student brings us a prototype that we can immediately see does not fulfill the success criteria, instead of telling the student that this is so, we can invite him or her into self-assessment and review the criteria together. In another example, if a student brings us a creative piece, and we sense he or she rushed and did not spend enough time in elaboration, we again work alongside the student to reflect on criteria. If we feel a learner has not interpreted the criteria with enough clarity, we may introduce mentor texts or work samples that push creative thought a little more. There may even be times when we have to accept the creative interpretation a student is making even though it does not reflect choices we would personally make. At these times, turn to discussions and reflection about what is informing elaboration decisions and look for new ways to approach the creative process (as opposed to the creative product). We can structure learning to invite consistent reflection, examination of examples, discussions, and responses from others (besides ourselves). In this way, assessment truly does inform a response but, as often as possible, the decisions continue to circle back to learners.

Final Thoughts

Elaboration can be the longest and most complex stage of the creative process. Students often find themselves wrestling with choices and decisions. At the same time, teachers help them navigate the waters of failure and missteps so they maintain hope and purpose in their quests for solutions to important problems. Together, students and teachers explore possibilities and potential, using assessment to help them along the way.

There comes a time, after exploring and elaborating, when we must make some decisions and share our work. The next chapter explains how expression can become an important way to help students make meaningful connections to the world around them. As we continue to walk alongside our learners while they refine their work, we can teach them the true importance of their creative endeavors.

Unlocking Elaboration: Observation and Self-Assessment

Teachers can use the following tool to self-assess the strengths and challenges of elaboration through observation. The following table contains the criteria for successful elaboration, descriptions of how these criteria look when lived out day-to-day, and suggestions for how educators can nurture these criteria within their instructional and assessment plans. The final column offers suggestions for how to respond when criteria are absent or need additional support.

Critical Action	Elaboration Targets	What the Teacher Sees	Teacher Facilitation Techniques	Teacher Response
Engaging in Research and Development	I can conduct research.	• Students who look to a variety of sources of information • Students who jot down ideas and information as they research • Students who have a clear purpose for their research	• Explicitly teach research processes. • Ensure students have access to the research items they need. • Allow enough time for learners to explore. • Introduce unique sources with new perspectives.	• Help the student find appropriate texts. • Provide an explicit process for gathering research information and translating it to creative work. • Reduce or expand the number of sources depending on student need.
Building a Knowledge Base and Developing Insight	I can seek help from others when I need it to build knowledge and insight.	• Students who ask for help • Students who can articulate why they are seeking help • Students who apply the help they receive in meaningful ways • Students who make decisions about what knowledge they need	• Designate a space in the classroom for students to seek and receive help. • Make yourself available to support as students need it. • Establish protocols for seeking help. • Do not solve problems that students can solve themselves with time. • Ensure there are multiple ways students can build knowledge and develop insight. • Activate people outside the class who might listen to student plans.	• When students are not asking for help when they clearly need it, make seeking help mandatory (for example, saying, "List one area where you need support," as opposed to "Do you need help?"). • Ask questions, instead of giving advice, as often as possible. • Help students who are struggling without judging them. • Help students list what they still need to know and choose from a list of places where they can gain insight.

Critical Action	Elaboration Targets	What the Teacher Sees	Teacher Facilitation Techniques	Teacher Response
Noticing, Describing, and Analyzing	I can notice, describe, and analyze important details and information.	• Students who collect ideas and then step back and reflect • Students who use descriptive language to capture their creative process • Students who can notice and describe their criteria for success • Students who use these criteria to self-assess • Students who connect their emotions to their success criteria (for example, I feel frustrated because this isn't the right texture)	• Pair students and have them spend time noticing and describing research, planning tools, mentor texts, catalysts, group processes, portfolios, and anything else that will lead to better decision making. • Use a journal or portfolio for capturing the creative process. • Use video, photographs, and artifacts to document learning. • Use mentor texts and work samples. • Show nonexamples. • Make time to reflect and adjust (self-assess).	• Provide students with descriptive word lists. • Plan for specific times to stop and notice; slow down the learning when needed (for example, What do you notice right now? What does it tell you?). • Confer and continue to ask questions to help students develop their own understanding of what is currently happening in their work. • As students create, innovate, and solve problems, have them continue to revisit criteria. Ask, "How is our understanding of these criteria changing?"
Refining Goals and Criteria Through Experimentation and Evaluation	I can generate and test multiple ideas, as needed.	• Students who can examine approaches, ideas, and strategies and determine effectiveness (in relation to goals and criteria) • Students who are willing to try things in more than one way • Students who actively seek alternate solutions and approaches • Students who make decisions that advance their creative work	• Encourage students to document their risks and results. • Build in time to reflect on results. • Build in time to recover from mistakes. • Deliver minilessons as needed to build skills and knowledge. • Invite at least two approaches to the same problem, when it makes sense to do so.	• Ensure students have enough time to explore. • Invite students to collaborate in groups. • Offer minilessons to introduce new possibilities. • Ensure students have criteria by which to determine effectiveness of approaches.

page 2 of 3

Critical Action	Elaboration Targets	What the Teacher Sees	Teacher Facilitation Techniques	Teacher Response
Experimenting With Form	I can generate ideas for the form my creativity might take.	• Students who are aware of possible forms creativity might take • Students who can list more than one alternative • Students who are beginning to think about audience and purpose	• Supply students with a list of possible products, performances, and services. • Have students make time to connect their ideas to form. • Make time to explore audience and purpose together.	• Help students explicitly connect their goals, audience, and purpose to possible forms. • Help students decide whether form will drive creativity or creativity and audience will drive the form. • Describe the role of elaboration.
Redesigning, Revising, and Revisiting	I can redesign, revise, and revisit materials and ideas.	• Students who continue to ask questions and explore • Students who analyze their work in relation to criteria • Students who seek and receive feedback • Students who show evidence of growth • Students who can adjust when needed • Students who reflect on possible future outcomes (forecast) • Students who use their goals to guide their decisions and actions	• Allow students time and opportunity to reflect and revise, revisit, and redesign. • Continually redirect students to their criteria. • Provide minilessons and feedback sessions as needed. • Use only formative assessment processes. • Use graphic organizers to facilitate decision making. • Have student goals front and center. • Celebrate decisions students make and have them elaborate on how they made them.	• Structure time to revisit work. • Ensure criteria and goals are visible. • Provide opportunities to offer feedback. • Guide students through not just what they need to adjust but how they might do it. • Spend time explicitly forecasting the impact of decisions. • Confer with students who are stuck. • Offer choices to students who need support. • Re-engage students in catalyst materials.

Elaboration Self-Assessment and Goal Setting

Students can use this tool to check in on their goals and progress toward those goals. This check-in can happen several times during elaboration if it is an extended process or just once during this stage if the creative work is brief. Teachers can implement this tool to slow down student thinking before moving to expression-stage decision making. Teachers and students can reflect on responses within this tool to plan supports and approaches, and store reflections and plans in creative portfolios.

Date:	What am I working on?	How am I feeling about my progress?	How will I know when I am successful?	What challenges am I experiencing?	What are my next steps?

Date:	What am I working on?	How am I feeling about my progress?	How will I know when I am successful?	What challenges am I experiencing?	What are my next steps?

Ingredients for Creativity

Directions: Teachers can use this tool to monitor their attempts at creating a strong elaboration process. Teams of teachers may also refer to this tool when planning assessment processes that will support the creative process.

The following are ingredients in the creative process.

◇ A willing partnership and a desire for productive conversation

◇ Trust and relationship between the participants

◇ Strong listening skills, including turn taking, eye contact, open body language, and paraphrasing

◇ Equality, where every person and all opinions hold equal weight

◇ A clear and shared purpose for the conference and a willingness to address that purpose

◇ Skill at choosing language carefully to support openness and safety

◇ Clarity about goals by both the person seeking feedback and the person offering it

◇ Clarity about decisions and the reasons for making them, to analyze these decisions

◇ The freedom to ask questions and seek to understand for all participants

◇ Specific criteria for success that can support careful reflection

◇ Enough time to linger on both successes and challenges and to plan next steps

◇ Artifacts of both process and product (when appropriate) to guide the conversation

◇ Final decision making and ownership of the product and processes resting in the hands of the person seeking feedback

Seeking Feedback

Students can use this tool to plan to seek feedback from others. The prompts allow students to form clarity about what they are hoping to learn from a feedback interaction.

The aspect of my work on which I am seeking feedback is:

To what degree have I been able to [list the criteria on which you are seeking feedback]?

How well did I [list the skill you are hoping to receive feedback about]?

Which of these is [list the specific criteria you were hoping to represent in your work]?

How might I address this concern?

What are my strengths?

Was I able to [list the skill, criteria, or quality you were hoping to develop]?

How could I shift my approach in this area?

How would you tackle this problem?

Creative Focus Tracker

This tool is intended primarily for teacher use, but teachers and students may complete the Current Area of Focus column together. This tool can assist teachers in tracking both student focus areas (most often short-term goals) and teacher plans to support students in their work. See the first row for an example.

Student Name	Current Area of Focus (Skill or understanding student is developing with teacher support)	Teacher's Strategic Approach
Mary Jones	Attempting to use materials that are less familiar (risk taking)	✓ Introduce new materials available for use in her project. ✓ Invite her to try one or two (practice and explore). ✓ Offer two minilessons based on materials of choice. ✓ Give her time to apply them and decide if she wants to continue or abandon (purposeful reflection).

Observations by Target

Teachers can use this tool to document their observations of students. When students are working for an extended time on elaboration, this tool can help teachers keep track of what they are seeing in relation to specific learning targets that either students or teachers have set.

Student Name	Target:	Target:	Target:	Target:
	Date: Observation:	Date: Observation:	Date: Observation:	Date: Observation:
	Date: Observation:	Date: Observation:	Date: Observation:	Date: Observation:
	Date: Observation:	Date: Observation:	Date: Observation:	Date: Observation:
	Date: Observation:	Date: Observation:	Date: Observation:	Date: Observation:

Observation and Action

Teachers can use this tool to keep track of their formative assessment observations as students work through the creative process. It also helps teachers document their instructional decisions in relation to their observations and questions. The first row offers an example.

Date	Student	What I Saw	What It Made Me Wonder	Actions Needed
May 7	Carlos	Today, Carlos was able to begin immediately, but he ran into difficulty with his presentation prep because he couldn't figure out how to insert images.	What might be the best way for Carlos to learn this in a timely fashion?	Present Carlos with options. ↳ YouTube video ↳ Skilled partner ↳ Minilesson with me ↳ Trial and error

Unlocking Expression

The teacher and her students file into the gymnasium, past the parents waiting in the lobby. They have three short minutes to get ready to receive family members and friends. Today, the fifth-grade arts education students are going to show their guests some of the things they have been doing in class, and the students are buzzing in anticipation. Every student has someone whom he or she will receive as soon as the doors open. The teacher has made sure of this, so not one student is left out.

Among other things, the class has been creating a couple of dances—one as a whole group and one in smaller pods of students. The work leading up to this hour of performance has been rigorous, and the students are satisfied they are ready to share with people who matter to them. In addition, the students decide to follow up their performances with a participation component by teaching their guests the class dance.

Even the most reluctant students are prepared. Their creative process ensures they had a hand in crafting the elements of the dance they will be performing, and the group spent some time during each class over the past few weeks rehearsing and refining skills. The group performed for another class and shared the small-group dances with each other, allowing time for feedback and short-term goal setting. The students and the teacher have explored how to make their movements communicate the emotions they desire. To help visualize possibilities, they have been watching video segments of a variety of creative movement routines. The class is ready.

As audience members file in and find the students they are there to see, the teacher hands them a feedback frame, designed around a couple of prompts. She will provide time at the end of the shared time for guests to sit with students and communicate some aspects of the dances they enjoyed and ask questions about how students created the dances. This will give students the chance to celebrate their creative processes and reflect out loud to someone other than their teacher.

Expression, like all other stages of creativity, is complex. There are times during this stage when learners are readying themselves to share a performance. At other times, it is a stage for final revisions of a product and preparation for display. Perhaps students are searching for an audience with whom to share, or perhaps the audience has been built into the creative process from the very beginning. The context of the creative act determines how this stage unfolds, the components that will compose student focus, and the length of time spent in expression. Further, because creativity can occur during large-scale, extended projects or it can occur during moments of practice in short time periods, expression might take the form of a story, a song, a solution to a problem, or a prototype. The products may be polished or they may simply be works in progress. Expression is about making final preparations for sharing. It rounds out the creation of products, performances, or services, and it also invites learners to negotiate how the results of their creative efforts will be expressed to others.

One of the most vulnerable moments in the creative process occurs when we put our work out into the world—when we make the decision to share it and place it in the hands of an audience. It is in this moment that our own level of investment and the huge risk involved in moving from private to public creativity become clear. Indeed, it is often not until sharing our creative efforts that we realize how much of ourselves we invest in our work. It is for these reasons that paying careful attention to expression of creativity is so important; the audience reception to students' expressions of their creative work can impact future creative efforts and learners' understanding of who they are as creative individuals. Teachers shouldn't take this stage lightly.

It does not take much effort to recall the feelings of deep nervousness I had prior to dramatic performances with my community theatre or before the opening of my first art show. I can just as easily recall the visceral fear I experienced on the day my first book was released to the public. The very first time I delivered a keynote speech to a crowd of educator colleagues, I spent weeks rehearsing in rooms by myself, working hard to believe that I had something interesting to say. Indeed, it would seem that my experience at sharing my creative work would make me immune to anxiety and vulnerability over time, but these feelings do not disappear. When we (as people) share something that has become part of who we are, we are sharing little pieces of our inner selves. This is rarely easy for anyone—much less our learners. Students want their peers to accept them, and when our learners run the risk of not fitting in because of creative choices they have made, the pressure can be intense for some students. This can result in learners' creativity becoming locked up more permanently.

That said, I have also witnessed students hopping excitedly from foot to foot as they await their turn on the stage before a performance. I have seen students grin from ear to ear as their parents walk into the gym to see their artwork on display. I have known students to stand with pride beside their science displays, waiting for the chance to explain their work to an interested visitor. Whether the expression is large (a performance or speech) or small (sharing a method for solving a problem or sharing a story with a friend), creative expression, it seems, is a mixture of uncertainty and pride, of desire for acceptance and understanding, and of confidence that creative efforts will yield a favorable audience response.

Creative expression is the perfect platform on which to nurture belonging in our classrooms, and to help our learners develop the sense that they have something to say that matters to others. By sharing their creative efforts (products, ideas, performances, services) in meaningful ways, learners can enhance their confidence, and we can ensure their risks result in a reward. Creativity, in this sense, is the vehicle for building tremendously important long-term skills through engagement in activities that have personal meaning. Carol A. Kochhar-Bryant (2010) explains, "Meaningful participation [of youth] means activities through which young people have opportunities to make significant decisions, develop and practice leadership skills, and experience a sense that they belong or matter to others" (p. 19). Creative expression is an important way to develop all three capacities in our students. When students learn to express their creativity successfully, they build a repertoire of success that will equip them to tackle many of life's challenges.

In this chapter, we will explore the critical actions for unlocking expression, the teacher's role in this stage of students' creativity journey, and how creative expression and assessment intersect.

Critical Actions for Teachers and Students When Unlocking Expression

In order to ensure that expression within the creative process is heavy on positive anticipation and light on paralyzing anxiety, there are three important actions that teachers and students must take to ensure success.

1. Establishing method and confirming the reason for sharing
2. Confirming product, performance, or service
3. Clarifying audience and ensuring emotional safety

Each consideration supports creative expression and the assessment to advance it. After reviewing these critical actions, see the reproducible "Unlocking Expression: Observation and Self-Assessment" (pages 163–165) for guidance in navigating self-assessment and observation related to these critical components.

Establishing Method and Confirming the Reason for Sharing

The expression of creative ideas or products can occur in diverse contexts and under a myriad of conditions. Sometimes, expressing creativity simply means turning to a partner and sharing an original thought about something. At other times, it may involve serving an innovative dish to a group of seniors or writing a possible solution to a mathematics problem on the whiteboard. Perhaps learners are demonstrating to their parents how well their boat prototype floats, or sharing their acting skills in a big performance. They may be using Skype to show distant peers a documentary they created, or they may be teaching another group of students a game they invented. No matter the context, the method in which students choose to express creativity and their personal reasons for doing so can be a powerful learning opportunity as students find ways to share pieces of themselves with others.

The expression stage of creativity is often when learners truly commit to sharing the ideas and goals they have been pursuing. It is when they decide that their creative efforts (in whatever form they may take) are worth putting out into the world. As audiences engage with these creative products, students have the opportunity to see their creativity reflected through the eyes of consumers. They may watch for general reactions or seek formal feedback. The relationship between the creator and the audience is an important aspect of creative expression. Sawyer (2006) explains, "Artistic meaning isn't only put into the work by the artist, but is often a creative interpretation by the viewer" (p. 172). How creative efforts are received by those who consume them is an important developmental aspect of creative thinking. The shift from creating for oneself to creating for others is often (although not always) a natural step. The audience and the student (creator) share responsibility for the meaning drawn from a creative product or performance. Offering students personal, safe time to wrestle with their own creative ideas, and the chance to share the results of this creative work with others, adds complexity to their creative goals. By sharing creative efforts with others, students can begin to shift from criteria that reflect their own motivations and preferences to criteria that encompass the responses of others. It invites students to invest because their creative process will offer them the chance to connect to other people in meaningful ways. This is a powerful driver of strong learning and the accompanying goal setting.

It is important that when students express their creative efforts, they receive positive reinforcement for doing so. This does not mean that the audience always offers an enthusiastic response, regardless of its feelings and interpretations, but it means that we have to teach students how to seek feedback appropriately from an audience. It also means that teachers and students will need to work together to choose audiences carefully and, in turn, teachers will need to equip these audiences with the skills and understanding needed to be thoughtful in their responses.

Having learners prepare carefully for sharing by reviewing their success criteria is one way to ensure they are satisfied with their efforts before they become public. This preparation also ensures students are clear about their method for sharing and the reasons for doing so, enabling them to enter expression with efficacy and confidence. Gura (2016) explains:

> *They should understand the creative process as one of ongoing improvement in which testing and evaluating their work is embraced and feedback, including feedback from an audience responding to their presentation of a final version, is collected and accepted and made the basis of "next step" creative work. (p. 11)*

Our students also become comfortable with gauging their confidence. This is an important indicator of whether they have reached their creative goals. In this way, expression is not the end of creative effort but rather another step in the creative process.

It is equally important to prepare the chosen audience for what it is about to receive. Teachers can work with students to communicate to their audiences the purpose for the creative work, the reason for sharing, and the criteria each student used to guide his or her creative process. Both the students who are sharing their creative work and the audiences with whom they are sharing need to have a mutual understanding of the purpose of the creative work and the reasons for sharing it with others. Are our learners inviting the audience simply to enjoy what they are sharing, asking the audience to offer feedback, or hoping audience members will react or respond creatively or emotionally in some way? Do students need the audience to build on the ideas they share? Clarity about the reason for expression of the creative effort is critical for creating safety for both the audience and the student.

The reasons for sharing and the methods for expressing creative ideas inside the classroom echo real-world contexts. Artists display their artwork and then hold openings for targeted audiences. Authors publish and share their writing with others. Scientists discuss their research questions in panels and publish their work to journals. Carpenters sell their creations at craft fairs. Audience affects the decisions creative individuals make in both the direction their creative work takes and the reasons and methods for sharing it. It not only is important to the development of message and meaning but it also contributes to quality control. Sawyer (2006) explains, "After a person creates a product, it's submitted to the field for consideration, and the field judges whether or not it's novel, and whether or not it's appropriate" (p. 190). In most fields, creative pursuits are vetted among experts in order to determine the degree of creativity, the inherent skills expressed, and the value of the work to the broader community.

It may be helpful to think about expression as a way to continue collaborative processes. If the audience contributes to the meaning making for the student, and if the results of sharing lead to reflection, then an audience could serve as a means by which to work with others to develop ideas. Audience interaction with creative expression can lead to new creative processes. For example, students may observe their audience disengaging in their presentation at a specific time, and analyze the reasons for this, leading to a refined process next time. Perhaps a learner may share a creative idea with a partner and, based on feedback, return to the creative process to work on a different solution to his or her problem. It is through the expression of creative ideas that students develop new ideas. Frost (1997) describes this symbiotic relationship between expression and new creative thinking when she states, "It is no wonder that the teachers place such a high value on the children's ability to communicate in as many ways as possible; because in the process of communicating, new ideas are formed" (p. 180). Creativity leads to expression, which, in turn, leads back to creativity.

Figure 5.1 offers a list of questions to support students establishing their method of sharing and their reasons for doing so.

Questions to support students establishing their method of sharing and their reasons for doing so:

- How will I know when I am ready to share?
- Why am I sharing my work? What am I hoping will happen?
- How might I build my confidence to share my creative work?
- Did I address the needs I was hoping to address?
- What problem does my product, performance, or service solve? What question does it answer for a potential audience?
- How will others see my work?
- Is my work important, appropriate, and relevant?
- What am I hoping to learn by sharing?
- Which criteria define a strong creative expression? Do I know what I am hoping to achieve?
- How might I best share my creative work?

Figure 5.1: Select and reflect—Questions to support students establishing their method of sharing and their reasons for doing so.

Visit go.SolutionTree.com/assessment for a free reproducible version of this figure.

Confirming Product, Performance, or Service

As students work their way through elaboration, part of their investigation and the decision making that follows centers on how their creativity will manifest. It is during expression when these decisions are confirmed and products, performances, or services are then prepared for sharing. Their choices will depend on their own goals and the contexts the teacher establishes. Additionally, sometimes the audience or the form will dictate the direction of the creative work, and sometimes the creative process will lead to decisions about form and audience. Either way, how students choose to express their ideas will be a key factor driving the work in creative classrooms. Students may engage in creating tangible objects like books, poems, paintings, maps, charts, or research papers. At other times, they may be working toward performance-based outcomes, like a dramatic presentation, a speech, a dance, a game, or an experiment. Creative expression may also address a service need, like designing a recreational program, a food drive, a flower garden, or an informational panel discussion. Table 5.1 (page 150) identifies some possible products, performances, and services—organized by written, oral, and visual forms—students may choose to use to express their creativity.

Teachers can use this table to connect the learning goals to the creative process and curate options for students. For example, if teachers are focusing on a learning goal that requires students to evaluate various physical activities for the degree to which they support cardiovascular fitness, they may look to appropriate options such as an editorial, a debate, or an essay. In instances when the form is negotiable, teachers could share this table (or parts of it) with learners to assist with experimentation (in elaboration) and then decision making and refinement (in expression). Whether these types of products, performances, or services *drive* the creative process or whether they emerge as a *result* of the creative process, they are the means by which our students will ultimately connect to a strong purpose and an authentic audience for their creative efforts.

Products

Students express many creative endeavors through a tangible *product* that they can share. They can express themselves in writing, orally, or in visuals and can share their product in digital or traditional formats. These products reflect the results of a much longer creative process. They are often the culmination of exploration and research, wonder, and experimentation. The products learners choose to use to convey their creative messages will hinge on the purposes they hold for working creatively, the audience with whom they plan to share, and their own skills and interests. For example, a student exploring butterflies will have engaged in books and images of butterflies in exploration, perhaps discussing what she discovered with a friend. In elaboration, she decided to try to find a way to represent her favorite butterflies doing all the things that butterflies do. She cut out some images from an old calendar and searched for images to print off the internet. She then may have realized she wanted to try drawing and painting a butterfly as part of her representation. As she moved into expression, she placed the images she had collected and painted side-by-side on a table. With the help of her teacher and the criteria they had co-constructed, she chose a form that would allow her audience to see all the butterflies at once instead of one after the other (like in a book). The student settled on making a poster and began to work on organizing her images. This is an example of how students can move toward a product over time as they explore, elaborate, and make decisions about expressing themselves.

Table 5.1: *Possible Products, Performances, and Services That Express Creative Learning*

Written	Oral	Visual
◆ Advertisement	◆ Audio capture	◆ Advertisement
◆ Biography	◆ Author's chair	◆ Altered book
◆ Book report or review	◆ Chant	◆ Assemblage
◆ Brochure	◆ Conversation	◆ Banner
◆ Collection	◆ Debate	◆ Cartoon
◆ Compare and contrast	◆ Demonstration	◆ Collage
◆ Crossword puzzle	◆ Discussion	◆ Computer graphic
◆ Digital story	◆ Dramatic reading	◆ Connections graphic
◆ Editorial	◆ Dramatization	◆ Cultural artifact
◆ Essay	◆ Feedback session	◆ Dance
◆ Experiment record	◆ Fishbowl discussion	◆ Data display
◆ Flowchart	◆ Informative display	◆ Design
◆ Graphic organizer	◆ Interview	◆ Diagram
◆ Historical fiction	◆ Instruction	◆ Digital story
◆ Infographic	◆ Oral examination	◆ Diorama
◆ Journal	◆ Oral presentation	◆ Display
◆ Lab report	◆ Oral report	◆ Drawing
◆ Letter	◆ Panel discussion	◆ Filmstrip
◆ List	◆ Poetry reading	◆ Flyer
◆ Log	◆ Program	◆ Functional products
◆ Magazine article	◆ Promotion	◆ Game
◆ Memo	◆ Puppet show	◆ Graph
◆ Newscast	◆ Radio script	◆ Installation
◆ Newspaper article	◆ Rap	◆ Map
◆ Personal communication	◆ Running record	◆ Model
◆ Play	◆ Scored discussion	◆ Painting
◆ Poem	◆ Skit	◆ Photograph
◆ Position paper	◆ Song	◆ Poster
◆ Proposal	◆ Speech	◆ PowerPoint
◆ Research report	◆ Tableau	◆ Prototype
◆ Script	◆ Volunteer drive	◆ Questionnaire
◆ Social media posting (tweet, status update)		◆ Scrapbook
◆ Story		◆ Sculpture
◆ Test		◆ Slideshow
◆ Website		◆ Storyboard
◆ Wiki, blog		◆ Venn diagram
		◆ Video capture
		◆ Website

*Visit **go.SolutionTree.com/assessment** for a free reproducible version of this table.*

Teachers can support students in making these choices by guiding them to products that reflect their needs while introducing them to *new* ways of sharing their ideas and then allowing students to make a decision. For example, students may start out believing the only way to share an idea is through a written piece, but the teacher may introduce them to the idea of a digital story that combines visual images, written text, and recorded spoken word as a possibility for communicating their message. Now the learners can decide which option addresses their personal goals the best. During elaboration, they may have experimented with both forms so that the decision, during expression, is based on personal experience. Conversation between students and teachers can lead to exploring creative products that are less familiar to students while still accomplishing the same creative goals. We then follow up by introducing and developing the critical skills and understanding necessary for creating these products in ways that echo the students' goals. The important work of creative classrooms functions as a bridge between what students are working toward and areas where their work needs development. By employing flexible groupings (groupings that shift based on the needs of the members) and frequent self-assessment and feedback processes, we can work alongside learners in ensuring they realize their vision for their chosen products.

Performances

There are times when *performances* are the expression of creative work. Perhaps, after a period of exploration and elaboration, students want to share their work through a speech or a demonstration. In other situations, they may have created stories that are best shared through dramatic presentations or tableaus. Maybe they need to share their ideas through song or dance, or perhaps they want to engage in a debate or create a documentary performance.

While both products and performances are expressions of creativity, they function quite differently in some respects. Products are tangible, and performances are ephemeral. Sawyer (2006) clarifies this difference in this way:

> *To explain performance, we have to focus on the creative process rather than the created product. Composition is a creative activity that results in a created product, like a musical score or a studio recording; performance is temporary, and exists only while the band is playing. (p. 351)*

This means the audience, or consumer of creativity, must share a physical space with the creator while the expression of creativity is occurring. All observations and subsequent feedback are based on in-the-moment engagement. The exchange of message and meaning is in real time. This intimate exchange of creativity is powerful for both the student and his or her audience. It speaks to the collaborative nature of creativity and reinforces the skills we work hard to build in students—the need for preparation, revision, and hard work, driven by a strong investment.

Services

There are times when creative products and performances come together for the purpose of *service* to others. These kinds of creative outputs address the audience's specific needs. In this way, the future consumers of a product drive the expression of creativity, and the relationship between the student and the audience is even more important. In this case, creative expression meets a need. The following are some examples of questions that drive this kind of creative expression.

◇   How might we communicate the impact of ageism to community members?

◇   How might we advertise the importance of a skate park in our community to people who already oppose it?

◇   How might we design a public service campaign that addresses the connection between poverty and school readiness?

◇   How might we care for the plants in our school?

◇   What kinds of activities might we organize to meet the needs of grades 1–3 students who feel alone at recess?

As students exercise their creative muscles to solve problems like these, the audience is always at the front of their consciousness, whether it be community members, leaders, or fellow students. The needs they are trying to meet in serving others will sculpt how learners share their creative thinking. The form that they use to express their creativity might be through a product or performance (as discussed in the previous two sections) but the intent, in this case, is to meet a specific need of a group. They may design brochures, documentary videos, advertising campaigns, games, schedules, programs, presentations, and so on. Creativity that serves others gives us the opportunity to teach students the power of their voices, the importance of their efforts, and the impact they have on a broader community.

Figure 5.2 offers a list of questions to support students confirming their product, performance, or service.

Questions to support students confirming their product, performance, or service:

  ◆ What risks am I willing to take?
  ◆ How might I best share my ideas?
  ◆ Are there approaches I did not consider?
  ◆ If my creativity is serving a need, what form does my creativity need to take?
  ◆ Why does form matter?
  ◆ How does my audience affect how I express my ideas?
  ◆ How could I share my ideas in a different way?

- How do I know when I select the correct way to share my creative ideas?
- What might make this product, performance, or service more valuable? Interesting? Engaging?
- What is my main challenge before sharing, and how might I solve it?
- How might I achieve the greatest emotional impact?
- If I change my audience, how might my product or performance shift?
- Do I need to add elements to my work (written, oral, visual) to enhance my message?
- How does my work serve a need?

Figure 5.2: *Select and reflect—Questions to support students confirming their product, performance, or service.*

*Visit **go.SolutionTree.com/assessment** for a free reproducible version of this figure.*

Clarifying Audience and Ensuring Emotional Safety

Audience, as I am using the term here, refers simply to anyone who engages in the creative work of others. The audience may be three hundred people at a performance or it may be the person sitting next to students as they talk through a problem. This is important because, in order to facilitate expression that honors both students and their creative work, teachers and students have to work together to choose audiences that fit the reasons why students are creating. If students are working to resolve the dilemma of littering in their town, the audience might be people who would benefit from this work—community members, community leaders, or the student body. If students are designing a set for a school play, the audience is those who attend the play and the students who will construct and engage in the set. If learners are looking for creative solutions to solve a mathematical dilemma involving the cost of materials needed for a construction project, the audience may simply be their group members or their teacher. If students are creating a puppet show to model how to solve a problem on the playground, the audience might be a select group of peers. The size of the audience can vary. The important thing is that students understand that creative work is important work, and it leads to shared understanding. It is what drives innovation, exploration, and growth.

Not only does the need for an audience communicate the importance of creative expression, but also it plays a critical role in the creative process itself and the resulting expression of creative ideas. The relationship between the audience and the learner ensures a meaningful purpose, a strong investment, a considered form, collaboration, and effective communication, all of which are important to learning, no matter the context. Further, when students share their creative ideas, skills, and understanding with a meaningful audience, they may find themselves improvising and adjusting in the moment. They may observe their audience and make decisions based on what they see. For example, they may notice peers laughing at specific times during a performance and so may choose to linger on a comedic moment longer than planned. Alternatively, students may listen as questions emerge when readers engage with a story they wrote and so they may decide to discuss a certain element of their text within expression. These improvisational moments involve quick assessment and response, and the abilities to read an audience and adjust in the moment are great skills for students to develop. Developing these skills within the creative process also enhances other aspects of students' growth and development. Learning to forgive themselves for less-than-successful in-the-moment adjustments, celebrate connection with others, notice the world around them, and remain flexible but focused are all important life skills. Expression is a great time to practice them. The audiences teachers and students choose for this stage of creativity are very important in determining whether our students achieve these kinds of benefits.

When students compose the audience for their peer's creativity, it is important for us to nurture and develop strong listening, viewing, and responding skills in all learners. Sharing creativity is an experience that places students in the vulnerable position of needing to trust their audience to respond in ways that demonstrate empathy, kindness, and critical thinking. Renzulli (2000) clarifies, "The very nature of creativity requires that students be allowed to express their thoughts and ideas in a warm and open atmosphere" (p. 10). Helping students understand that their role as an audience member is as important as their role of creator is vitally important. The items in the following list can help us attend to and teach students how to be effective audience members. Teachers can use this list as a tool for establishing, teaching, and reinforcing the criteria for effective audience participation. Students can refer to this list to practice, reflect on, and refine these skills in many contexts. Visit **go.SolutionTree.com/assessment** for a reproducible version of this list. Good audience members have the following qualities.

- ◇ **Effective listening skills:** Eye contact, nonverbal engagement, positive facial expressions, and open body language
- ◇ **Self-regulation skills:** The ability to refocus with minimal distraction for the person sharing and the other audience members
- ◇ **Empathy:** The ability to relate to a peer's nervousness and the desire to connect and respond accordingly
- ◇ **Interest:** Interest in the topic, the person sharing, and the purpose for the creative work
- ◇ **An understanding of criteria for success:** Understanding that leads to critical listening and appropriate feedback and questions

By preparing our classroom audience, we can also ensure that both the creative learner and the audience members experience the mutual gains of creative expression. This enhances creative output, a willingness to take risks, and the possibility of future collaboration, all of which are critical for creative classrooms. David Culberhouse (2014) explains, "When we feel anxious, when we focus our thinking on the wrong things, our mental capacity is soaked up on that which has nothing to do with creativity and innovation." We want our students to feel comfortable in being vulnerable and thinking outside the box, knowing their decisions will not influence their sense of belonging. We can therefore also support the creative process by recognizing the relationship between students and classroom audiences as holding potential for further collaboration. We can leverage this relationship to build empathy, critical thinking, and deep engagement.

There are times when the audience that makes the most sense for creative expression is not within the walls of the classroom. For example, when students are engaging in creativity that serves the needs of others, those others may be members of our communities. These kinds of audiences offer rich opportunities for students to make a difference through their creative efforts. Further, these audiences drive creative processes like revision, feedback, and goal setting, because the student is accountable to someone besides the teacher. This is just the kind of motivation that can move even the most resistant creative students to become highly invested creators. Table 5.2 outlines just some of the possible audience members teachers and students might consider as part of creative expression. Teachers can use this list in discussions with students about potential audiences for their work. They could also post this list somewhere in the classroom and allow students to add their own ideas to it.

Table 5.2: *Possible Audiences for Creative Expression*

Classroom and School	Community and Beyond
• Teachers	• Parents, grandparents, elders, or other relatives
• Support staff members	• Community leaders or elected officials
• Classmates	• Community professionals
• Self	• Community volunteers
• Younger class or students	• Community tradespeople
• Older class or students	• Students in other schools
• Administrators	• Artists, dancers, musicians, or actors
• Librarians	• Journalists
• Custodians	• Media specialists
• Bus drivers	• Community business owners
• Safety personnel	• Health and safety workers
• Health personnel	• Postsecondary personnel
• Administrative assistants	• Authors and poets

continued ⇒

Classroom and School	Community and Beyond
• Coaches • Artistic directors • Referees • Counselors	• Tourism personnel • Athletes • Food service industry personnel • Agricultural services personnel • Environmentalists, researchers, or scientists • Law enforcement personnel • Fire protection workers • Transportation service workers • Customers

Visit **go.SolutionTree.com/assessment** for a free reproducible version of this table.

It is important to understand that because creativity is not always a drawn-out affair, expression within the creative process might look a lot like collaboration or conferring. It may follow rapid exploration and elaboration stages, and the expression of the creative work may simply be the beginning of the next iteration of creative thinking. This means that the reason for sharing a creative product or performance might simply be to receive feedback or work with another person to get new ideas that propel students into their next creative endeavor. For example, if the creativity is happening in the context of solving a mathematics problem, exploration and elaboration may involve individuals working alone or in small groups to generate solutions. The expression of ideas may simply occur when the individuals turn to each other and share their approaches before settling on one. With this type of small c creativity, expression is simply making a product public by sharing it with another person. However, in cases where the expression of creativity occurs after considerable revision and elaboration, the audience can vary and so can the method for engaging the audience. Table 5.3 offers a number of alternatives for sharing creative products, performances, or services with an audience.

Table 5.3: *Possible Sharing Formats*

Fishbowl	Students form a circle around the group sharing its creative work. The group in the middle shares either its individual creative ideas or its products, or, if the group engaged in the creative work together, it may share as a group. The students on the outside observe without interacting. They may jot down observations or strengths, or form questions they may ask following the session.
Author's Chair	A special time and place are set aside for students to share their creative work (usually writing but it can be other creative forms), with the authors or creators taking a seat in a place where they can see their classmates and receive their feedback. The primary response from the audience comes in the form of celebrations and in-depth questions.

Panel	A small group of people share with the intention of discussing a particular creative effort, especially one that has implications outside the group. (For example, the group may discuss whether a service project will meet the needs of the group it's aiming to serve.) The discussion is highly reflective in nature.
Topic Talk	A group of people gathers to engage in a specific learning conversation related to the area of creative inquiry. Teachers expect the group to use domain-specific language and elevated discussion based on a deep understanding of the topic. During this discussion, the group also explores the methods it uses to create and the processes that enhance products or performances.
Hot Seat	The student adopts the persona of another person, often a historical or literary figure or someone who is otherwise well known. The audience asks questions, and the student answers based on his or her chosen persona. This strategy requires a good deal of background knowledge.
Discussion Circle	Small groups of students gather to discuss a topic in depth. This creative expression strategy is most useful in contexts where learners are moving quickly between exploration, elaboration, and expression, often returning to the beginning again following the discussion. Each member takes a turn at responding to either the problem itself or the previous person's reflection on the problem.
Read and Respond	In this strategy, the chosen method of expression is written form. After a student shares a creative product, performance, or service (expression), each audience member responds in writing to the experience, directly addressing the author. The author has time to respond verbally or in writing to each audience member.
Chalk Talk	In this strategy, students do all their thinking silently, on paper. In a creative context, the audience offers responses to work through the written word or through images only. Verbal responses are withheld.
Digital Sharing	This strategy works when it is impractical or perhaps not possible for the audience to physically be in the room. The creative work is shared digitally, and the audience responds digitally as well. Many programs and apps facilitate this kind of sharing.
Peer Response Groups	Groups of students give and receive feedback on creative tasks. Each student has a specific role in the response. For example, one student may collect evidence of success, while another may formulate questions.
Presentation With Q and A	The audience asks questions about either the student's *creative process* (how he or she arrives at the driving questions, how the student uses materials, or how he or she resolves challenges) or the *end result* (product, performance, or service).
Carousel	Multiple students place their work around a classroom space and students rotate through each sample, offering suggestions, connections, and questions on sticky notes.

Visit go.SolutionTree.com/assessment for a free reproducible version of this table.

Figure 5.3 offers a list of questions to support students selecting an audience.

Questions to support students selecting an audience:
- Who needs to hear my message?
- With whom do I feel most comfortable sharing?
- How does what I am saying affect who I choose to share it with?
- Do I feel ready to share this with someone else?
- What do I need from my audience?
- How would I like to receive feedback?
- What can the audience learn from my work? How will they learn it?
- What am I hoping to change by sharing with this audience?
- How can I prepare my audience?
- When do I feel safe enough to share?
- How do I feel about sharing my work with others?
- How might I prepare to share?
- What response am I hoping for?
- Why might audience response matter to me?

Figure 5.3: *Select and reflect—Questions to support students selecting an audience.*

Visit **go.SolutionTree.com/assessment** *for a free reproducible version of this figure.*

The Role of the Teacher

The role of the teacher during expression is multifaceted. First, we need to ensure learners have created products, performances, or services that adequately address their creative goals. We may need to work with our students when, after a self-assessment, they discover that they are not yet satisfied with their results. Minilessons, further research, targeted feedback, or more time to refine may be in order. Next, we have to balance the roles of assessor, audience member, and encourager. We need to create a safe space for students to share while still encouraging high standards and a devotion to both short- and long-term goals. When an audience is made up of other students in our charge, we may need to explicitly teach and reinforce strong audience skills. We may task our students with responsibilities (such as offering constructive feedback, celebrating strengths, or responding appropriately, for example) as audience members and follow up by offering support with these tasks as needed (such as through feedback scripts, graphic organizers, and explicit modeling and teaching). Our understanding of our learners and their creative goals equips us to employ the instructional and assessment agility required in creative classrooms.

Following are some important roles for teachers when unlocking expression that can support some challenges students experience in this stage.

◇ **Audience:** While we know we don't want to be the only audience for students' creative pursuits, the truth is we often hold that role in some capacity as the teacher. We need to engage in students' work to collect formative data, to offer feedback, and to decide when a student is approaching readiness for a summative assessment. We may be asking further questions or helping students to connect the work of several learners. Maybe we are an audience member to offer support for students who have anxiety over sharing.

◇ **Agent for sharing:** When the teacher is the primary consumer (audience) of student work, the opportunity for diverse feedback and responses is diminished. Often, the reason for sharing creative efforts is related to summative assessment alone and any feedback comes in the form of a grade. This paradigm prevents the opportunity for increased investment through engagement with authentic audiences.

◇ **Encourager:** Once again, during expression praise can stall creativity. Focusing on the development of skills and knowledge to advance personal, creative goals is essential.

◇ **Skill enhancer:** Creative expression is difficult for some students. They may feel confident in their products, but sharing them with others creates anxiety. In other cases, even when students prepare for a performance, the idea of sharing with a crowd of people can be overwhelming. They may worry that their efforts have not produced something good enough. They may fear receiving negative feedback and may lack confidence in being able to move through this discomfort.

Table 5.4 suggests specific actions that a teacher can take to overcome the challenges of these roles.

Table 5.4: *The Role of the Teacher and Key Actions in the Expression Stage*

Role of the Teacher	Key Teacher Actions
Teacher as Audience	◆ Respond with compassion when the expression of creativity falls short of expectations. ◆ Support students through failures as they engage in risky tasks where failure can occur again. ◆ Re-engage students in tasks and refocus them on their successes. ◆ Use observations and feedback to build a bridge between creative expression and reflection and response.

continued ⇒

Role of the Teacher	Key Teacher Actions
Agent for Sharing	• Work with students to decide who would benefit the greatest from their expression of ideas, skills, and knowledge. • Provide students the means by which to engage audiences both within and beyond the classroom (for example, Skype with a scientist or dance for a group of seniors).
Encourager	• Assess learners' needs. • Support students when they need it. • Reassure students that they are capable of sharing their creativity in meaningful and appropriate ways. • Invite students to elaborate on their options and their decisions. • Provide the needed materials and supports.
Skill Enhancer	• Offer guidance and explicit teaching on topics (for example, how to listen, how to be respectful, how to manage stress, how to prepare for sharing, how to celebrate a job well done, how to revisit and refine, how to speak, and any number of skills associated with the chosen method of expression). • Utilize flexible grouping based on student need (as determined by formative assessment through observation, artifact analysis, and conversation). • Connect emerging evidence and instructionally agile responses.

Assessment and Expression

Assessment within expression serves many purposes. First, it helps both students and teachers build toward readiness for sharing. Next, it determines degrees of success both during the sharing process and afterward, as students consider next steps. Depending on the timing of when a student moves from elaboration to expression, students may re-engage in the creative process, further elaborating, or they may decide the work is worthy of summative assessment and plan to apply what was learned to the next creative learning endeavor. As in the other stages, assessment propels the learning forward and can continue to support students as the primary decision makers. Ostroff (2016) explains, "Assessment can be enhanced (rather than diminished) when the process of representing their work is in the hands of the students" (p. 152).

As was the case for exploration and elaboration, ensuring students engage in effective expression requires attention to formative assessment (information gathering), feedback (dialogue with others), and self-assessment (dialogue with self). Early in this stage, formative assessment will focus on determining readiness for expression. It is critical that teachers assess the degree to which students are prepared to share so they can ensure success and increase confidence in learners as creative individuals. Later in the expression stage, once the product, performance, or service has been confirmed and prepared, teachers should adopt an observer stance to continue to nurture students who can self-assess. Teachers will watch students as they share with and gain feedback from others, and they will collect formative assessment information, but they will withhold their own feedback until the formal reflection and response stage.

Determining Readiness for Expression

Prior to sharing, students and teachers should engage in self-assessment and formative assessment to determine students' readiness for expression. We will review students' criteria for success and allow them to rehearse or refine areas where it would be beneficial. For example, if the creative expression is a performance, assessment (either formative or self-assessment) near the beginning of the expression stage may indicate a need to practice a portion of the performance a little more. Or prior to an assembly presentation focused on the power of volunteering, it may show a need to rehearse transitions to make them smoother. Formative assessment will inform educators about student progress in establishing their method and reasons for sharing. It will also assist them in ensuring that the creative products, performances, or services themselves are nearing creative resolution. Teachers can structure feedback during the early parts of this stage to address gaps in preparedness by the students doing the expression and by any students who will form the audience. This will support the emotional safety needed to ensure confidence and trust.

Adopting an Observer Stance

The most important assessment strategy for teachers in the latter part of expression is to step back from feedback or instruction and listen (or read, or view) when students are ready to express their creativity. When students decide to share their creative thinking and skills, their teachers need to step back from instruction and let the students speak. This nurtures the respectful learning relationship that is so important for creative classrooms. As we listen to, read, or view the creative work, we may find it helpful to have the student goals beside us, along with the criteria for success. (These criteria may relate to the product itself, the processes accessed to develop the end creative result, or both.) We may also note strengths and areas needing growth so we can support not only short-term steps but also long-term creative development. These kinds of assessment data increase our ability to be instructionally agile and responsive to learners' creative needs. Once students finish sharing their work, teachers can embark on a formal reflection and response, which may include feedback, revision, or celebration as well as summative assessment decision making.

Using the reproducible tools at the end of this chapter (pages 163–167) can help teachers facilitate these assessment processes within the expression stage of the creative process. The reproducible "Expression Self-Assessment and Reflection on Goals and Success Criteria" (page 166) invites students to self-assess and reflect on goals and criteria as they prepare to share their work.) "Observation During Expression" (page 167) is a tool that teachers can use to observe and plan next steps while students are engaged in expression.

Final Thoughts

During the expression stage of the creative process, students make plans for and then share their creative efforts with a wider audience. While audience size can vary, the importance of sharing remains immense. This is the time of greatest risk for some students, and our job is to help them navigate this vulnerability and match them with a meaningful audience.

Following expression, there is a time to step back from the busyness of creativity and reflect on the decisions made throughout the whole creative process. Students will connect past work to future work and will design approaches to their next creative pursuits. Chapter 6 explores reflection and response, providing supports for both teachers and students as they navigate this final and very important stage.

Unlocking Expression: Observation and Self-Assessment

Teachers can use the following tool to self-assess the strengths and challenges of expression through observation. The following table contains criteria for successful elaboration, descriptions of how these criteria look when lived out day-to-day, and suggestions for how educators can nurture these criteria within their instructional and assessment plans. The final column offers suggestions for how to respond when criteria are absent or need additional support.

Critical Action	Expression Targets	What the Teacher Sees	Teacher Facilitation Techniques	Teacher Response
Establishing Method and Confirming the Reason for Sharing	I can identify why I am sharing my creative work (purpose) and with whom.	◆ Students who can share the reasons for why they are engaging in creative processes ◆ Students who can identify who would benefit from their work and why	◆ Structure discussions or templates that facilitate decision making around audience and purpose. ◆ Connect students to meaningful audiences. ◆ Work with students to contemplate the implications of audience and purpose.	◆ Return to exploration to connect students to a strong purpose. ◆ Offer many alternatives for audience and ensure students are making strong choices.
Confirming Product, Performance, or Service	I can choose a meaningful way to share my creative ideas.	◆ Students who can identify ways to share ◆ Students who can choose a way to share that is meaningful and appropriate ◆ Students who engage in positive self-talk about sharing	◆ Provide students with alternatives for products, performances, and services as well as methods for engaging audiences. ◆ Allow students choice in how and with whom they will share.	◆ Limit choices or expand choices depending on why a student feels challenged. ◆ Be clear about the reason for expression. ◆ Reduce the risk if necessary (for example, by adjusting audience size, timing, and so on).

Critical Action	Expression Targets	What the Teacher Sees	Teacher Facilitation Techniques	Teacher Response
Confirming Product, Performance, or Service	I can appropriately prepare for sharing.	• Students who can practice and revise in preparation for sharing • Students who invest in products that address their goals	• Offer time to prepare. • Allow collaborative preparation, where students can offer each other feedback before sharing with a broader audience. • Offer additional skill and knowledge support when students need it.	• Build checklists to guide preparation. • Confer and coach as necessary. • Draw attention to criteria and goals. • If students aren't invested, reflect on the root cause and address it.
Clarifying Audience and Ensuring Emotional Safety	I can address my audience's needs.	• Students who are visibly aware of their audience • Students who can adjust in the moment as they need to • Students who examine their audience for a response (feedback)	• Document audience responses when appropriate (for example, through video, photo, audience feedback). • Invite students to respond, both during and after sharing.	• Facilitate an analysis of audience response. • Confer with students when they need it. • Cease the sharing and address safety when a student struggles with audience response.

Critical Action	Expression Targets	What the Teacher Sees	Teacher Facilitation Techniques	Teacher Response
Clarifying Audience and Ensuring Emotional Safety	I can be a respectful audience member.	• Students who listen well and demonstrate interest and respect • Students who ask questions • Students who offer positive and constructive feedback at appropriate times	• Share criteria for being a respectful audience member. • Be clear about the purpose for being an audience member. • Ensure the students who are sharing their work plan appropriately (remove the temptation to be disrespectful). Build in formal reflection and targeted revision if needed.	• Address disrespectful behavior immediately and without interrupting the student who is sharing, if possible. • Reteach respectful behavior and allow the student to try again.
	I can safely and respectfully collaborate and share with others.	• Students who can receive feedback • Students who can reflect on their own work • Students who can apply feedback and the ideas of others to their own work (when appropriate)	• Plan collaborative processes to facilitate shared refinement. • Explicitly teach criteria for effective collaboration. • Ensure this work is grounded in the goals and criteria. • Allow time for students to do this work.	• Be selective about groups when needed. • Ensure feedback is clear and concise so students can take the necessary action. • Use video capture or photography to capture creative work without the face-to-face engagement for students who have deep anxiety.

page 3 of 3

Expression Self-Assessment and Reflection on Goals and Success Criteria

This tool invites students to reflect on their creative work and determine the degree to which it is ready for sharing. It brings students back to their goals and their success criteria in order to ensure readiness for expression. Students can store completed versions in a creative portfolio.

My goal for this creative work:		
My anticipated audience:		

Criteria for Success	Current Strengths	What I Still Need to Do to Get Ready

From my audience, I need:

I think I will be ready to share on _____

Observation During Expression

The teacher or audience members can use this tool to record what they observe to prepare to give feedback following expression.

Date:			
Student:			
Goal, problem, or guiding question (or questions):			
Criteria	**What I Notice**	**What I Wonder**	**Next Steps**

6

Unlocking Reflection and Response

I ask students to post their service plans on the bulletin board next to their goal sheets. Today is reflection day. We have completed our plans and enacted them in the school and the community over the last two weeks and now it is time to reflect on how it all went. The emotions that emerged from the acts of service have passed, and the students are quiet and pensive. They know that reflection day means they will examine their creative efforts as a whole and decide what they might do differently next time.

To begin, I ask each student to take a turn briefly restating the purpose of his or her service project, whom he or she was attempting to serve, and when he or she actually enacted the plan. The purpose of this review is to help students re-orient themselves to their work and review the variety of services the class was able to complete. This is a celebration, and it is a great way to start our reflections.

Next, I ask students to work with someone else for the remainder of the reflection. Their partner will serve as a resource for advancing their reflection skills. This person is not offering feedback at this time, but rather is asking questions to deepen metacognition. Asking good questions is yet another skill we are working on developing as a class. The students have been adding to a class list of great questions for reflection, and this list shows a growing understanding of how to frame questions in a more open fashion to encourage expansion and deep reflection.

By the end of reflection day, I expect students to document the process they took to arrive at their service project plan and compare it to the process their partner used in a Venn diagram. They need to clarify their actions and decisions as they explored, expanded on, and shared their plan with the group that actually received their service. They also need to decide, with their partner, to what degree their plan met their service goal. This reflection will be another source of data to help me make summative decisions when I assess their efforts after today.

Tomorrow, we will end our creative project with a class discussion about how to create a successful service plan. We will generate a list of tips and techniques for strong planning, which I will use with my class next year. The reflections today will help us arrive at a strong list tomorrow.

I have moved several times in my life. Anyone who has done the same can understand my temptation to eliminate "stuff" from my home so my moves will be less of an ordeal. I have given away or sold books, clothing, kitchenware, and furniture, but the items never purged are the portfolios of my creative work, collected over many years. I have folders of writing dating back to my early childhood. I have high school and university art collections packed into fraying portfolios. I have albums of photography from the years when I was trying to capture my life in black and white. I have books of poetry, story ideas, and journals filled with daily musings. All this creative output is almost sacred to me because it represents not only my work but also who I was at various stages of my life. My creative work and my identity connect inextricably.

As a classroom teacher, I have witnessed the same important connections in my students. Watching learners take deep pride and ownership in their creative work has been one of my greatest pleasures. When students spot their parents waiting to pick them up after art classes, and rush to the door to show off their latest artwork, I know creative expression means something to them. Witnessing high school students effortlessly toss notebooks into the garbage at the end of the year while they stuff their writing portfolios in their backpacks reveals the importance of creative work to them. In end-of-course student meetings, I have seen the flush of pride students have when they lay out their work in preparation for our reflective discussion. Creativity matters.

The power of creative work to reveal, express, and explore aspects of ourselves, including who we are as learners in creative contexts, is a key reason why a formal reflection and response is so important in creative classrooms. Hall and Simeral (2015) assert, "We don't learn from experience. We learn from reflecting on that experience" (p. 80). Students deserve the opportunity to reflect and adjust not only throughout the creative process (through self-assessment during exploration, elaboration, and expression), but also at the end of a creative endeavor, as part of their development as creative human beings. By looking at the artifacts, performances, and services they generate, students can determine which conditions best support their creative instincts. They can explore how their creative ideas develop, how insight is supported, and how creative sharing leads to long-term growth. Gura (2016) asserts, "Our goal as educators must be to produce reflective creators who understand the mental processes behind their creativity and how they can be applied to other situations, problems, and challenges beyond the context of the arts" (p. 5). When we make time for deep reflection and response in our classrooms, our students have the opportunity to internalize those processes that support their creative growth, so they can plan to replicate them in future creative endeavors.

It is critical to build reflection into every stage of creativity because it launches students from one stage to the next. The reflection and response described in this chapter is slightly different from the reflection and response (formative assessment, self-assessment, and feedback) that occurs during the other stages of creativity. In exploration, students generate questions and problems to guide their creative pursuits. During this initial stage, learners reflect on their interests and curiosities and revise questions and frameworks as needed. In elaboration, students research and explore, reflecting and adjusting their efforts as needed to get closer to their goals. During expression, students see their work through others' eyes and make in-the-moment decisions and responses, in order to enhance their message and support engagement.

However, the kind of reflection and response that occurs after all these embedded reflections is a deeper and longitudinal examination of creativity over time. This reflection connects products and performances to strategies and approaches. It invites students to view their work from beginning to end and use what they learn to imagine new creative pursuits. It allows them to synthesize their creative work and make decisions that affect how they will approach learning in the future. This reflection is about who they are as creative learners and how they will decide next steps, whether it be moving back into the creative process or moving on to something new.

This rich reflection and considered response supports the development of some of the most critical skills students require for success throughout life. Sean Slade and David Griffith (2013) explain:

> *The skills that will be essential in the future will be those that allow the individual to navigate conceptual learning: social skills of empathy, communication, and understanding; team skills of collaboration, leadership, and contribution; and creative skills of problem-solving, ideation, and synthesis. (p. 26)*

By mindfully planning this final, deeper reflection, we can help our students see beyond the immediate task and beyond this moment in time. Julia Marshall (2010) explains the importance of reflection that moves students into metacognition and self-awareness:

> *Because creativity includes venturing into the unknown, knowing what one is doing may seem antithetical to creativity. However, knowing that one is venturing and how one is going about it facilitates this process. Therefore, reflection on how one learns through creative processes not only makes an art investigation a true learning experience, but also promotes creativity. (p. 21)*

Whether this reflection follows an art investigation or it follows a prototype design in science, a construction project in practical and applied arts, a business plan in business education, or a social studies simulation, it becomes the bridge between the immediate creative experience and all other future creative endeavors. When we linger long enough to facilitate this kind of reflection, we are ensuring we support creative learning both now and in the future.

In this chapter, we will explore the critical actions for unlocking reflection and response, the teacher's role in this stage of students' creativity journey, and how creative reflection and response and assessment intersect.

Critical Actions for Teachers and Students When Unlocking Reflection and Response

In order to ensure that the reflection and response stage of the creative process gets at the heart of deep thinking about how creativity works for our students, there are six important actions teachers and students need to take to enhance their creative processes.

1. Illuminating
2. Verifying whether work meets established goals and criteria
3. Internalizing creative mindsets and practices
4. Re-engaging and refining
5. Demonstrating forgiveness and empathy
6. Choosing reflection methods

Each consideration supports creative reflection and response and the assessment essential to advance them. After reviewing these critical actions, see the reproducible "Unlocking Reflection and Response: Observation and Self-Assessment" (pages 194–197) for guidance in navigating self-assessment and observation related to these critical components.

Illuminating

The act of reflection following creative work can provide *illumination*—a clarification and deeper awareness that results from students unpacking their feelings about their creative efforts and the processes they use to get there. In some ways, it is a trip into their own creative minds, but it combines that journey with the idea of seeing their creativity from a distance. This reflection might occur after a little time passes, so the immediate emotions a student feels following creative expression recede somewhat. Students can step back from their creative process a little and seek a closure of sorts.

While they may decide to either move on to something new or re-engage in their products, performances, or services, illuminating lets them do so with a different lens. Instead of focusing solely on their success criteria, they may focus on *how* they arrived at their creative work. For example, they may decide that they are not yet happy with their use of the materials and conclude that they need to spend more time exploring the skills associated with them. Perhaps, when they step back from their work, they see that seeking feedback earlier on may have been beneficial, and they resolve to do that next time. In the end, students will decide the best course of action to take, based on their reflections. This decision is important for all creative people.

Decisions like these are the result of insight, which purposeful examination of documented creativity supports. Mary Catherine Bateson (1994) defines insight in this way: "*Insight*, I believe, refers to that depth of understanding that comes by setting experiences, yours and mine, familiar and exotic, new and old, side by side, learning by letting them speak to one another" (p. 14). Inviting students to compare their creative work to their other works, or alongside their peers' work, allows them to develop this kind of insight that leads to purposeful action.

It is not enough to simply ask students to reflect—like with any practice, the implementation determines impact. There has to be finesse—teachers guide students to reflect on the right questions at the right time to ensure students benefit from the process. To facilitate this process, teachers select questions that stimulate metacognition. They will then provide time and a method or methods by which students might record their thoughts. Some teachers may choose to employ a creativity journal or blog. Others might invite students to record themselves digitally, thinking on their own or with a trusted partner. Perhaps learners and teachers have photographed the creative process and the reflection occurs through a visual essay supplemented by captions. With young learners, this illumination might occur through conversation. Any variety of methods of thinking about the process of creativity can be productive but facilitating reflection processes that lead to illumination is an important aspect of creative classrooms. Figure 6.1 offers a list of questions to support students during illumination.

Questions to support students during illumination:
- How did I get here?
- How am I feeling about my creative processes? Why am I feeling this way?
- What do I notice about my work? How does that connect to how I approach things?
- How does this work compare to other creative work I have done? Why?
- What else is my product or process like? Where have I seen something like this before?
- What could I do instead?

Figure 6.1: *Select and reflect—Questions to support students during illumination.*

continued ⇒

- What is the effect of the choices I made when approaching this task, experience, or problem?
- How did I expand my understanding of my challenge? Where did I go for help?
- What else do I know or what else can I do that this work didn't allow me to show or demonstrate?
- When I step back from my creative efforts, what do I see?
- How does this work fit in my overall learning and growth?
- Why was this work important to me, to others, or to what I was trying to say?

*Visit **go.SolutionTree.com/assessment** for a free reproducible version of this figure.*

Verifying Whether Work Meets Established Goals and Criteria

While self-assessment will have been the driver of many decisions throughout the creative process, the reflective process that comes after students commit to form, audience, purpose, materials, and criteria allows them to really come to terms with their products, performances, or services in relation to their goals and criteria for success. Certainly, they may choose to re-engage in their current work to refine it further, but a more likely outcome might be to reflect on how they approached their creative work and verify whether it meets the goals and criteria they established during exploration and refined during elaboration and expression. Like at other stages of the creative process, this means students re-engage in the goals and criteria they have been recording, refining, and reflecting on during their repeated self-assessments. At this point, they have the benefit of having experienced a creative effort from conception to expression and their reflection means really investigating the degree to which it did what it was intended to do. At this stage, it is also appropriate to ask students to support their verification with evidence from their product, performance, or service. They may describe specific aspects of their products, discuss audience response during performances, or relate the evidence they have of helping others in their service projects. Before they make any subsequent decisions, they need time to explore their efforts and the results they yielded. The "Reflection and Response Self-Assessment" reproducible (page 198) is a tool students can use to facilitate this process.

If students have had the opportunity to work through each component of the creative process, chances are high that they will have something to celebrate. Stopping to consider not only the aspects of their creative work that need refinement but also those that invited a strong manifestation of their vision is important. It is from this platform of strength that students build the confidence to move into future creativity with increasing independence, as they realize their developed skills will help them in their next effort. They may reflect on a performance and acknowledge that the emotions that both they and their audience experienced during expression were rich and impactful. They may think about how they were able to draw these emotions from themselves and others and they plan to do so in their next performance. It is important to ask students to document and acknowledge their newly found and deeply developed skills. They may use checklists, photo essays, journals, vlogs, or other methods of recording to celebrate these skills. The time we spend on this documentation alone will remind our learners that they have indeed come a long way during their creative expression.

Reflecting at this time also allows students to consider the degree to which they have been independently innovative. It allows them to evaluate which aspects of their work were of their own design and which derive from others' work. As Johnson (2015) says:

> *A good assessment asks the student to formally consider if all required elements of the task were completed. It should ask why their approach was the best one. And it can and should ask if the thinking that went into the effort was their own—not just a regurgitation of others' ideas. (p. 93)*

As discussed earlier, encouraging students to use others' work to act as catalysts to their own work is a healthy approach to early creativity. However, inviting students to reflect on which aspects of their work were of their own design is an important celebration. Without purposeful reflection, students may not even realize their own innovation. They may not see how their decisions were unique and reflect their personal tastes and goals.

As students reflect on their creative efforts, they will likely verify that they have developed strengths through their work and perhaps still have some unresolved aspects in their products, performances, and services as well as the approaches they took to get to those results. Reflecting on these strengths and challenges will allow them to make decisions about where their creative work will go next. Often, creativity breeds further creativity as elements of a newly completed project inspire new questions, new ideas, and new approaches. Students may realize, when attempting to verify their work, that they did not meet certain goals, and are then able to identify these items when brainstorming goals for the next creative activity. In this way, verification leads back into creativity, and brainstorming future approaches is yet another creative act. Figure 6.2 offers a list of questions to support students verifying whether their work meets their established goals and criteria.

Questions to support students verifying whether their work meets their established goals and criteria:

- How closely did I come to a result I hoped for?
- Do I feel satisfied with my efforts? To what degree?
- Did I encounter any problems while I was building (or creating)? How did I recognize these problems?

Figure 6.2: *Select and reflect—Questions to support students verifying whether their work meets their established goals and criteria.*

continued ⇒

- Did I produce what I set out to?
- What is the most original aspect of this piece? How do I know?
- What problem does my product solve? What question does it answer?
- Did my prototype give me the results I was looking for? Why or why not?
- What were the criteria for a good solution to the problem? How do I know when I achieve what I hope to achieve?
- How were my decisions my own? To what degree did others influence me? Am I happy with those influences?
- What questions remain unanswered? How might I continue my exploration?

Visit **go.SolutionTree.com/assessment** *for a free reproducible version of this figure.*

Internalizing Creative Mindsets and Practices

Creativity changes us. It opens up our potential; it empowers us to make decisions; and it allows us to take risks in ways that speak directly to our own desires, hopes, and dreams. The more experience students have with creativity in all its forms, the more confident they will become in engaging in the processes that support deep thinking, wonder, and creative problem solving. Theresa Anderson (2014) calls this long-term relationship between reflection and creativity "essential green spaces for the mind" (p. 45). Making time to reflect and respond to creative work ensures that these "green spaces" that offer a place to reflect and imagine yield long-term rewards in the areas of self-regulation, persistence, and curiosity. Watching young learners develop the ability to access these green spaces is truly one of the greatest joys of teaching.

As students develop not only their creative prowess but also their ability to reflect on their processes, products, performances, and services, they increase their ability to self-assess and, in turn, self-regulate. The combination of deep investment and confidence in their ability to overcome obstacles and solve their own problems means our students can determine their own strengths and challenges and make decisions to address their goals. This ability to self-regulate goes hand-in-hand with the development of self-assessment skills (Andrade, Du, & Mycek, 2010). As students gain experience in selecting materials, choosing their learning environments, asking their own questions, seeking sources of knowledge and skill, and shifting their approaches based on need, they enhance their ability to self-regulate to ensure maximum productivity and focus.

The ability to self-assess and self-regulate contributes to the development of the ability to persist. By inviting students to step back from their creative work and reflect on their processes, we can help them see that creativity manifests in many ways. Sometimes, it is straightforward with clear insight leading the way, and other times, it is messy and filled with twists and turns. Guided reflection at the end of creative work allows students to recall decisions they made along the way that were successful and those that were not. It allows them to see that most mistakes are not final and that creative people often end up in a different place from where they imagined they would be when they started. In truth, sticking with creativity through the difficult times is important for many reasons. Johnson (2015) explains a critical benefit of this kind of reflection: "there is always a way, if one is sufficiently innovative and persistent, to get around, over, under, or through any obstacle" (p. 12). We want our students to approach challenges with optimism. We want them to see difficulty as something to move through as opposed to something to avoid. We want them to experience light after darkness and know that life is filled with both joy and struggle. These can be some of the lasting benefits of reflecting on creativity.

Another lasting benefit of reflection following creativity is the generation of new curiosity and ensuing questions. As students explore what they learn and how they learn it, their reflections can lead to new questions and new goals. For example, a student may express satisfaction at his or her attempt to create an imaginary city within a geographic setting that addresses trading and transportation needs. However, the student may now wonder why cities exist in areas without water or plentiful natural resources. This may catapult the student into a subsequent exploration of the connection between population settlement and political events. A creative exploration builds future creativity and wonder. Students may find themselves asking questions like, "What happens if I use a different tool?" or "How might my product change if I create it for a different audience?" Hall and Simeral (2015) highlight the relationship between creativity and wonder when they explain, "You'll find that the more you reflect on what you know, the more you'll realize what you don't know" (p. 47). Teaching students how to recognize what they don't know and why this is important is part of our creative work in schools. We must make sure that students have the time to consider new questions that arise from creative work. We may offer prompts that invite students to explore their work more deeply, with consideration for how it fits in a broader context of learning. Over time, we want students to see that curiosity is critically important for deep learning. We want to honor student curiosity as one of the most favorable attributes of strong learners.

Figure 6.3 offers a list of questions to support students internalizing creative mindsets and practices.

Questions to support students internalizing creative mindsets and practices:
- What strategies did I use in the past that could help me in the future?
- Given my results, what goal might I set for myself in my next creative endeavor?
- What do I still wonder?
- How might this work lead to future creative ideas and questions?

Figure 6.3: *Select and reflect—Questions to support students internalizing creative mindsets and practices.*

continued ⇒

- What problems did I solve along the way? How did I solve them?
- What did this teach me about myself?
- How would I compare this to what I did last time?
- What aspects of my creative process are most important to me?
- Did I have enough time? Would I use my time differently if I could?
- How might a different tool impact my results?
- How might my product change if I create it for a different audience?
- Why do people quit? How might I avoid this choice?
- What did I need to do to increase my productivity? How did I know I needed to do that?
- What habits do I have that support my creativity?

*Visit **go.SolutionTree.com/assessment** for a free reproducible version of this figure.*

Re-Engaging and Refining

The idea of the "end" in creative work is somewhat elusive. Like with most learning within our school systems, deadlines are manufactured and "finishing" something is a somewhat arbitrary decision based on factors quite separate from the learning itself (for example, bells that signal the end of class, end-of-term dates, and unit timelines). Indeed, true learning is recursive and expansive, with ideas building on ideas, and skills building on skills. Sawyer (2006) explains, "The difference between creating a completely new work and simply varying an existing one is a matter of degree" (p. 213). So, in some ways, saying that this type of creative reflection comes at the end of creative output is inaccurate.

There are times when students will reflect at a time they presume is the end, only to find that they want to return to their work and re-engage in and refine aspects that have not brought clarity or satisfaction. This drive to continue to grow and enhance is natural and is one reason why portfolios can be so important to creative processes. Portfolios serve as a holding place for work and can act as an invitation to revisit and even re-invent creative products. Peta Gresham (2014) explains, "Creativity refers to the processes of deep thinking, crafting, revising and refining, just as much as it relates to originality or inspiration" (p. 48). Reflection on creative efforts may drive students into future questions and investigation or it may push students back into pre-existing questions. In this way, reflection serves as a bridge between discrete creative efforts and acts as the gateway to enhanced investment in creativity over time. Kelly (2012) says, "The greater the personal relevance of the creative work to the student, the greater the potential for the sustained development of this work over time" (p. 18). We establish the importance of creative work when we honor it by documenting it, storing it in a portfolio, and reflecting on it.

Students can use portfolios to invite reflective thought about how creative work evolves over time. By comparing past work to present work, students can consider risks they took, consider the ensuing results, and plan for future work. They can explore material differences or different perspectives they may attempt and decide which yield the best results. They can identify approaches to creativity that produce the greatest success and those that distract them from their goals. Stepping back and exploring creative work over time is an essential step in unlocking creativity.

Students often use portfolios to share their work with their families, and this practice is important for building relationships and communicating growth. However, as mentioned in a previous chapter, creative portfolios often look different from more polished versions teachers often use for school-home communication. Creative portfolios will contain documentation that shows success but also artifacts that show failure. There may be samples that are unfinished or samples that show quite visible adjustments, and this is important for the purposes explained in the previous paragraphs. However, for this reason, it is important to explain to families what to expect when students share the portfolios and why they look the way they do. Further, it may be helpful for teachers to share questions with parents that they could ask their children when looking at the children's creative portfolios. These questions provide opportunities for conversations between students and their families about the creative work, and facilitate greater partnership between families and schools. Figure 6.4 includes some suggestions to help family members guide the conversation as they explore creative portfolios with their students.

Questions to help family members guide the conversation as they explore creative portfolios with their students:

- What is happening here? Tell me more about this.
- What decisions did you make as you were working on this?
- What risks did you take? Show me what happened as a result.
- What was a problem you had and how did you solve it?
- How might you do things differently next time?
- What strategies work best for you? What helps you be most creative?
- What makes creativity hard for you?
- How have you grown?
- What do you want to improve?
- Which artifact feels incomplete to you?
- Which artifact are you proudest of and why?
- What is your next project?
- What questions do you have now?

Figure 6.4: *Questions to help family members guide the conversation as they explore creative portfolios with their students.*

*Visit **go.SolutionTree.com/assessment** for a free reproducible version of this figure.*

Deep reflection allows students a process to explore not only *what* they did as a result of creative processes but also *how* they chose to approach a problem. In this way, we can work with students to affirm successful creative approaches while exploring strategies and tools that may allow them to create a different result next time. In fact, learning strategies (the actions students take to advance their learning) ground this aspect of reflection and response—they speak to *how* students will shift their approaches and further develop their work. This component of creativity invites students to consider strategies that invite creative productivity—different ways of thinking, representing thinking, and sharing thinking. By considering how creativity happens and the strategies that support it, we are adding to the students' toolkit and advancing their creative skills. Table 6.1 lists some of the strategies students might consider when thinking about past creative efforts and planning for future endeavors. They may ask themselves what parts of their creative process were particularly difficult and whether additional strategies may help their next effort.

Table 6.1: *Creative Strategies*

Exploration	Elaboration	Expression	Reflection and Response
• Generate questions. • Clarify the purpose or reason for the creative effort. • Visualize possibilities. • Imagine alternatives and approaches. • Activate prior knowledge. • Make predictions, estimations, and hypotheses. • Confer with others. • Look at things from a different perspective. • Explore relationships between ideas. • Group or classify ideas.	• Prepare a plan to gather and critically consider ideas and information. • Consider tone, mood, voice, and point of view. • Consider feedback. • Set goals. • Explore message and meaning. • Generate possible solutions or ideas. • Experiment with technology. • Find and apply patterns and connections. • Use reference tools. • Make inferences. • Revisit texts and resources.	• Consider possible audiences. • Revise for meaning and effect. • Consider the impact. • Adjust to audience response. • Appraise for clarity. • Rehearse. • Refine details. • Check responses. • Seek alternate ways of communication. • Enhance presentation. • Access technology. • Seek feedback. • Offer feedback.	• Examine feedback. • Compare efforts. • Consider processes. • Review audience response. • Generate new questions. • Set new goals. • Revisit and revise as needed. • Explore emotional responses (self and others). • Map process from start to finish. • Imagine alternate perspectives. • Confer with others. • Document ideas.

Exploration	Elaboration	Expression	Reflection and Response
• Engage in and explore the catalyst. • Explore materials. • Choose an effective learning space. • Consider the prompt. • Offer reactions and opinions. • Set goals and establish criteria.	• Speak with experts. • Confer with others. • Make notes. • Organize thoughts and ideas. • Elaborate on details. • Consider and plan for timelines and deadlines. • Map an approach and set goals. • Reflect on criteria.	• Set or refine goals. • Reflect on criteria.	• Reflect on criteria.

Figure 6.5 invites learners to consider the options before them as they decide how to respond after reflecting on their creative efforts. By choosing a next step, they are setting a new goal for re-engagement and refinement.

Date:

After today, your next steps might include:
  ❏ Self-assess and set a new goal
  ❏ Revise your work
  ❏ Restart
  ❏ Submit for summative assessment
  ❏ Collaborate with someone else
  ❏ Do a little more research
  ❏ See me for a minilesson on _____ [list a concept or topic that needs clarifying or explicit instruction]
  ❏ Start something new
The action I plan on taking is:

Figure 6.5: *Goal setting after reflection.*

*Visit **go.SolutionTree.com/assessment** for a free reproducible version of this figure.*

UNLOCKED

Figure 6.6 offers a list of questions to support students re-engaging with and refining their work.

Questions to support students re-engaging with and refining their work:

- Which aspects of my work meet my goals?
- Which aspects of my work fall short of my goals? Why?
- Would I prefer to return to my work and revisit it, or do I want to start something new?
- How do I approach this creative task?
- What decisions did I make along the way, and what happens as a result of those decisions?
- Which strategies did I use? Which strategies might I try using next time?
- Did I spend enough time in the right places?
- How might I document my thinking next time?
- How does my portfolio help me think about my own creative processes?
- Could I order my efforts from most satisfying to least? Which criteria am I using?
- What challenges do I have during the learning? How do I know they are a challenge? What do I do? Why do I make that decision?
- How might I change the outcome? What might I try differently?
- What will I do next time?
- Did my new approach result in an accurate answer, a strong product, or both? If not, why? If so, why?
- Which strategies do I want to keep in my creative toolbox?
- What do I want to stay the same in my work, even if I try again?
- What are my best approaches? What should I celebrate?
- What could I tell others about becoming more creative?

Figure 6.6: *Select and reflect—Questions to support students re-engaging with and refining their work.*

*Visit **go.SolutionTree.com/assessment** for a free reproducible version of this figure.*

Demonstrating Forgiveness and Empathy

Despite our students' best efforts at working their way through the creative process, there may come a time when they need to exercise their very best skills at forgiveness and empathy. These skills come into play when students reflect after creative work and recognize criteria they have not met, goals they have not reached, and visions they have not realized. It is important to remember that creativity promotes deep investment by learners and, as a result, when efforts fall short, the disappointment students feel can be more profound than in other circumstances when they may have less of an emotional stake in the outcome. Students may feel tempted to give up and retreat from creativity because it makes them feel too vulnerable. They may want to overgeneralize their lack of capacity. Reeves (2015) goes even further by stating, "Creativity fails to offer the immediate positive feedback, to which generations of students have become accustomed. Few students persist in the face of failure—the inevitable result of creative efforts" (p. 1). It is our job, as their teachers, to make sure that none of these outcomes occur.

This stage of the creative process rests in building an understanding of both failure and success as not only tolerable but critical for future creativity. Miller (2015) explains, "If failure is the end of the road in some instances, it can be the beginning of an innovative journey in others" (p. 1). It is equally important to help students learn to accept not only their difficulties but also their strengths. Both sides of the coin are parts of creative work. By designating a time and place for extended reflection within the creative process, we can teach students how to examine the choices they make and the strategies they employ and plan to adjust them as needed. We can help them identify decisions that led to small successes and decisions that led away from this. By finding time to reflect, we can have students identify questions they still have and unresolved actions. This is part of the purpose of reflection at this point in the creative process.

It is important to share with students the journeys of experienced creative people. Telling the stories of creativity that accompany some of the most creative products, performances, and services in our world helps students see how failure is embedded within creative success. For example, inviting a published author to share the iterations of a final product or a scientist to share experiments that led to inconclusive results can help students see the importance of failure. Hearing stories of tenacity and unrelenting vision illustrates the power of revisiting work. The development of this kind of growth mindset means students will continue to take risks and persevere in the face of challenge (Dweck, 2006). By learning others' stories, our students can develop a greater empathy for the shared struggles of creative individuals and learn to forgive their own missteps as part of this empathy. Miller (2015) explains, "Educators need to create sacred spaces for students to continually reflect on what's working, what isn't, and why. Reflection focused on analyzing failure can help students to reframe it as a positive and meaningful experience" (p. 22). Employing processes that invite students to do this kind of failure analysis will build confidence in the midst of challenge.

Figure 6.7 offers a list of questions to support students developing forgiveness and empathy.

Questions to support students developing forgiveness and empathy:
- What parts of my work make me feel best or proudest?
- What parts of my work disappoint me? Why?
- How do other people create? What does creativity look and sound like for other people?

Figure 6.7: Select and reflect—Questions to support students developing forgiveness and empathy.

continued ⇒

- How often do others experience challenge?
- How do I overcome challenges?
- What do I do when I feel proud? How do I celebrate?
- What do I do when I feel frustrated? Does my response help me?
- What do I say to myself when things are working?
- What do I say to myself when things aren't working?
- How do I keep going when I want to quit? What strategies do I use to keep going?
- How do I respond when I see others struggling?
- How is my creativity like the creativity of other people?
- What do I need to do to get excited about something?
- How do mistakes teach us something?
- What makes a mistake a good mistake?

*Visit **go.SolutionTree.com/assessment** for a free reproducible version of this figure.*

Choosing Reflection Methods

Through personal action research I have undertaken throughout my career, I have identified four critical methods for facilitating strong, meaningful reflection that teachers can implement.

1. **Prompts:** Ensure that we (as teachers) provide strong prompts—questions that guide thinking. The questions students will explore at this stage of creativity should invite thinking about the creative work in its entirety, including processes used, decisions made, and the impact on the final product, performance, or service.

2. **Time:** Make the time to engage in reflection and response. At this stage of creativity, students will need additional time to explore creative portfolios, to consider all decisions they made, and to connect explicitly to goals for future work.

3. **Portfolios:** Use portfolios or collections of artifacts to facilitate deep introspection that spans the entire creative project. Reflection at this stage is longitudinal.

4. **Safety:** Find methods or tools for reflecting that support intellectual and emotional safety. At this stage, students may experience additional vulnerability because time may have run out. Students may not experience closure for every creative effort. Helping students begin to think about next time can reduce these feelings.

Prompts

In my experience, the prompts we choose to frame reflection time will largely determine the depth of response. We may find that the responses are limited in their depth and perception when we ask questions like, "Did you like your project?" or "What part of this activity was your favorite?" (*No, I hated it. The last part was my favorite.*) However, we may find that the responses are more thoughtful when we ask questions that encourage higher levels of thinking—questions like, Compare this product to one you have done previously. Which one met your expectations to the greatest degree? Why do you think this happened? The prompts included in the select and reflect reproducibles throughout this book elicit strong reflection when aligned with the work students have been doing.

Time

My action research in this area also revealed that even when students were to reflect in writing, allowing them to verbalize their thoughts ahead of time increased the depth of their written responses. Combining oral reflection with written reflection can help our learners develop both their thoughts and their ability to reflect in general. This means teachers and students must give the reflective process enough time to ensure that it yields strong goal setting, question generation, and overall response. Building in this time is critical, and it need not come at a cost to other kinds of learning. Reflection can often meet the process standards several courses require (speaking and listening, writing, hypothesizing, problem solving, analyzing, practicing), and it also enhances content and skill standards in the long run by encouraging learners to revisit, revise, and relearn.

Portfolios

Collecting artifacts that represent the creative process from start to finish is vital for ensuring that reflections are grounded in the actual experiences of our students. Portfolios containing items such as planning guides, brainstorming sheets, lists of questions, practice efforts, and drafts help students recall the decisions they have made and weigh them against the outcomes they desire. Portfolios are an essential element of purposeful reflection and planned response.

Safety

Lastly, safety is critical for honest reflection. If students are concerned about being judged or evaluated, they will be far less willing to be vulnerable. This is not a time for summative assessment. We can save that for later once students have completed their reflections. If learners fear repercussions from teachers, family, or peers, they may inflate their assessment of themselves and reduce their ability to be truly reflective about both successes and failures. We need to create conditions for sharing reflections that protect students and help others understand the purpose reflection serves in the creative process. Getting families on board with students' work in unlocking their creativity supports their feelings of safety and improves the success of the shift toward creative initiatives in the classroom. When we decide to unlock creativity, we need to make sure we share our vision of student-directed goal setting and learning and the development of creativity with families. Explaining the benefits and the processes helps families see not only why creativity itself is important but also how it facilitates the development of key ways of navigating learning that equip students with skills and dispositions essential for long-term success. When family members understand the significance of creative work, students will feel the safety of a supportive environment.

Another strategy to support students' comfort levels is to have students share with peers who make them feel safe; there is value in allowing students to assess one another's work (Wiliam, 2018). Collaborative reflection can be a very powerful way to invite meaningful introspection. Other options include offering clear criteria for being a listener when students share reflections orally, or assuring students that reflections are personal and you will not share them with others. When students have to reflect in ways that challenge them too greatly (for instance, in written or oral form), they will spend far too much time trying to produce the reflection and far too little time actually engaging in metacognition. To avoid this, we can offer multiple ways to engage in reflection, including journals, blogs, video diaries, photo essays, letters, graphic organizers, and annotated notes. When students feel safe to think about their creative processes, their introspection can lead to profound insight and can help us have a window into who our students are as creative people.

Figure 6.8 offers a list of questions to support student reflection.

Questions to support student reflection:
- What advice would I give to someone else attempting this practice, skill, or creative pursuit?
- How might I address my next creative project?
- What did I learn?
- How did I learn?
- How do I feel about this work in relation to others?
- What is my favorite way to reflect?
- Do I prefer to reflect orally or in writing?
- How might I support my ideas with details and examples?
- What kinds of questions make me think most?
- How might I get ready to reflect? What materials do I need?
- Who is someone I enjoy reflecting with?
- What conditions help me to be the most honest I can be about myself?

Figure 6.8: *Select and reflect—Questions to support student reflection.*

Visit go.SolutionTree.com/assessment for a free reproducible version of this figure.

The Role of the Teacher

The role of the teacher during reflection and response is critical. During this time, teachers:

◇ Ensure that students have collected their work in a portfolio and that they have it in front of them at the time of reflection

◇ Provide them with strong prompts and time to examine their efforts

◇ Pair them with peers or mentors who make them feel safe

◇ Reassure students that their reflections are still part of their formative work and that teachers will not judge (grade) their thoughts

◇ Offer them gentle feedback

◇ Confer with them when they need assistance

◇ Witness their successes and coach them through their failures

◇ Introduce them to creative individuals and help them see what creativity looks and sounds like

Our role during this aspect of the creative process leads students into future creative attempts with the assurance that confidence and optimism remain.

Following are some important roles for teachers when unlocking reflection and response that can support a few challenges students experience in this stage.

◇ **Listener, observer, and feedback agent:** When students examine their creative work, they may feel waves of emotion that they find difficult to channel into productive reflection. Without intervention, they might make decisions that are detrimental to their development as creative individuals.

◇ **Facilitator of collaborative processes:** If we aren't careful, students can feel shame, frustration, and even humiliation when they face their peers' work in relation to their own work. Witnessing what others produce can replace our students' feeling of pride in their own work with frustration and the urge to withdraw. It may be tempting to protect our learners by never exposing them to their classmates' work and never asking them to reflect with another person. However, this temptation would reduce the potential learning that occurs during effective collaborative reflection.

◇ **Facilitator of reflective processes:** The structures we provide students during reflection and response determine the strength of this work for our students. Without facilitation, reflection can dissolve into judgment, emotional response, and lack of action. It can become an empty exercise where students disengage or simply seek to offer the reflection and response they think we want.

◇ **Facilitator of creative processes:** Students may be tempted to dive into a new creative venture without pausing for reflection. Alternately, they may abandon creative work because it makes them feel too vulnerable. They may draw conclusions about their own creative worth based on false pretenses.

◇ **Assessor:** Up until this point, summative assessment has not been part of the equation because creative exploration reflects the process of learning as opposed to the verification of learning. However, there is a time, after students reflect, when teachers need to engage in summative assessment.

Table 6.2 suggests specific actions that a teacher can take to overcome the challenges of these roles.

Table 6.2: *The Role of the Teacher and Key Actions in the Reflection and Response Stage*

Role of the Teacher	Key Teacher Actions
Listener, Observer, and Feedback Agent	• Listen carefully to the students as they reflect. Watch their responses to their own and others' work, and assess degrees of confidence and skill both in creative work and in the ability to self-assess and reflect. • Confer with the learners; point out aspects of both their processes and products that possess strength and those that hold challenges. • Help students acknowledge strategies they use and those they miss so their responses, whatever they may be, are fruitful.
Facilitator of Collaborative Processes	• Teach students to respond to each other effectively. Use conversation or prompt frames (such as the one in figure 4.8, page 122) to guide students through the process. • Model this process with your own work, and invite students to observe. • Introduce collaborative reflection by setting criteria as a class. • Begin by asking students to only focus on strengths. • Have the work in front of learners, and insist that they limit commentary to the work and not the person. • Ensure the person responsible for the work does the majority of the talking.

Facilitator of Reflective Processes	• Offer effective processes that support meaningful reflection and response. • Nurture safe conditions. • Provide strong prompts. • Give adequate time to this aspect of creative learning. • Invite students to think about their thinking, and teach them how to do this. • Draw their attention to decisions they made and the goals they set.
Facilitator of Creative Processes	• Help students see the role reflection plays in creativity. • Help students see that the most important factor in whether creative work is successful is their own perceptions based on their own goals. • Model that when creativity is part of your classrooms, self-assessment is the most important assessment. • Provide needed supports.
Assessor	• Allow students to drive goal and criteria setting while ensuring that this process reflects the learning intentions of standards, outcomes, and competencies. • Construct catalysts that position students within required learning. • Engage in feedback that further orients students to the needs of coursework. • Construct minilessons that develop the skills and knowledge of your domains, and orchestrate an alignment of exploration with key resources. • Prepare to assess student products, performances, and services in a summative fashion. • Make a verification of understanding and skill based on your learners' work.

Assessment and Reflection and Response

Reflection and response is a critical part of the learning journey, and the role of assessment in unlocking the journey continues to be of the utmost importance. As in the previous creativity stages, formative assessment (information gathering), feedback (dialogue with others), and self-assessment (dialogue with self) are the assessment approaches that advance strong reflection and response by learners. In particular, this final self-assessment supports the critical actions of illumination and verification of success and challenge. It promotes the internalization of creative mindsets and practices, and it facilitates re-engagement and final refinement when needed. As teachers formatively assess, they can use reflection as a springboard for discussions around forgiveness and empathy and encourage learners to set future goals based on what they have learned about themselves as creative individuals. In addition, once reflection and response has provided some closure for our learners, teachers can then engage in summative assessment when appropriate (when they are ready to verify degrees of learning in relation to specific learning goals).

The reproducible tools at the end of this chapter (pages 194–200) offer practical strategies and processes for inviting the kinds of assessment that support reflection and response. Teachers can invite students to use the reproducible "Reflection and Response Self-Assessment" (page 198) to self-assess and set new goals during this stage of the creative process. Teachers can offer "Comparing Creative Work" (page 199) to learners when they want them to engage in a comparison between two creative artifacts. "My Portfolio" (page 200) can facilitate reflection while students examine their creative portfolio.

Self-Assessment

The reflection and response that occurs when students step back from the immediacy of their creative work and reflect in more holistic ways is self-assessment that moves past in-the-moment decision making to decision making that supports long-term growth. This type of self-assessment leads our students to examine their products as the manifestation of decisions they made along the way. It allows them to connect what they do to the results they achieve. It invites learners to imagine how a current creative effort connects to a future one, moving them from short-term goals to long-term creative approaches.

As students examine artifacts that represent their creative journey, we ask them to consider criteria for success that guided their creative work. We prompt them to think about whether these criteria apply to other work they have done and work they wish to do. For example, we may offer students the choice of whether certain criteria will apply to their next project, either because they need to try again to achieve success in this area or because these criteria transfer across contexts. It's important to note that criteria can crop up in future projects even if students were successful in an earlier attempt. This is how we reinforce learning in the long term. As another example, we could ask them to decide whether a criterion at this stage is the same criterion they established for a previous creative attempt, and if the criterion shifted over the creative process, why this was the case. When students explore criteria in a more longitudinal way, it may help them think about how their decisions about which criteria to emphasize or focus on in their work (for example, attention to patterns; novel use of materials; functional design) contributed to the personal nature of their creative products, performances, or services. As a result of this kind of reflection, self-assessment moves from a determination of success for grading purposes to a determination of success for creative growth, development, and the expression of self.

We, as teachers, want to facilitate our students' exploration of their own creative processes in ways that promote autonomy, resilience, and measured responses. We want to really think about what drives their creative work and maximizes their efforts. It is very easy for any learner to decide the value of creative work based solely on how hard he or she tries. Ross (2006) explains that "student self-assessments are frequently driven by their perception of the effort expended on the assignment, an important criterion but it should not swamp attention to other dimensions of performance" (p. 9). With that in mind, educators want to teach students how to reflect on their own learning based on criteria that extend beyond the effort they expend. Creativity teaches our students that sometimes the greatest efforts still yield uncertain results. Sometimes the questions we ask are too big for the resources we have. Some problems are larger than a single attempt. This is an important understanding to develop in the learners who are going to be responsible for some very big changes in our world. Creativity must move us past easy success and immediate answers; it should push the limits of our current understanding and comfort. This is creativity that changes our world.

Formative Assessment

As in all other components of the creative process, there is a strong place for formative assessment and teacher response at this stage. By watching our students reflect, by listening to them process their thinking, and by examining the reflections they are producing, we can come to understand how comfortable they are with their own creative process and, in particular, how comfortable they are with the reflection stage. We work alongside our students to determine their clarity about criteria and help them consider challenging questions. For example, a teacher may read a student's journal reflection and notice that she did not reflect deeply enough on a key success criterion. The teacher may then re-engage this learner in her reflection by asking her a question related to that specific criterion (for example, "I notice you stated very early on that you were trying to create a product that was structurally stable for an extended period of time. In your reflection, you noted that your product collapsed. Could you reflect a little more on the reasons why this might have occurred and what decisions you might have made to avoid this result?").

Formative assessment processes such as these allow us to collect information that can help us facilitate metacognitive conversations. Educational psychologists Stephen N. Elliott, Thomas R. Kratochwill, and John F. Travers (1996) explain, "By making students aware that they can 'think about their thinking,' you will also help them to improve those cognitive behaviours that result in better classroom performance" (p. 270). As teachers formatively assess during the reflection and response stage, they observe students connecting their creative work to their next steps, assessing their strength in considering how aspects of their current work might apply to future creative goals. When students need support with this reflection work, teachers may confer with them, offering them guidance in transferring strategies and success criteria to personal goals. Finally, we teachers work with our students to reflect on portfolios that represent their growth. We use these artifacts as documentation of decision making and as a spring-board for discussions about thinking and learning.

Summative Assessment

One question we may still wrestle with, after all is said and done, is *What do I actually put in my gradebook?* This is a fair question in regard to the reality of our current education system and the need to communicate with families about student learning. So, let us answer this question in a practical sense.

First, when we assign student work a grade, it is the result of a professional judgment. In order to make this judgment with accuracy, we need to draw information from multiple sources and apply it to our evaluation. Given that we have spent time throughout creative learning observing students, conferring with them, teaching them, guiding them, and reflecting with them, we are in position to have real clarity about student strengths. In other words, we really know our learners. This is no small by-product of unlocking creativity and we should acknowledge and celebrate it. More than with many other ways of approaching learning, we will have had the chance to see inside our students' minds and watch learning as it develops. When we increase our levels of observation, conversation, and documentation, we are able to see the criteria we will use to measure and verify learning very clearly.

Second, we have not left students to their own devices. We step in when students struggle. When students need support, we are there. This is critical in a discussion about summative assessment because we can feel increasingly secure that when we make a summative decision about learning in relation to learning goals, we will see students' amazing results. Not only will we see evidence of proficiency on specific, critical learning targets, but we will also see proficiency on a whole host of additional outcomes that enhance overall learning.

Lastly, we can use creative processes, products, performances, and services to address any number of learning goals our states, provinces, and other educational authorities require. As this book explains, creativity is *not* an add-on. It is not something we do in addition to the learning goals. In fact, it is how we get to those goals and how students make choices around applying required knowledge and skills. It is about deepening engagement in the things we already do in our classrooms. When learners engage in creative processes, they develop skills like communicating, collaborating, problem solving, critical thinking, analyzing, assessing, researching, calculating, designing, reading, writing, exploring, experimenting, and the list goes on and on. We can find all these skills in our mandated learning goals in a variety of subject areas. If they do not exist within our own subject areas, they certainly exist within the subject areas others are responsible for. With this in mind, collaborating with our teacher colleagues can open amazing opportunities for cross-curricular learning and assessment. When we assess in order to verify degrees of proficiency (summative assessment), we can very tightly align data we have been collecting, the observations we have been making, and the criteria we see reflected in the work of our students with required learning goals in any number of subject areas. This is why it is important for teachers to deeply understand their learning goals and why they also benefit from collaborative work with their colleagues. Going into creative contexts with this kind of refined understanding of our learning goals equips us to allow learning to emerge from our learners, knowing we can facilitate creative experiences in ways that benefit student learning in mandated areas.

Final Thoughts

Reflection and response can help our students turn short-term creativity into long-term personal creative understanding. Through careful consideration of decisions made and challenges overcome, our students can begin to see that creativity is a muscle that needs exercise like any other. They can begin to recognize their own strengths and strategies. They can also begin to imagine new questions they might have and new problems they may wish to solve. This final stage of the creative process can often serve as a catalyst for the next creative pursuit.

Unlocking Reflection and Response: Observation and Self-Assessment

Teachers can use the following tool to self-assess the strengths and challenges of reflection and response through observation. Teachers can also use this tool for summative purposes if they are assessing the skill of reflection (for example, some learning goals directly require students to reflect on their work). The following table contains the criteria for successful reflection and response, descriptions of how these criteria look when lived out day-to-day, and suggestions for how educators can nurture these criteria within their instructional and assessment plans. The final column offers suggestions for how to respond when criteria are absent or need additional support.

Critical Action	Reflection and Response Targets	What the Teacher Sees	Teacher Facilitation Techniques	Teacher Response
Illuminating	I can explore decisions I made and strategies I used and reflect on their effectiveness.	• Students who can refer to samples and artifacts that show their creative process • Students who can identify when they made decisions and whether those decisions were effective (relate to goals and criteria) • Students who can name a variety of strategies • Students who can identify personal preferences and approaches to creativity that yield success and focus	• Make sure artifacts are front and center. • Make sure goals and criteria are readily available. • Provide a space for students to track successful or preferred approaches to creativity. • Engage students in discussions about approaches and preferences (help students see how others approach creativity). • Provide cause-and-effect templates to guide reflection. • Provide time to stop and think (have students consider, "What decisions did I make today and what happened?"). • Use photographs and video to help students recognize decisions in the moment.	• Draw student attention to a video clip or photograph and facilitate a discussion about what is happening. • Ensure students reference goals and criteria frequently so students are comfortable with them by the time they get to reflection. • Co-construct an effect rating scale. • Interview people whom students would immediately identify as creative (like writers, singers, painters).

page 1 of 4

Critical Action	Reflection and Response Targets	What the Teacher Sees	Teacher Facilitation Techniques	Teacher Response
Verifying Whether Work Meets Established Goals and Criteria	I can explore my work in relation to goals and criteria.	• Students who are aware of their criteria for success • Students who can analyze their own work in relation to goals and criteria	• Ensure criteria are always front and center. • Provide time for self-assessment. • Ensure students reflect on their actual creative work; they connect reflections to examples. • Invite the use of sticky tabs, annotated notes, and tables to guide strong reflection.	• Confer and coach with the student if he or she needs it. • Narrow the focus if the student feels overwhelmed. • Reflect on one criterion at a time. • Provide a template that connects aspects of the work directly to criteria.
	I can identify strengths.	• Students who can confidently point to aspects of their work that show strength • Students who can explain why a strength is a strength	• Explain how strengths are connected to goals and criteria. • Explore how strength ties to audience. • Model strength finding.	• Explore how identifying strengths is different from bragging. • Explore how strengths are specific and not general statements. • Confer with the student when he or she needs it.
	I can identify challenges and unresolved aspects of my work.	• Students who can confidently point to aspects of their work that show challenge • Students who can explain why a challenge is a challenge • Students who can share ideas about moments they stopped looking for solutions to a creative problem and were left with unresolved aspects	• Explain how challenges connect to goals and criteria. • Explore how challenges tie to audience. • Model how to use criteria to identify unresolved aspects of creative work. • Explain what *unresolved* means and why it is a natural part of creativity. • Work with students to make sure they are aware of problems they may have been working to resolve. • Explore times when students felt dissatisfied and connect this to a lack of resolution.	• Confer with the student when he or she needs it. • Help students connect their feelings of unhappiness or frustration to challenges. • Ensure students understand that a lack of resolution and challenges lead into new creativity. • Help students set new goals based on unresolved elements.

page 2 of 4

Critical Action	Reflection and Response Targets	What the Teacher Sees	Teacher Facilitation Techniques	Teacher Response
Internalizing Creative Mindsets and Practices	I can identify newly acquired skills and knowledge.	• Students who can identify skills they have developed and knowledge they have gained • Students who can relate these skills and knowledge to their actual creative work	• Encourage students to work together to list all the skills and knowledge they needed to engage in their work. • Define skill and knowledge and explain their role in creativity. • Relate skills and knowledge development to learning goals (standards, outcomes). • Encourage students to keep a running record of developing skills and knowledge over time. • Use a portfolio or collection to illustrate new skills and knowledge.	• As a class, brainstorm skills and knowledge students could gain and then have them select those they acquire. • Provide a ready-made list from which to choose. • Use video and photos as well as artifacts to illustrate skill and knowledge. • Use a celebration board to document the development of skills and knowledge.
Re-Engaging and Refining	I can identify and plan a response to re-engage and refine.	• Students who can choose a course of action (return to old work, start new work) • Students who can identify steps they plan on taking	• Provide a checklist of possible responses from which students can choose. • Work to identify possible responses. • Determine areas that need refining. • Pair students up for next-step discussions. • Provide a planning template.	• Work through plans step-by-step. • Reduce the number of actions to the first next step. • Help students "let go" of dissatisfaction and abandon projects when necessary (sometimes starting fresh is the best course of action).

page 3 of 4

Critical Action	Reflection and Response Targets	What the Teacher Sees	Teacher Facilitation Techniques	Teacher Response
Demonstrating Forgiveness and Empathy	I can forgive myself for my mistakes. I can empathize with others when they experience success or challenge.	• Students who demonstrate positive self-talk • Students who can show evidence of compassion (comforting others) • Students who celebrate their own achievements • Students who celebrate the achievements of others	• Openly discuss how the messages we tell ourselves affect our success. • Model positive self-talk (aloud). • Openly discuss growth mindset and communicate that, in most cases, failure is not permanent. • Celebrate growth and achievement in all aspects and stages of the creative process. • Celebrate process as much as product, performance, or service (find strength in many places).	• Openly address negative self-talk and provide suggestions for how to adjust to positive self-talk. • Address students who are struggling to be empathetic. Teach empathy, model it, reinforce it. • Keep discussions future focused. • Model optimism. • Connect with creative people and have them share how they manage forgiveness.
Choosing Reflection Methods	I can choose a method for reflecting that helps me reflect well.	• Students who can show evidence of reflection • Students who can name various ways to reflect • Students who are aware of prompts and use them to guide their reflection • Students who show comfort in reflecting and refer to their actual work • Students who can reflect with others	• Ensure students have many options. • Have students decide how to reflect, and then monitor those decisions based on effectiveness. • Have students try reflecting in a variety of ways and discuss the results. • Provide students with strong prompts. • Build a safe environment, where honesty holds more value than success. • Teach students how to reflect with others.	• Limit the number of choices when a student feels overwhelmed. • Work with students to choose methods that match current skills. • Guide the process step-by-step until students build independence. • Limit the number of prompts. • Form collaborative reflection groups based on comfort.

page 4 of 4

Reflection and Response Self-Assessment

Students can use this tool to reflect on their creative products, performances, and services. It invites them to consider strengths and challenges of their work relative to their success criteria. It also helps them consider unresolved aspects of their work or questions they may still have. Lastly, it encourages students to think about future goals.

My goal was:			
	Possibilities for the Future		
	Questions I Still Have		
	Challenges (With Evidence)		
	Strengths (With Evidence)		
	Criteria for Success		

Comparing Creative Work

Students may find this tool useful when exploring their portfolios. Using this tool, learners compare two artifacts (they could be different versions of the same work or two completely separate creative samples) side-by-side and consider what the samples tell them about creative choices they are making, creative goals they may be exploring, and questions they may still have about their own creative processes.

Sample description:	Sample description:
My goals for this sample are:	**My goals for this sample are:**
What I learned:	**What I learned:**

When I look at both samples, I can see:
I still wonder:
This makes me think I might:

My Portfolio

In my portfolio, I identify the following criteria, and I can explain why the samples I chose fit these criteria.

- ◇ Something that makes me proud
- ◇ Something that meets my goals
- ◇ Something that still frustrates me
- ◇ Two samples that show I got better at something
- ◇ A sample showing how I revise my work
- ◇ A sample that shows inspiration or innovation
- ◇ A sample that leads to new ideas and questions
- ◇ A sample that I would like to take and make into something new
- ◇ A sample that I would give to someone else because I think he or she would like or need it
- ◇ A sample that I will never give away or throw out because it really means something to me
- ◇ A sample that reflects my own voice and my own thoughts
- ◇ A sample that shows who I am and what I believe
- ◇ Something I need help with
- ◇ A sample I think some people may not understand
- ◇ A sample that shows an answer to a specific question

APPENDIX A

Table A.1 explores qualities of creative people and provides explanations that can help both teachers and students develop these qualities within themselves. Teachers can use this table to generate a class discussion around a question (such as, What are the qualities of creative people, and why is this so?), to reinforce student understanding of creative qualities (for example, I can see you are showing real *persistence* today even though you are frustrated), and to incorporate such qualities into lesson plans (for example, Today, we are going to practice being curious).

Table A.1: *Qualities of Creative People*

Curious	The interest in questioning the conventional, seeking information, questioning reasoning, and exploring both the known and unknown
Integrative Thinker	The ability to perceive connections, rhythms, patterns, and relationships between a variety of ideas across content and domain
Persistent	The tendency to be driven by a strong purpose or passion; a willingness to return to ideas and expand, develop, and embellish
Collaborative	The willingness and ability to work with others, forming ideas, solutions, and opinions in an interdependent manner
Imaginative	The ability to conjure vivid imagery, create fiction, daydream, and visualize; the ability to stretch and reach beyond what is obvious
Critical Thinker	The ability to examine the evidence and information available and form opinions, ask questions, analyze, and synthesize
Risk Taker	A willingness to test and experiment; to move past comfort into the unfamiliar; to try something new despite the possibility of failure

continued ⇒

Tolerant	The ability to function in the presence of ambiguity and disorder; the ability to remain stable amid uncertainty or unfamiliarity
Flexible	A willingness to use different approaches to solve problems; a willingness to change direction, adapt, and shift
Fluent	The ability to generate a flow of ideas, possibilities, consequences, and objects; to explore further than the information given
Divergent Thinker	A willingness to experiment and break away from conventional thinking; to think in unique ways, and use nontraditional approaches
Convergent Thinker	The ability to structure and organize diverse ideas; to make decisions and evaluations; to formulate a solution
Courageous	The willingness to break barriers, be vulnerable, and continue to act and think, even in difficult or challenging circumstances
Reflective	The ability to learn from past experiences and apply that to new contexts; to ask important questions and consider alternatives
Intuitive	The ability to exhibit a depth of feeling, heightened sensibilities; hunches; observation and discrimination; reliance on senses
Observant	The ability to see the world in many ways; to notice surroundings and emotions; to describe experiences

Source: Adapted from Dacey & Conklin, 2004; Renzulli, 2000; Sawyer, 2006; Wagner, 2012.

APPENDIX B

Figures B.1 (pages 204–208) and B.2 (pages 208–212) are intended to provide clarity about the creative process and assessment approaches that support it by offering examples of how to integrate creative processes into learning experiences within a classroom setting. Each example is based on a specific learning goal (standard or outcome). The first section describes a traditional instructional approach to this particular learning goal. While this approach is not incorrect, it does not provide students with creative opportunities. The second section provides examples for integrating creative approaches into learning in smaller ways. These take far less time, but they open up opportunities to practice creative skills. The left column explores an ideal creative approach that is more complex and invites students to work for extended time in each of the four stages. The right column describes how the three key assessment processes (formative assessment, feedback, and self-assessment) connect to each stage of the broad creative approach example and offers teachers direction for facilitating assessment within the contexts provided.

Learning Goal: Standard 7.G.B.6—Solve real-world and mathematical problems involving area, volume, and surface area of two- and three-dimensional objects composed of triangles, quadrilaterals, polygons, cubes, and right prisms.

Traditional Approach

The teacher introduces the topic by writing "solving geometry problems" on the board and asking students to write the same heading in their notebooks.

The teacher teaches each topic in sequence.

- Linear measurement (review)
- Perimeter (review)
- Units and conversions (review)
- Geometric shapes (review)
- Area formulae
- Surface-area formulae
- Volume formulae

For each topic, the teacher provides an explanation using direct instruction, shows examples to students, gives students a problem or question to solve in pairs, and then has students independently practice problems from their textbook. The teacher gives homework to reinforce learning and scores the homework at the beginning of the subsequent class.

The class completes a review of the topics and the teacher provides an outline for the exam.

Students take the exam.

Smaller Creative Approaches

The teacher invites students to create sketch notes explaining what they already know about geometry, problem solving, or both.

The teacher has students photograph real-life examples of geometric shapes, examples showing when solving these kinds of mathematics problems is important, or both.

The teacher shows students a variety of images and asks them to create a list of mathematics geometry terms they feel the images represent.

The teacher shows students solutions to problems and has them generate ideas about what the problem itself might be.

Students work in pairs to create problems relating to area, volume, and surface area.

Students take regular geometric shapes and combine them into irregular shapes, and then propose a context when those shapes may exist in the real world.

Students create their own formulae for making various calculations.

Students design an anchor chart to help them think about solving complex geometric problems.

Students create a defense for a particular answer within a set of possible answers.

Students turn a problem and solution into an image that reflects the context of the problem.

Students create incorrect approaches to problems and challenge other students to identify the errors and misconceptions.

Students write an advice column for students who need to solve specific problems.

Students share their work in flexible ways.

Students debate solutions with each other.

Students trade self-generated problems and discuss approaches.

Students trade problems with another class.

Students reflect in a mathematics journal about personal approaches to mathematics problems.

Students track their knowledge of targets over time in a self-created graphic.

Students write advice to future mathematics students, explaining tips, tricks, or information they find helpful.

Broad Creative Approach	Assessment
Exploration	**Formative Assessment**

Catalyst:
 	
Share a letter from a regional curling organization that grants hosting duty of the regional curling playoffs to its community. A local rink will be the location of this tournament, and the letter outlines the competition area needs and equipment requirements for converting the rink to multiple sheets of ice so several teams of students can compete at the same time. The students are invited to create a proposal of how this conversion and preparation of the ice surface might occur, the human resource needs, the possible cost of preparation, and the specific design of the competition area, complete with measurements.
 	
Students form groups of three and brainstorm specific measurements they will need to make and things they will need to know about the local facility in order to successfully meet the requirements the letter outlines.
 	
As a class, generate a cumulative list of prior knowledge: What do we know about measurement? What do we know about solving problems? What do we know about curling?
 	
Students then work together to list all the questions they still need to answer in order to ensure a successful event.
 	
The class establishes criteria for a successful response to the letter. The teacher posts these criteria, making them accessible for all groups.
 	
Groups collect their work in a portfolio. They understand that all sketches, calculations, measurements, and research must stay in the portfolio.
	• Engage in formal observation, keeping in mind the following questions for successful exploration:
	  • Which groups are struggling to get started?
	  • Which groups would benefit from extra challenge?
	  • What questions and needs do some groups still need to identify?
	• Utilize success criteria (related to the learning goal and related to the creative process), such as the following:
	  • Engagement and comfort with the proposed task
	  • Ability to work effectively in groups
	  • Absence or presence of background knowledge, including understanding about the game of curling
	• Engage in conversation to gather information.
	
	Feedback
	• Confer with students.
	• Invite peer dialogue and feedback when appropriate.
	
	Self-Assessment
	• Engage students in criteria setting by asking them questions such as the following:
	  • What are the qualities of a strong proposal?
	  • How will you know when you have prepared a proposal that offers enough detailed information?
	  • What are the qualities of effective collaboration?
	  • What kinds of artifacts do you need to collect in your portfolios?
	  • How do you know when you are ready to begin your research and investigation?
	  • Do you understand the criteria?

Figure B.1: *Unlocking creativity—Grade 7 geometry example.*

continued ⇒

Elaboration	Formative Assessment

Elaboration

Students generate a list of to-do items in their groups of three, with help from the teacher, such as these:

1. Determine the area of the rink surface and calculate the number of ice sheets, based on dimension requirements.
2. Determine placement of rings, hog line, and sponsor decals on ice sheets.
3. Calculate the volume of water necessary to flood the ice surface (and potential cost).
4. Determine placement and design of scoreboards.
5. Design a round-robin play schedule, and so on.

Members decide who will be responsible for which aspects of the calculations and planning, and each person sets short-term goals.

Teams then begin to search for necessary information, make calculations, and design a model of the facility with dimensions and calculations.

The teacher offers short instructional lessons for the whole class or small groups as needed.

The class pauses frequently to share its work, offer feedback, and adjust goals and actions as needed.

Formative Assessment

- Engage in formal observations and conversations. Look for some of the following criteria for successful elaboration:
  - Ideas students generate indicate understanding of the catalyst.
  - Students have an adequate understanding of the game of curling.
  - Students have an adequate understanding of geometry as related to the project.
  - Groups are able to organize themselves.

Feedback

- Consider the following questions as you work to guide feedback conversations:
  - Which groups are struggling?
  - Which groups need additional instruction?
  - When does it make sense to stop and reflect?
  - How might I guide research?

Self-Assessment

- Engage students in goal setting. Look for the following as indicators of progress:
  - Students break the proposal into manageable chunks and students set goals to direct their work.
  - Students are clear about where they will need to make decisions.
- Engage students in criteria refinement by asking:
  - Are there aspects of this proposal that you didn't consider earlier?
  - Are your criteria specific enough? Are they too limiting?
  - Are the criteria guiding your investigating and creation?
- Engage students in planning next steps by asking questions such as the following:
  - Are you working according to timelines?
  - Is your process working for you?
  - Have you done the necessary research?
  - Are you coming up with ideas? Do you need supports?

Expression	Formative Assessment
Groups post their models and engage in a carousel activity to check for consistency in calculations. The class debates differences and groups return to adjust as needed. Each group then shares its finalized proposal with a panel, explaining what it created to plan for this event.	• Engage in formal observations and conversations to gather information. Look for the following criteria for successful expression: • Adequate preparation • Comfort with sharing • Awareness of revision needs and successes **Feedback** • Consider the following questions as you work to guide feedback conversations: • Which groups need additional practice or revision? • How might I help them prepare for sharing? • What needs do the chosen audience(s) have? • What needs do the presenting groups have? **Self-Assessment** • Engage students in goal and criteria refinement while preparing for expression. Ask the following questions to guide the process: • Did you address your original goals? • Is your proposal complete? • Did you explain yourselves enough? • Did you meet the criteria? • Do you need to set another goal? • Are you ready to share? If not, what do you need to do to prepare? • Engage students in reflection immediately following expression. Ask the following questions to guide the process: • How did your audience respond? • Did you address all your criteria? • Did you meet your goals?
Reflection and Response	**Formative Assessment**
In their groups, students reflect on their successes and challenges within the task. They look for areas of innovation and areas where they needed supports. They identify unresolved understanding. Students then complete a journal reflection on their own creative processes during this project. They consider how they approached their goals and whether they met the criteria. They make decisions about the next challenge they may face.	• Engage in formal observations and conversations to gather information. Look for the following criteria for successful reflection and response: • Successful collaborative reflection • Identification of successes, challenges, and unresolved elements • Successful individual reflection • Engagement and ease with prompts

continued ⇒

	Feedback
	• Consider the following questions as you work to guide feedback conversations:
	• Do groups or individuals need help with reflection or understanding the prompt?
	• Are there additional questions I might ask to activate deep reflection?
	Self-Assessment
	• Prepare students for reflection. Ask the following questions to guide the process:
	• Can your group accurately identify successes and challenges?
	• How might you make your reflections thorough and contain supporting evidence?
	• How might your portfolio help you with your reflections?
	• Are you able to look at your portfolio and notice patterns, successes, and challenges?
	• Do you remember the decisions you made? Do you recognize their degree of effectiveness?
	• Which approaches and strategies will serve you in your next creative effort?
	• How well did you work with others? Why?

Source for standard: National Governors Association Center for Best Practices & Council of Chief State School Officers (NGA & CCSSO), 2010b.

Figure B.2 provides a second example of how a teacher might integrate creative processes into learning, this time for a specific English language arts learning goal.

Learning Goal: Standard W.4.1—Write opinion pieces on topics or texts, supporting a point of view with reasons and information.

Traditional Approach

The teacher gives students a prompt that requires an opinion.

The teacher gives students a graphic organizer to work through organizing an argument.

The teacher works with students who seem to be really struggling.

Students then turn their graphic organizer into a short essay.

Students trade papers to correct errors.

The teacher edits those papers that need much work.

Students complete a "good copy."

Students hand in their writing.

Smaller Creative Approaches
Students generate their own opinion topics after engaging in a variety of texts.
Students view emotionally impactful photographs and generate opinions based on them.
Students collect and display examples of effective introductions.
Students create oral arguments on a variety of topics and give two-minute persuasive talks.
Students explore advertisements and develop opinions about how persuasive they are.
Students create methods for organizing thoughts when planning persuasive writing.
Students add visual images to their persuasive writing.
Students choose music that suits the mood of their opinion writing.
Students create opinion writing as a group in order to develop confidence.
Students experiment with creating feedback in unique ways.
Students design a method for sharing their opinion writing.
Students write two opinion pieces and compare them based on criteria.

Broad Creative Approach	Assessment
Exploration	**Formative Assessment**

Catalyst:
 	
Teachers give students envelopes filled with provocative statements (for example, All students in fourth grade should have to work outdoors for two hours each day; All students in fourth grade should focus on learning how to deal with money instead of having physical education; All students in fourth grade should have no sugar in their diet).
 	
Students then order the statements from those that they feel strongest about to those they feel least strongly about.
 	
Teachers invite students to choose one statement and form an opinion about it, so they can write a letter that will be published in a class newsletter.
	◆ Engage in formal observations and conversations to gather information. Look for the following criteria for successful exploration:
	  • Engagement in the catalyst
	  • Ability to form an opinion about the rating of the topics
	  • Ability to form an opinion about a topic
	
	Feedback
	◆ Consider the following questions as you work to guide feedback conversations:
	  • Is there a student who is having trouble making a decision?
	  • Is there a student who needs affirmation?
	
	Self-Assessment
	◆ Engage students in goal and criteria setting. Ask the following questions to guide the process:
	  • Which topics lead to a well-formed opinion?
	  • How do you know when you have an opinion? What does it mean to have an opinion?
	  • How might you support your opinion?
	  • Do you feel strongly about one of these topics?
	  • Do arguments and support immediately come to mind?
	  • Do you already know where you might look for ideas to support your opinion?

Figure B.2: *Unlocking creativity—Grade 4 writing example.*

continued ⇒

Elaboration	Formative Assessment
Teachers share a variety of samples of opinion writing and, in pairs, students create a list of tips and tricks for people who want to be convincing (criteria setting).	• Engage in formal observations and conversations to gather information. Look for the following criteria for successful elaboration:

The teacher guides the pairs through the elements of opinion writing, and students debate the best and worst ways to convince other people of their belief.	• Comprehension of the texts
	   • Ability to identify persuasive elements
	   • Engagement with a partner and creation of a list

Students then take what they learn and begin to map out their argument. The teacher asks the students to pause and discuss possible methods for organizing persuasive thinking.	• Ability to defend a point of view
	   • Organization of ideas
	   • Idea generation

Students stop periodically and share their work in small pieces (for example, reading just the introduction). They offer feedback. The teacher may introduce new mentor texts if students need inspiration.	• Ability to give and receive feedback
	
	Feedback
	• Consider the following questions as you work to guide feedback conversations:
	   • How are the students progressing in forming an opinion and in their planning?
	   • Do students need support with idea generation, research, organization, and mechanics?
	
	Self-Assessment
	• Engage students in refining goals and success criteria. Ask the following questions to guide the process:
	   • Are you clear about what you are trying to do?
	   • What are some goals you need to set to be able to complete this task?
	   • What do you need to consider?
	   • What are the elements of strong opinion writing?
	   • How might you convince others of your point of view?
	   • How do you organize your opinion so it makes sense?
	   • How do you make sure you have the right information?
	• Engage students in planning next steps. Ask the following questions to guide the process:
	   • Do you have an opinion and supporting arguments?
	   • Are you organizing your writing in a way that makes sense?
	   • Are you using language that is convincing?

Expression	Formative Assessment

Students engage in final revisions, following structured conferring either with the teacher or in peer groups.
 	
The class compiles the opinion writing into a class newsletter.
 	
The students share their writing and discuss pieces that present opposite opinions.
	• Engage in formal observations and conversations to gather information. Look for these criteria for successful expression:
	  • Ability to confer effectively
	  • Ability to apply feedback
	  • Clarity about opinion and the way to communicate it through writing
	  • Time management
	
	Feedback
	• Consider the following questions as you work to guide feedback conversations:
	  • Is there a student who needs assistance with organization, revision, and editing?
	  • Are students working effectively with each other, or do I need to coach?
	  • Did I teach students how to refine their work on their own and with others?
	
	Self-Assessment
	• Engage students in goal and criteria refinement while preparing for expression. Ask the following questions to guide the process:
	  • Is your message strong?
	  • Did you organize your thoughts clearly?
	  • Are your language choices clear and appropriate?
	  • How do you think your audience may respond?
	  • Are you ready to share? What do you still need to do?
	• Engage students in reflection immediately following expression. Ask the following questions to guide the process:
	  • Did you do what you set out to do?
	  • How well did you attend to the criteria?

continued ⇒

Reflection and Response	**Formative Assessment**
Students engage in collaborative reflection in circles of four students. The teacher issues one prompt at a time and each student offers thoughts on the prompt. The second time around the circle, students offer thoughts about each other's reflections. Students then return to their writing portfolios and engage in individual reflection about their opinion writing and their creative writing process. They then set a goal for next time, focusing on repeating effective strategies and adopting a new one as well.	◆ Engage in formal observations and conversations to gather information. Look for the following criteria for successful reflection and response: • Success of collaborative and independent reflection • Identification of successes, challenges, and unresolved elements • Engagement and ease with prompts **Feedback** ◆ Consider the following questions as you work to guide feedback conversations: • Are there groups or individuals who need help with reflection or understanding the prompt? • Are there students who need affirmation? **Self-Assessment** ◆ Prepare students for reflection. Ask the following questions to guide the process: • Did you identify your successes and challenges? • Have you supported your reflections with evidence? • Look at your portfolio and the final writing. Do you notice any patterns, successes, and challenges? • Do you remember the decisions you made? Do you recognize their degree of effectiveness? • Which approaches and strategies will serve you in your next creative effort? • How well did you work with others? Why? What might you do the same and differently next time?

Source for standard: NGA & CCSSO, 2010a.

REFERENCES AND RESOURCES

Amabile, T. (1996). *Creativity in context: Update to the social psychology of creativity* (2nd ed.). Boulder, CO: Westview Press.

Anderson, T. D. (2014). Making the 4Ps as important as the 4Rs. *Knowledge Quest*, *42*(5), 42–47.

Andrade, H. L., Du, Y., & Mycek, K. (2010). Rubric-referenced self-assessment and middle school students' writing. *Assessment in Education: Principles, Policy and Practice*, *17*(2), 199–214.

Batchelor, K. E., & Bintz, W. P. (2013). Promoting creativity in the middle grades language arts classroom. *Middle School Journal*, *45*(1), 3–11.

Bateson, M. C. (1994). *Peripheral visions: Learning along the way*. New York: HarperCollins.

Black, P., & Wiliam, D. (1998). Inside the black box: Raising standards through classroom assessment. *Phi Delta Kappan*, *80*(2), 139–144, 146–148.

Boud, D. (2003). *Enhancing learning through self assessment*. London: RoutledgeFalmer.

Csikszentmihalyi, M. (1990). *Flow: The psychology of optimal experience*. New York: HarperCollins.

Csikszentmihalyi, M. (1997). Happiness and creativity: Going with the flow. *The Futurist*, *31*(5), 8–12.

Csikszentmihalyi, M., Abuhamdeh, S., & Nakamura, J. (2005). Flow. In A. J. Elliott & C. S. Dweck, *Handbook of competence and motivation* (pp. 598–608). New York: Guilford Press.

Culberhouse, D. (2014, May 24). *The creative leader series: Part 5* [Blog post]. Accessed at https://dculberh.wordpress.com/2014/05/24/the-creative-leader-part-5 on January 9, 2018.

Dacey, J., & Conklin, W. (2004). *Creativity and the standards*. Huntington Beach, CA: Shell Education.

Davies, A. (2011). *Making classroom assessment* work (3rd ed.). Bloomington, IN: Solution Tree Press.

Drapeau, P. (2014). *Sparking student creativity: Practical ways to promote innovative thinking and problem-solving*. Alexandria, VA: Association for Supervision and Curriculum Development.

Dueck, M. (2014). *Grading smarter, not harder: Assessment strategies that motivate kids and help them learn*. Alexandria, VA: Association for Supervision and Curriculum Development.

Dweck, C. S. (2006). *Mindset: The new psychology of success*. New York: Random House.

Elliott, S. N., Kratochwill, T. R., & Travers, J. F. (1996). *Educational psychology: Effective teaching, effective learning*. Madison, WI: Brown & Benchmark.

Erkens, C., Schimmer, T., & Vagle, N. D. (2017). *Essential assessment: Six tenets for bringing hope, efficacy, and achievement to the classroom*. Bloomington, IN: Solution Tree Press.

Frost, J. (1997). *Creativity in primary science*. Philadelphia: Open University Press.

Greene, M. (1995). *Releasing the imagination: Essays on education, the arts, and social change*. San Francisco: Jossey-Bass.

Gregory, K., Cameron, C., & Davies, A. (2011). *Self-assessment and goal setting* (2nd ed.). Bloomington, IN: Solution Tree Press.

Gresham, P. (2014). Fostering creativity through digital storytelling: "It's a paradise inside a cage." *Metaphor*, (*1*), 47–56.

Gura, M. (2016). *Make, learn, succeed: Building a culture of creativity in your school*. Washington, DC: International Society for Technology in Education.

Hall, P., & Simeral, A. (2015). *Teach, reflect, learn: Building your capacity for success in the classroom*. Alexandria, VA: Association for Supervision and Curriculum Development.

Hattie, J. A. C. (2009). *Visible learning: A synthesis of over 800 meta-analyses relating to achievement*. London: Routledge.

Hattie, J. A. C. (2012). *Visible learning for teachers: Maximizing impact on learning*. London: Routledge.

Hattie, J. A. C. (2015). *What works best in education: The politics of collaborative expertise*. London: Pearson.

Hattie, J. A. C., & Donoghue, G. M. (2016). Learning strategies: A synthesis and conceptual model. *Science of Learning, 1*. Accessed at www.nature.com/articles /npjscilearn201613 on June 21, 2018.

Hattie, J. A. C., & Timperley, H. (2007). The power of feedback. *Review of Educational Research, 77*(1), 81–112.

Hume, K. (2008). *Start where they are: Differentiating for success with the young adolescent*. Toronto: Pearson Education Canada.

Johnson, D. (2015). *Teaching outside the lines: Developing creativity in every learner*. Thousand Oaks, CA: Corwin Press.

Kelly, R. (Ed.). (2012). *Educating for creativity: A global conversation*. Calgary, Canada: Brush Education.

Kirschner, P. A., Sweller, J., & Clark, R. E. (2006). Why minimal guidance during instruction does not work: An analysis of the failure of constructivist, discovery, problem-based, experiential, and inquiry-based teaching. *Educational Psychologist, 41*(2), 75–86.

Kochhar-Bryant, C. A. (2010). *Effective collaboration for educating the whole child*. Thousand Oaks, CA: Corwin Press.

Levenson, E. (2011). Exploring collective mathematical creativity in elementary school. *Journal of Creative Behavior, 45*(3), 215–234.

Marshall, J. (2010). Thinking outside and on the box: Creativity and inquiry in art practice. *Art Education, 63*(2), 16–23.

Marzano, R. J. (2007). *The art and science of teaching: A comprehensive framework for effective instruction*. Alexandria, VA: Association for Supervision and Curriculum Development.

Maslow, A. H. (1954). *Motivation and personality*. New York: Harper & Row.

Maslyk, J. (2016). *STEAM makers: Fostering creativity and innovation in the elementary classroom*. Thousand Oaks, CA: Corwin Press.

Miller, A. K. (2015). *Freedom to fail: How do I foster risk-taking and innovation in my classroom?* Alexandria, VA: Association for Supervision and Curriculum Development.

Mitra, D. L. (2004). The significance of students: Can increasing "student voice" in schools lead to gains in youth development? *Teachers College Record, 106*(4), 651–688.

Morgan, G. (2015). *Innovative educators: An action plan for teachers.* Portsmouth, NH: Heinemann.

Mumford, M. D., Medeiros, K. E., & Partlow, P. J. (2012). Creative thinking: Processes, strategies, and knowledge. *Journal of Creative Behavior, 46*(1), 30–47.

Murray, D. M. (1981). Making meaning clear: The logic of revision. *Journal of Basic Writing, 3*(3), 33–40.

National Governors Association Center for Best Practices & Council of Chief State School Officers. (2010a). *Common Core State Standards for English language arts and literacy in history/social studies, science, and technical subjects.* Washington, DC: Authors. Accessed at www.corestandards.org/assets/CCSSI_ELA%20Standards .pdf on August 2, 2018.

National Governors Association Center for Best Practices & Council of Chief State School Officers. (2010b). *Common Core State Standards for mathematics.* Washington, DC: Authors. Accessed at www.corestandards.org/assets/CCSSI _Math%20Standards.pdf on August 2, 2018.

Olivant, K. F. (2015). "I am not a format": Teachers' experiences with fostering creativity in the era of accountability. *Journal of Research in Childhood Education, 29*(1), 115–129.

Orr, A. M., & Olson, M. (2007). Transforming narrative encounters. *Canadian Journal of Education, 30*(3), 819–838.

Ostroff, W. L. (2016). *Cultivating curiosity in K–12 classrooms: How to promote and sustain deep learning.* Alexandria, VA: Association for Supervision and Curriculum Development.

Pink, D. H. (2009). *Drive: The surprising truth about what motivates us.* New York: Riverhead Books.

Pintrich, P. R. (2000). Multiple goals, multiple pathways: The role of goal orientation in learning and achievement. *Journal of Educational Psychology, 92*(3), 544–555.

Porosoff, L., & Weinstein, J. (2018). *EMPOWER your students: Tools to inspire a meaningful school experience, grades 6–12.* Bloomington, IN: Solution Tree Press.

Reeves, D. (2015). *Inspiring creativity and innovation in K–12.* Bloomington, IN: Solution Tree Press.

Renzulli, J. S. (2000). *New directions in creativity: Mark 2.* Mansfield Center, CT: Creative Learning Press.

Reynolds, L. (2012). *A call to creativity: Writing, reading, and inspiring students in an age of standardization.* New York: Teachers College Press.

The Right Question Institute. (n.d.). *Teach students to ask their own questions.* Accessed at http://rightquestion.org/education on October 19, 2017.

Ritchhart, R., Church, M., & Morrison, K. (2011). *Making thinking visible: How to promote engagement, understanding, and independence for all learners.* San Francisco: Jossey-Bass.

Ritchhart, R., & Perkins, D. (2008). Making thinking visible. *Educational Leadership, 65*(5), 57–61.

Ritter, S. M., & Dijksterhuis, A. (2014). Creativity—the unconscious foundations of the incubation period. *Frontiers in Human Neuroscience, 8,* 215. Accessed at www.ncbi.nlm.nih.gov/pmc/articles/PMC3990058 on September 13, 2018.

Robinson, K. (2009). *The element: How finding your passion changes everything.* New York: Viking.

Robinson, K., & Aronica, L. (2015). *Creative schools: The grassroots revolution that's transforming education.* New York: Viking.

Rogers, C. R. (1954). Toward a theory of creativity. *ETC: A review of general semantics, 11*(4), 249–260.

Rogers, C. R. (1961). *On becoming a person: A therapist's view of psychotherapy.* Boston: Houghton-Mifflin.

Ross, J. A. (2006). The reliability, validity, and utility of self-assessment. *Practical Assessment, Research, and Evaluation, 11*(10), 1–13.

Rothstein, D., & Santana, L. (2014). The right questions. *Educational Leadership, 72*(2). Accessed at www.ascd.org/publications/educational-leadership/oct14/vol72/num02/The-Right-Questions.aspx on September 13, 2018.

Sawyer, R. K. (2006). *Explaining creativity: The science of human innovation.* New York: Oxford University Press.

Schimmer, T. (2014). *Ten things that matter from assessment to grading.* Boston: Pearson.

Shute, V. J. (2007). *Focus on formative feedback.* Princeton, NJ: Educational Testing Service.

Simonton, D. K. (1988). Creativity, leadership, and chance. In R. J. Sternberg (Ed.), *The nature of creativity: Contemporary psychological perspectives* (pp. 386–426). Cambridge, MA: Harvard University Press.

Simonton, D. K. (1999). *Origins of genius: Darwinian perspectives on creativity.* New York: Oxford University Press.

Slade, S., & Griffith, D. (2013). A whole child approach to student success. *KEDI Journal of Educational Policy*, 21–35.

Smutny, J. F., & von Fremd, S. E. (2009). *Igniting creativity in gifted learners, K–6: Strategies for every teacher.* Thousand Oaks, CA: Corwin Press.

Spacey, J. (2016). *What is domain knowledge?* Accessed at https://simplicable.com/new /domain-knowledge on October 12, 2017.

Tan, A. (2004). *Exploring children's perceptions of learning.* New York: Marshall Cavendish.

Thompson, M., & Wiliam, D. (2007). *Tight but loose: A conceptual framework for scaling up school reforms.* Paper presented at the annual meeting of the American Educational Research Association, Chicago, IL.

Torrance, E. P. (1965). *Rewarding creative behavior: Experiments in classroom creativity.* Englewood Cliffs, NJ: Prentice-Hall.

Wagner, T. (2008). Rigor redefined. *Educational Leadership, 66*(2), 20–25.

Wagner, T. (2012). *Creating innovators: The making of young people who will change the world.* New York: Scribner.

White, K. (2017). *Softening the edges: Assessment practices that honor K–12 teachers and learners.* Bloomington, IN: Solution Tree Press.

Wiggins, G. (2017). *How to create a rubric that does what you want it to.* Accessed at www.teachthought.com/pedagogy/assessment/how-to-create-a-rubric-that-does -what-you-want-it-to on October 3, 2018.

Wiggins, G., & McTighe, J. (2005). *Understanding by design* (2nd ed.). Alexandria, VA: Association for Supervision and Curriculum Development.

Wiliam, D. (2018). *Embedded formative assessment* (2nd ed.). Bloomington, IN: Solution Tree Press.

INDEX

Softening the Edges
Katie White
Discover how to design, deliver, and differentiate instruction and assessment to address learners' diverse intellectual and emotional needs. By creating an effective assessment architecture, you can ensure your students are invested in their own learning and have the confidence to face any learning challenge.
BKF781

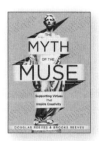

The Myth of the Muse
Douglas Reeves and Brooks Reeves
The authors argue that creativity is not spontaneous or inborn but a process that can be cultivated. Ideal for team study and discussion, the book outlines seven "virtues" that inspire creativity and includes activities and guidelines to encourage and facilitate creativity.
BKF655

The New Art and Science of Classroom Assessment
Robert J. Marzano, Jennifer S. Norford, and Mike Ruyle
Shift to a new paradigm of classroom assessment that is more meaningful and accurate. Step by step, the authors outline a clear path for transitioning to a holistic mode of assessment that truly reflects course curriculum and student progress.
BKF788

Growing Tomorrow's Citizens in Today's Classrooms
Cassandra Erkens, Tom Schimmer, and Nicole Dimich Vagle
For students to succeed in today's ever-changing world, they must acquire unique knowledge and skills. Practical and research based, this resource will help educators design assessment and instruction to ensure students master critical competencies, including collaboration, critical thinking, creative thinking, communication, digital citizenship, and more.
BKF765

"Excellent engagement
in what truly matters
in **assessment**.

Great examples!"

PD Services

Our experts draw from decades of research and their own experiences to bring you
practical strategies for designing and implementing quality assessments. You can choose
from a range of customizable services, from a one-day overview to a multiyear process.

Book your assessment PD today!
888.763.9045

Solution Tree